EDUCATION OF WEAKER SECTIONS

Policies and Problems

EDUCATION OF WEAKER SECTIONS

Policies and Problems

(Essays in Honour of Prof. K.S. Chalam)

Edited by

Prof. D. PULLA RAO

AKANSHA PUBLISHING HOUSE
NEW DELHI • GUWAHATI • VISAKHAPATNAM

AKANSHA PUBLISHING HOUSE
4649-B/21, Ansari Road
Daryaganj, New Delhi-110002
Phones: 23268193, 09435116718
Email: ektabooks@yahoo.com
visit us: www.akanshapublishinghouse.com

Education of Weaker Sections: Policies and Problems

First Published 2010

ISBN 978-81-8370-227-0

PRINTED IN INDIA

Published by Akansha Publishing House, New Delhi-110002 and printed at S.N. Printers, Delhi.

Prof. K.S. Chalam

Member, U.P.S.C, New Delhi.

Prof. K.S. Chalam in whose honour the present book is edited is an alumni of Andhra University. Noted scholar and renowned Educationist, Political Economist and an innovator of Staff Development Programme in India, he entered the U P S C as a Member in 2005 after a brief stint as Vice- Chancellor at Dravidian University, A.P.

He served the Department of Economics, Andhra University as a Lecturer, Reader and Professor for more than three decades with dedication and distinction. He was trained as an Economic Planner at Central School of Planning and Statistics, Warsaw, Poland during 1981-1982. He has obtained first rank in the international diploma programme of the school. As a student of Prof. B. Sarveswara Rao, he has strengthened the teaching of Economics of Education and Human Development. He has delivered endowment lectures on Public Sector and on issues relating to educational development at several universities and institutes in the country. He has published so far 20 books in English and 6 in Telugu and about 90 research papers covering areas of Economics of Education, Political Economy, Public Economics, Dravidian Studies etc. Some of his articles published in the *Economic and Political Weekly* are still cited in several reference works. In his book on "Economic Reforms and Social Exclusion" he has made an attempt to bring interdisciplinary approach to study the impact of reforms on the socially excluded groups in India. His book on "Caste-based Reservations and Human Development in India" (2007) was reviewed in around 20 leading newspapers and journals including the *Hindu*, the *Tribune,* etc. appreciating the author for the innovative approach used to understand and solve the contentious issue of our times. The reviewers in Pakistan and DFID commended the book as "immense topical relevance, this book will be of interest to students and scholars of development studies....useful to policy makers and practitioners working in this area". The book is being translated into Tamil and Telugu. An honours diploma thesis was submitted by Natasha Azad to California University on this book.

Prof. K.S. Chalam is known in the country as the father of the famous Academic Staff Colleges Scheme as he was the one who initiated the concept in 1985. At a time when the professors of the university system were not given any structured training to improve the quality of higher education, Prof. Chalam initiated a training course with UGC support in 1985. The UGC has recognized his contribution and asked him to conduct the first national workshop to design the proposed Academic Staff Colleges in India. He himself founded the college in 1987 and organized the first orientation course. It became an important part of the system of higher education to improve the Quality of Higher Education. The UNESCO has appreciated the scheme as one of the largest schemes of Staff Development in the world. He was responsible in strengthening the scheme with his 3 important publications on staff development. The latest (2006) book on 'Modern Techniques of Teaching and Staff Development' is a reference volume for all teachers in higher education. He has delivered lectures on Staff Development and participated in deliberations of the Prof. Rastogi Committee. It has helped consolidate the scheme in the interest of Quality of University Education.

Chalam was the first student trained formally in a university system in Economics of Education in 1972 at Andhra University under Prof. B. Sarveswara Rao. Late J.P. Naik inaugurated the specialization. He has worked for his Ph.D. on 'Finances, costs and productivity of higher education'. The study published as a book was reviewed both in India and abroad. Late Dr. Malcolm Adiseshiah acclaimed it as 'an excellent analysis of the economics of education in Andhra Pradesh as such is an important addition to the limited literature in India'. Another reviewer Dijon Jean-Claude Eicher commended it as a "courageous and useful book". He was Professor of Economics in Andhra University and taught the specialization both in the Departments of Economics and Education for a generation of students. He has pioneered interdisciplinary research and published 'Education and Weaker Sections' in 1988. Prof. P.R. Panchamukhi in his review of the book mentioned that 'the interdisciplinary approach to the study of educational problems is a useful framework'. Some of his books are offered as Text books for P.G students. He is one of the very rare research guides who has trained a dozen research students on a variety of issues starting from Human Development in A.P (before HD Report, 1990), Child Labour, Primary Education, Dalit Poverty, Impact of Technology on Agriculture, Liberalization to name a few. He is a prolific writer in Telugu. Apart from 6 Books in Telugu, scores of edit page articles were published in all leading dailies. He has supervised 12 scholars successfully to obtain their Ph.Ds in Economics, conducted research studies funded by UGC, Govt. of A.P, UNICEF, etc.

The contributions of Prof. Chalam are cited by scholars and activists across the globe. He has kept a legacy of teaching at Andhra University. One of the citations of an award rightly remarked that he is a 'scholar with social consciousnesses'. A Volume of papers were contributed in his honour in the name of 'Development of Weaker Sections' in 1998. As the third Vice-Chancellor of Dravidian University for a brief period, he has produced a programme of action for the university. He is also known as the first Director of Swamy Ramanand Teertha Rural Institute, the first institute of NCRI, Govt. of India. His experiments with rural higher education for one year at Pochampally published later in a book are useful as a reference work. He is the founder Editor of 'South India Journal of Social Sciences'.

Prof. K.S. Chalam commands respect among the academicians and activists due to his committed service in public affairs over a period of three decades. He is not an armchair scholar. He has been actively involved in public affairs relating to education and social development. All his studies in economics are interdisciplinary in nature and contain social issues with economic analysis of development. Therefore one of his biographers Avinash Misra called him as Simon Kuznets of India.

He has single handedly projected the underdevelopment of North Andhra with his publications and lectures for the last three decades making the Govt. of Andhra Pradesh to appoint a separate development board for the region in 2007. He is not an idealist but a practical person who got himself married outside his caste and implemented the same principle for the entire family. He has performed more than hundred social marriages in A.P.

Prof. Chalam is not only a serious scholar and teacher, but also a social activist. He served as the National Secretary, Amnesty International during 1984-85, Secretary and Vice-President of Professional bodies like A.P. Economic Association, Indian Political Economy Association etc. He has participated in international debates on caste and race at Durban, Cairo etc. He has presented papers on Education, Poverty, Political Economy at Cambridge, Wisconsin, Manchester, Colombo, Bangkok and at other international fora. He has been on several expert committees at center and State levels and has served on the World Bank teams. He is a builder of institutions. The Academic Staff College that he has nurtured at Andhra University became a model for the entire country. He has started Mahendra Degree College in his native place, Pathapatnam a decade ago to provide higher educational facilities in a remote tribal region. He got his Economics honours from S K C G College, Parlakhemundi, Orissa. He was the first Telugu person to receive honours degree from Utkal (Berhampur) University in 1968 at an age of 19. He became a Lecturer at a very young age that helped him develop passion for teaching and research. The passion for teaching made him to continue his advice to the UGC as Hon. Chairman of a 'High Power Committee on Academic Staff Colleges' even after joining the UPSC. He is on several committees including NCRI, ICPR on an advisory capacity. He has an impeccable character and sound knowledge in social sciences that helped him become Member, UPSC. It is said that his presence in the UPSC made people from lower socioeconomic background to get inspired to enter into civil services to serve the country and people. This is reflected in the results of recent Civil Services Examination.

CONTENTS

SECTION C
EDUCATION OF WEAKER SECTIONS

FOREWORD

I am very happy to write a few words about the book edited by Prof. D. Pulla Rao in honour of his teacher who was a great teacher and scholar.

Education, according to Babasaheb Ambedkar gives the greatest material benefit to those who possess it. In his Bombay Legislative Council debates in 1927 he said that, "we may forego materials benefits of civilizations, but we cannot forego our right and opportunity to reap the benefit of the highest education to the fullest extent". Though he wanted the expansion of opportunities for education of the dalits about 80 years ago, the weaker sections of the society including scheduled castes, tribes and other disadvantaged groups have not been able to reap the benefits of education the fullest extent, yet. It is only to achieve these objectives, the present government is going to enact a Bill for compulsory education for the age group of 6-14 very soon. In this context, the present volume on education problems and prospects of weaker sections is a welcome attempt.

I have gone through the pages of the volume containing 25 papers divided into 3 sub-themes. The first part of the book is devoted to literacy and primary education. It is pointed out that despite of planned effort, the country could not achieve universal literacy. Therefore, it is suggested that additional allocation of resources for education in the budget. There is a case study of the experience of the residential schools for weaker sections in Andhra Pradesh. It has given a very encouraging account of the role played by these schools in moulding the character of the students of the weaker sections. The case studies of enrollment and retention of S.C. children in selected districts in Andhra Pradesh has brought out very interesting results indicating that in some districts the school enrolments are declining due to the increase in the number of schools. It has also brought out how child labour in the country particularly in the agriculture sector is contributing for the dropouts among the boys and girls of weaker sections. The study has also focused on tribal enrolment and the disparities in enrolment between boys and girls.

The section on higher education has started with a paper narrating the historical role of the university system in India. I may mention here that Prof. K.S. Chalam in his recent book on Babasaheb Ambedkar, for the first time provided information how he has worked not only for the universalisation of education, but also gave concrete suggestions for the development of university education in India. Babasaheb Ambedkar was given the opportunity to draft the Constitution which he has eminently used to provide a structure to the emerging nation, but also provided directive principles to the state. It is in this connection, he has used the occasion to incorporate Article 45 for compulsory primary education. The other papers in this section contain the role of private sector, distance education, and the need for reforms in the examination system to bring improvements in Quality. There is an important paper on Academic Staff Colleges, the scheme that has revoluntionsed teaching in higher education. Prof. K.S. Chalam in whose honour this volume is edited is considered as the father of this scheme.

The section on the problems and policies of weaker sections education seem to have concentrated on women empowerment. I have expected concrete suggestions from this section. There are some papers which are repetitive in nature. It is however suggested that universal literacy and enrolment in education is possible through reservation in educational institutions and government jobs. It is also reported that the information relating to reservations is not reaching majority of the people and the author suggested that more publicity is to be given about jobs and seats among the reservation groups. There is a positive out look in some of the papers that indicate the progress of education among the weather sections is in the right direction. It is because of the fact that the present government has introduced several schemes like Midday Meal, success schools, pre- and post-matric scholarships etc, that are motivating the people to send their children to schools and colleges. We hope that the weaker sections will join the mainstream educated very soon through the policy of government aided programmes and schemes.

I have known Prof. K.S. Chalam, Member, Union Public Service Commission as a dedicated and committed scholar and now a bureaucrat. It is in the fitness of things that these essays are being published in his honour.

I congratulate Prof. D. Pulla Rao for bringing out a useful and purposeful volume.

Prof. B.L. Mungekar
Member, Planning Commission
Govt. of India, New Delhi

ACKNOWLEDGEMENTS

This book is an outcome of the Seminar on "Human Development and Social Exclusion" conducted in the Department of Economics, Andhra University, Visakhapatnam on the occasion of Shastiabdi Poorti Celebrations of my Guru and Director of my Ph.D. work Prof. K.S. Chalam, Member, UPSC, New Delhi. About 350 delegates participated and more than 250 delegates presented papers and participated in the discussion and deliberations. I am highly thankful to the paper contributors for helping me in bringing out this book which will be of some help to the researchers and also policy makers in India. I am very much beholden to the Prof. K. Rama Krishna Rao, Chairman, Indian Council of Philosophical Research, New Delhi, for his financial assistance. My special thanks are due to our honourable Vice-Chancellor Prof. Beela Satyanarayana and Prof. V. Satyanarayana, Honorary Director, Indian Council of Social Science Research, Southern Regional Centre, Hyderabad for their financial assistance.

My sincere thanks to Prof. L.K. Mohana Rao, Principal, College of Arts & Commerce, Andhra University for inaugurating the seminar session. I express my grateful thanks to Prof. Beela Satyanarayana, Vice-Chancellor, Andhra University, for his inaugural address to the seminar. My sincere thanks are due to Prof. K. Rama Krishna Rao, Chairman, Indian Council of Philosophical Research, New Delhi for sparing his valuable time for preparing and delivering the keynote address. My special thanks to Sri D. Raja, M.P (Rajya Sabha) for attending as a guest of honour and releasing the Souvenir. My sincere thanks to Prof. Y. Satyanarayana, Vice-Chancellor, Andhra Pradesh University of Law for attending as a guest of honour and delivering valuable message.

I am deeply beholden to Prof. B.L Mungekar, Member, Planning Commission, New Delhi for having kindly written the foreword to this book sparing his precious time. I express my thanks to Sri S. Reghupathy, Hon. Minister for Environment and Forests, Govt. of India for attending as the Chief Guest for Shastiabdi Poorti Celebrations of Prof. K.S. Chalam and valedictory function of the seminar session and released the book 'Dravida Udyamam Katha' written by Prof. K.S. Chalam.

I express my gratitude to Ms. Parveen Talha, Member, UPSC for attending the Shastiabdi Poorti Celebrations of Prof. K.S. Chalam and releasing the book 'Political Economy of Underdevelopment of Kalingandhra' written by Prof. K.S. Chalam.

My heartful thanks to Sri. P. Janardhana Rao, Mayor, Greater Visakhapatnam Municipal Corporation who presided over the function of the Shastiabdi Poorti Celebrations of Prof. K.S. Chalam.

I also thank to Prof. R. Sudarsana Rao, Head, Dept. of Economics and Prof. G. Ramachandrudu, Chairman, P.G. Board of Studies for their continuous support for the successful completion of the seminar.

Finally, my special thanks to the teaching and non-teaching staff, research scholars and students of the Dept. of Economics, Andhra University for their support for the successful completion of the seminar and Shastiabdi Poorti Celebrations of Prof. K.S. Chalam and also in bringing the book to the present shape. I place on record the excellent work done by publishers in bringing the book on time.

Prof. D. Pulla Rao

INTRODUCTION

Education is one of the important socio-economic inputs that brings economic growth. It is also an important component of human development. It is the United Nations through its organizations like UNESCO, UNICEF etc. that made education as one of the important human rights. The UN has also incorporated universalisation of elementary education as one of the Millennium Development Goals. Thus, the educational problems of the weaker sections of India need to be examined in the broad framework of the above factors that have emerged during the 21st century.

Education of weaker sections was considered as one of the important provisions of the directive principles of state policy. It was directed that the state should achieve free and compulsory education for the children of 6-14 within 10 years after the adoption of our Constitution. But the progress that we have achieved in this direction seems to be very little. Therefore, the government has formulated a Right to Education Bill in 2004. But this is not yet passed in the parliament to become a law. However, the most challenging problem before the Bill is the enrollment and retention of children from scheduled castes, tribes and other weaker sections. It was Prof. K.S. Chalam who in his pioneering study on 'Education and Weaker Sections' opened the debate for discussion about two decades ago in 1988. Therefore, the papers that contain in the book are arranged in such a way that they address the problems and policies of weaker sections in education.

The present book on 'Education of Weaker Sections: Policies and Problems' consisting of 25 papers were part of the national seminar on "Human Development and Social Exclusion', organized during 6-7 October, 2008. The seminar was organized in honour of Prof. K.S. Chalam on his 60th birthday on 7th October, 2008.

The book is divided into three sections. In the first section of the book, **P. Ramappa and V. Jagannatham** in their paper on "*Progress and Problems of Primary Education: A Study*' observed that despite its importance, education continues to be a neglected area at the policy level. After many years of planning and promises total literacy in India remains to be a distant dream. It is suggested that financial allocations for education are to be increased to solve its problem and to improve the performance of primary education. Otherwise the performance of primary education may not be up to our expectations.

R. Siva Prasad in his paper on "*Impact of Sex, Caste and Type of School on 'Adjustment' of Residential School Students*" observes that the type of school in which the student is studying, has nothing to do with social adjustment of the students. It is further found that, in respect of home and emotional adjustments there are significant differences among majority of the schools. This shows that the types of schools have impact on the home and social adjustments of students. The Andhra Pradesh Residential Schools and Andhra Pradesh Social Welfare are successful in promoting educational adjustment. Anyway, the main objective of these residential schools, to promote education among weaker sections of society is accomplished.

A. Vamsi Krushna, A. Archana Bala and R. Vijaya Krishna in their paper on "*Trends in the Growth of Primary Education in Visakhapatnam District*" observe that Article 45 of the Indian Constitution guarantees provision of free and compulsory education to all children up to the age of 14. The National Policy of Education (NPE), 1986 and the Programme of Action 1992 (POA) reaffirmed the national commitment of Universalisation of Elementary Education (UEE). It was concluded that the DPEP initiated by the government had a positive effect on the growth rate of schools and enrollment. The programmes thereafter deserves to be paid even greater attention if our intension is to draw the child to the school and to retain it there.

D. Pulla Rao, D. Francis and P. Raj Kumar in their paper on "*Urban-Rural Disparities in Literacy Rates in India: Some Dimensions*" observe that urban literacy, has, no doubt improved significantly. In rural areas more than two fifths of the population is still illiterate. It is concluded that urban-rural literate ratio still calls for more vigorous efforts especially among the rural female population. Rural women need to wake up and actively participate in the movement in universalisation of literacy. Special efforts need to be paid to promote rural literacy among various groups comprising SCs and STs especially among the females of these groups.

D. Narayana Rao, V. Seshagiri Rao and P. Arun Kumar in their paper on *"Educational Dropout of Children at Primary Stage in East Godavari District of Andhra Pradesh"* observe that the National Policy on Education (NPE), 1986 and the Programme of Action, 1992 reiterate the commitment of retaining the children in schools at least up to Class-VIII. It was concluded that excessive involvement of children in domestic work, negligence of parents towards education of their children, social customs, shifting of families from one place to the other and early marriages of children are the other causes for the higher dropout rates, in addition to the literacy levels of parents and poor economic conditions of the families as the two basic factors responsible for dropouts at the primary school level.

Mohammad Khasim Shaik, D. Francis and D. Pulla Rao in their paper on *"Status of Primary Education in Vizianagaram District of Andhra Pradesh"* observe that primary education occupies an important position in the entire structure of education. It is concluded that enrolment ratio varies for different categories in various management schools. The ratio is highest for Scheduled Castes and Scheduled Tribes in Government schools and the lowest in private schools due to their poor economic status. Number of children per school showed a declining trend at primary level because of increasing number of schools due to various programmes initiated by the government.

P. Jayanand Kumar and A. Vamsi Krushna in their paper on *"Development of the Primary and Upper Primary Education in India"* observe that one of the important characteristic features of democracy is that it presupposes an educated and enlightened society. Democracy, both as a form of the government and as a way of life, cannot function when the society is uneducated and ignorant. Education and modernization are the two wheels of the same cart. Both, when combined together, lead to a rapid socio-economic development of a nation. As a conservative estimate, the population of children in the age group 6-14 years, at present, may be about 200 million of which about 160 million (2001-02 estimate) might be attending elementary schools. This leads to the conclusion that about 40 million children are still out of school, which constitute about 20 per cent of the relevant age group. It is reported that 22 per cent of the total out of school children of the world are in India.

P.S.K. Sudheer, Y. Ravini and D. Pulla Rao in their paper on *Trends in the Growth of Secondary Education in India*" observed that according to the 2001 Census about 65 per cent of the people were literate. If the population aged 7 years and above is concerned, the level of illiteracy is 35 per cent. It is 46 per cent for women. The total enrolment in secondary stage in the year 1950-51 was 15 lakhs students of which 13 lakhs were boys and only 2 lakh were girls. Girls constituted only 13 per cent to the total enrolment. The total enrolment had increased gradually and reached 282.00 lakhs in 1999-2000. The enrollment of girls was 110.00 lakhs which constituted 39 per cent of the total enrolment. The annual compound growth rate of total enrollment at secondary stage was 6.04 per cent. The growth rate was 8.34 per cent for girls and 5.30 per cent for boys during 1999-2000 over 1950-51. The student-teacher ratio at the secondary level as it stood in 1999-2000 was 16:1, and a highly favorable situation.

G. Venkata Ramana in his paper on "*Child Labour: Perils and Preventive Strategies*" observed that ironically, India's child labour laws prohibit children being engaged in factories where wages are high, but not in cottage industries, restaurants in households and agricultural sector where wages are low. In fact, the agricultural sector stands out as the biggest single source of child labour in India. It is concluded that despite legislative measures, government efforts and sizeable NGO interventions, the problem of child labour continues.

S. Ramesh Babu, Y. Venkata Naidu and K. Ravi Kumar in their paper on "*Disparities of Females in Literacy Rates and*

Education in India" observed that education for women should always be directed towards their holistic development. Education enhances a women's sense of her own health needs and perspectives, and her power to take any health and family planning decisions. This in turn, helps to reduce child and maternal mortality and morbidity rates. Increased women education leads to greater empowerment of women, to a postponement of the age of marriage and to a reduction in the size of the families etc. The literacy rate among females has increased as a faster rate than among males. There was a successively decreasing trend of disparity index from 16.4 in 1901 to 1.4 to 2001 in the country. In literacy rate, Kerala retained its supremacy with a 90.9 per cent literacy rate in 2001 in the country. The rate among males was 94.2 per cent and among females it was 87.9 per cent. Bihar stood at the bottom with a literacy rate of 47.5 per cent with 60.3 per cent for males and 33.6 per cent for females.

D. Francis, S.M. Khasim and D. Pulla Rao in their paper on *"Dropouts in Primary Education in Vizianagaram District of Andhra Pradesh - Mandal Level Analysis"* observe that the universalisation of elementary education has been recognized as a constitutional obligation in India by the year 1960, but the target has not been achieved even after 48 years of the target year. It was concluded that except few urban mandals, the coverage of the concept of universalisation of primary education was almost only one third of the set target. Tribal mandals are not ready to realize the target of universalisation of primary education except Gummalakshmipuram which is a highly tribal populated mandal without any dropouts.

R.V.L.N. Ratnakara Rao and V. Krishna Murthy in their paper on "*Literacy in India – Some Observations*" remark that in the Census of 1991, the literacy percentage was calculated for the first time based on the total population including children below seven years. Elementary education in India as J.P. Naik says is "a promise to keep" so that India achieves its position in the developing world, as it is already ahead of others in computer education etc.

In the second section of the book, **I. Narendra Kumar, C.P. Kasaiah and A. Siva Sankar** in their paper on *"Role of Higher Education in Rural Areas of India"* observe that in India there has been a considerable demand for higher education since Independence. Democratisation of education system boosted the growth of higher education in India. It has been accelerating rapidly over the past 150 years since the inception of Calcutta, Bombay and Madras Universities in 1857. There has been significant quantitative expansion in terms of institutions, enrollment and teachers. It is concluded that the problems of higher education in rural areas were more. Efforts will be made to expand the quantity and quality of higher education in rural areas.

Rakesh A. Joshi in his paper on *"Need for Reforms in Examination System"* observes that after providing proper information and knowledge to the students, it is necessary to test their grasping power. If the student is not quite up to the mark, then he should not be upgraded to the next standard. It is concluded that actually examinations are necessary but some changes in the system and the changes in the aptitudes of the students are essential.

K.A. Rasure in his paper on *"Higher Education and Private Sector"* observed that higher education in India has evolved in divergent and distinct streams with each stream monitored by an apex body, indirectly controlled by the Ministry of Human Resource Development. According to the University Grants Commission only two per cent of Indian colleges have the potential for excellence. It was concluded that proactively liberalizing higher education and designing suitable policies to minimize adverse effects would go a long way in sustaining India's competitiveness in services.

P. Raj Kumar, N. Someswara Rao and P.S.K. Sudheer in their paper on *"Role of Open Universities in the Development of Higher Education in India"* observed that in order to ensure access and education of a reasonably good quality, we must think of some alternative system capable of supplementing the role of conventional system. The distance education is one of such alternatives. It was concluded that distance education institutes should supplement the efforts of traditional universities in promoting excellent higher education, particularly accessing the students from the rural areas. The planners, policy makers and decision makers will have to be very clear about the role of distance education in higher education development.

Sai Ramesh, Thota in his paper on "*Academic Staff Development in Higher Education: Role of UGC Academic Staff Colleges*" observes that colleges and universities are national institutions supported by the resources of the society. Therefore, the teachers in these institutions have a moral responsibility of maintaining a high degree of respect in the minds of the public. Hence, there is always a need for in service education for teachers for their academic development. It is concluded that since education is a life long process, certainly there is a need for the teachers to become life long learners. Due to the information explosion and rapid growth of knowledge in various disciplines, we are considered to be the learners only in the academic environment.

A. Pal Pandi, U. Surya Rao and D. Jeyathilagar in their paper on "Visionary Leadership in Higher Education" suggested that the visionary leadership concept must be instituted in the institutions and also to implement the model of Integrated Total Quality Management for improving quality level of performance in the academic activities for achieving quality assurance in institutions. Visionary Leadership is essential for educational and management system, leads to overall human development and social exclusion. Therefore Vice-Chancellors/Principals/ Administrators/directors have to play as a visionary leader role in setting the direction for human and organization development.

In the third section of the book, **J. Rama Rao and T. Tirupathi Naidu** in their paper on "*Women Empowerment through Education*" observed that education is one factor that plays the most crucial role in empowering women. Schools, colleges and other professional bodies are consistently trying to educate, motivate and train the women in their chosen areas of career through curriculum, training, field exposure and other practical methods. It was concluded that education would emancipate and endow women with ability to control her life, accomplish her dreams and enhance her status. The task is challenging yet not impossible. Education and the empowerment of women are both essential and indispensable for prosperous nation.

G. Syamala Rao and M. Sanyasi Rao in their paper on "*Women Empowerment through Education*" observe that women's empowerment is the issue of raising awareness about rights - legal literacy, right to education and health, and enhancing information sharing about basic issues. It was concluded that the organization and government must treat women as equal to men and give them the respect, responsibility to grow in leadership positions. Parents and family members also should encourage the girl child education equal to their boys.

E. Vanilla Kumari, E. Sharmila Hymavathi and G. Ratna Priya in their paper on "*Empowerment of Weaker Sections through Education*" observe that the preamble to the Constitution bears the testimony of the nation's solemn promise to secure social, economic and political justice and equality as well as opportunity for all. It is concluded that the Indian Constitution guarantees every help and support to all the socio-economically weaker sections and disadvantaged groups so that they be transformed into quality human resource to shoulder the responsibilities of mother and make it a forward nation as early as possible.

R. Vijaya Krishna, D. Pulla Rao and P. Jayanand Kumar in their paper on "*Policies and Programmes and Changing Employment Opportunities for Women in School Education –A Case of Andhra Pradesh*" observed that several strategies were adopted to promote education of girls as an integral part of the planned socio-economic development of the country. The removal of women's illiteracy and obstacles inhibiting their access to and retention in primary education will receive over-riding priority, through provision of special support services, setting of time targets and effective monitoring. It is concluded that unless all the ladies are totally educated we cannot expect them to play any effective role in the society.

S. Pulla Rao and P. Usha in their paper on "*Status of Education and Employment of Weaker Sections in India (in Relevance to Accessibility* *of Reservations)"* observed that reservation in most of the states is at a maximum of 50 per cent and for jobs in the government/ public sector, as reserved quota for the SC and ST candidates respectively for a period of five years, after which the situation was to be reviewed. It is concluded that the desired progress can be achieved only when these people are well aware about all those programmes initiated by the government which is possible through extended publicity towards the provisions available to these sections.

E. Vanilla Kumari, E. Sharmila Hymavathi and G. Ratna Priya in their paper on *"Educational Status of Scheduled Castes in India"* observe that the Scheduled Castes and underprivileged people are still lagging behind in all stages of education. It was concluded that despite the Constitutional provision and persistent efforts to improve the levels of education since Independence, these exhibit high degree of dispersion and disparities.

V. Krishna Murthy and R.V.L.N. Ratnakara Rao in their paper on *"Education of Weaker Sections in India"* observe that education of weaker sections like Scheduled Castes, Scheduled Tribes and women are to be improved. Primary education as the foundation occupies an important position in the entire structure of education. This is perhaps the reason that Article 45 of the Indian constitution guarantees provision of free and compulsory education to all children up to the age of 14 or 7 years of schooling i.e. 7-14 years of age. So that Universalisation of Elementary Education is achieved i.e. 100 per cent literacy at elementary level.

Prof. D. Pulla Rao

SECTION - A
SCHOOL EDUCATION AND LITERACY

1

PROGRESS AND PROBLEMS OF PRIMARY EDUCATION: A STUDY

P. Ramappa & V. Jagannatham***

It is the education that it would accelerate economic growth, that it would improve the levels of living and knowledge of the people and that it would encourage modern attitudes. Despite its importance, education continues to be a neglected area at the policy level. After many years of planning and promises total literacy in India remains to be a distant dream.

The literacy rate for the country as a whole in 2001 worked out to 65.38 per cent for the population aged seven years and above. The corresponding figures for males and females are 75.85 and 54.16 per cent respectively. Kerala with a literacy rate of 90.92 per cent holds the first rank while Bihar with a literacy rate of 47.53 per cent ranks last in the country. In 2001 the overall literacy in Andhra Pradesh stood at 61 per cent.

The present paper aims at understanding the progress and problems of Primary Education. This study has been divided into two parts. The first one explains the progress, problems and expenditure on primary education in Andhra Pradesh. The second part presents the features of the selected schools, problems and measures for improving the performance of primary education.

* Professor, Department of Economics, S.K. University, Anantapur, A.P.

** Research Scholar, Department of Economics, S.K. University, Anantapur, A.P.

Methodology and Data Base

The study is based on secondary data as well as primary data. The secondary data has been collected from different offices like District Educational Officer, DPEP, Department of Education, Govt. of A.P. and Director of Economics & Statistics, Hyderabad. Since it is not possible to take up the census survey covering the entire district due to the constraints of time and financial resources a Mandal namely Hindupur was selected purposively for empirical study. In the second stage, six primary schools, two from urban area, another two from semi-urban areas and the remaining two from rural areas are selected randomly. Discussions were held with the headmasters of the selected schools and the information relating to various aspects of primary education was collected with the help of structured schedules. Another schedule is prepared to canvas among the parents of dropout students. A total of 20 dropout students are selected from each school. All together 120 students are selected from six schools and the parents of these students are met to know the reasons for discontinuing the education of their children.

Primary Schools

Large number of primary schools are necessary to meet the demand and to achieve the objective of total literacy. The data presented in Table-1 clearly reveals that as high as 91.55 per cent of primary schools are being managed by local bodies like Mandal Praja Parishats, Zilla Praja Parishats and Municipalities. But the percentage of schools managed by local bodies declined from 91.55 in 1986 to 80.35 in 2005. The share of private aided schools in total schools is not so significant. The percentage of government schools increased from 2.55 in 1986 to 8.24 in 2005. In absolute terms the number of government schools rose from 1131 to 5085 during the same period. It is also interesting to note that the number of private unaided schools rose significantly from 643 (1.45 per cent) in 1986 to 4756 (7.71 per cent) in 2005. (Table-1).

Table-1: Primary Schools by Management

Management	*1986*	*2002*	*2005*
Government	1131 (2.55)	5666 (8.94)	5085 (8.24)
Local bodies	40599 (91.55)	51268 (80.91)	49559 (80.35)
Private aided	1973 (4.45)	2265 (3.57)	2280 (3.70)
Private unaided	643 (1.45)	4163 (6.57)	4756 (7.71)
Total	44346 (100.00)	63362 (100.00)	61680 (100.00)

Source: Statistical Abstracts, Directorate of Economics and Statistics, Govt. of A.P.

Basic Facilities

Availability of teachers and infrastructure facilities in schools is necessary to provide quality education. As high as seventy six per cent of the primary schools have pucca buildings. It is also evident that the percentage of schools having infrastructure facilities increased over a period of time. However there are schools without important infrastructure facilities. About 35 per cent of schools do not have drinking water, nearly 74 per cent of schools do not have separate toilets for girls and 58 per cent of schools are not having toilets.

Only 50 per cent of schools have library facility and more than fifty per cent of schools do not have playground facility. As high as 84 per cent of schools do not have electricity facility. Unless these basic facilities are improved in all primary schools we cannot expect teachers to succeed in accomplishing even the more modest aims of primary education. In a highly competitive world all schools must have good infrastructure facilities. Otherwise they cannot attract more students and the objective of universalization of elementary education cannot be achieved.

Enrolment

Accessibility of schooling facilities is no longer a major problem. As shown in Table-2 the number of schools in Andhra Pradesh increased from 29076 in 1956-57 to 63362 in 2002-03 registering 2.17 fold increase. Out of total primary schools 62800 (99.11 per cent) are for boys and 562 (0.89 per cent) for girls. The number of children enrolled in classes I - V rose significantly from 24.54 lakh to 63.51 lakh during the same period. The rate of enrolment also improved from 57.94 per cent in 1956-57 to 117.74 per cent in 2002-03. Gender wise enrolment ratios for classes I - V are calculated separately to know the differences in the enrolment ratios of boys and girls (not shown in Table-2). These statistics reveal that the enrolment ratios of boys and girls increased during the period from 1992 to 2003. The enrolment ratios of boys increased from 86.2 to 118.07 while the enrolment ratio of girls rose from 58.9 to 117.41 during the same period. In 1992 and 2000 the enrolment ratio of girls was less than that of boys.

Table-2: Growth of Primary Education in Andhra Pradesh

Year	*No. of Schools*	*No. of children enrolled (in lakhs)*	*Rate of Enrolment (in %)*	*No. of enrolled (in lakhs)*
1956-57	29076	24.54	57.94	84
1977-78	38836	46.76	70.55	120
1984-85	41702	64.12	89.10	153
1989-90	49000	69.21	88.52	141
1995-96	49125	76.40	94.92	155
2002-03	63362	63.51	117.74	100
2004-05	61680	55.24	109.88	90

But in 2003 the enrolment ratios of boys and girls are more or less equal to each other and they are greater than 100 per cent. It is due to the inclusion of under age and over age children. Here enrolment is simply the percentage of enrolment in classes

I – V to the estimated child population in the age group of 6-10 years. It is observed that there is no steady growth in the average number of children enrolled in each school. The average number of children per school varied from 84 in 1956-57 to 155 1995-96. In 2002-03 the average number of children per school is 100. This implies the fact that on an average there are only 20 students in each class.

Student-Teacher Ratios

The number of teachers in the primary schools of Andhra Pradesh increased from 78521 in 1960-61 to 166935 in 2004-05. At the same time the percentage of women teachers also rose from 18.62 to 45.02 during the same period. One of the important indicators that influence classroom transaction is the student-teacher ratio. Student-teacher ratio rose from 27.5 in 1981 to 51.9 in 1991. Afterwards the student-teacher ratio in the state as a whole started declining and reached to 33.1 in 2005. Among the three regions the student-teacher ratio in 2005 ranged between 31.1 in coastal Andhra and 35.9 in Telanga. This indicates that the regional disparities in student-teacher ratios have narrowed down over a period from 1991 to 2005. The heaviest pupil-teacher ratio in primary schools is observed in Bihar (76.1), followed by Uttar Pradesh (74.1), Jarkhand (54.1) and West Bengal (50.1). While the lowest pupil-teacher ratio is found in Sikkim (10.1), Jammu & Kashmir and Nagaland each with 15:1. (Arun C. Mehta, 2004-05).

Dropout Rates

In Andhra Pradesh the dropout rate in classes I–V was recorded at 31.95 per cent in 2004-05. It is observed that the difference in the dropout rates of boys and girls declined. For instance in 2004-05 the dropout rates of boys and girls were recorded at 31.77 per cent and 32.14 per cent respectively. In 2002-03 the dropout rates in classes I – VII and I – X were recorded at 53.17 per cent and 63.19 per cent respectively. It means only 37 per cent of the total students enrolled in class I reached Class X. The dropout rate of girls in classes I – VII and I – X is high compared to that of boys. The dropout rates of both boys and girls are increasing from primary to upper primary and to high school.

District-wise data for 2004-05 reveals that the dropout rates in classes I–V are very high in Mahaboobnagar district (53.02 per cent) followed by Medak district (52.34 per cent) and Warangal district (52.13 per cent). While the dropout rates in classes I - V are very low in Kadapa district (8.34 per cent) followed by Hyderabad district (8.53 per cent) and Chittoor district (9.71 per cent). Gender-wise dropout rates are also high in the districts of Mahaboobnagar, Medak and Warangal.

Expenditure on Education

The trends in the expenditure on education in Andhra Pradesh reveal that the percentage share of primary education varied from 44 in 1980-81 to 57 in 1999-00. These allocations for primary education are below the requirements (above 60 per cent). The ratio of total expenditure on education to G.S.D.P., remains more or less at three per cent. (V. Ratna Reddy & R. Nageswara Rao, 2003). Therefore the investment in education needs to be increased and a greater allocation to primary education is necessary if every child is to be got into school.

Primary Education in Anantapur District

As shown in Table 3 the number of schools in Anantapur district increased from 2770 in 1996-97 to 3212 in 2004-2005. While the enrolment in classes 1-5 declined from 401287 to 263197 during the same period. The number of teachers also increased considerably. It is interesting to note that the gross enrolment ratios rose significantly from 84.64 in 1996-1997 to 107.90 in 2004-2005. The gap between the enrolment ratios of boys and girls also declined. In 1996-1997 the dropout rate of boys and girls in classes 1-5 were 46.08 and 52.44 per cent respectively. The main reason for high dropout rates was due to ill-health, low income, household works, illiteracy of parents, lack of interest etc. But this position improved by 2004-05. Because the dropout rate of both boys and girls declined to 19.72 and 19.12 per cent respectively.

Table-3: Primary Education in Anantapur District at a Glance

Items	*1996-1997*	*2004-2005*
No. of Schools	2,770	3,212
Enrollment	4,01,287	2,63,197
No. of Teachers	5,552	8,071
Gross Enrollment Ratio		
Boys	87.58	106.42
Girls	81.63	109.47
Total	84.64	107.90
Dropout rate		
Boys	46.08	19.72
Girls	52.44	19.12
Total	48.99	19.42

Source: Selected Educational Statistics of Anantapur District, Director of School Education, Hyderabad, 1996-97, Statistical Abstract, Directorate of Economics & Statistics, Govt. of A.P., 2004-05.

Pupil-Teacher Ratios

In 1997-98 the pupil-teacher ratios in primary, upper primary and high schools stood at 52, 46 and 37 respectively. But we find a different picture in 2004-05. In primary schools the enrolment and the number of teachers declined significantly. But in the case of upper primary schools both enrolment and number of teachers increased compared to those of 1997-98. In 2004-05 the pupil-teacher ratio for primary and upper primary schools was estimated to be 33 each. These pupil-teacher ratios in primary and upper primary schools are in better position, because these are below the ideal pupil-teacher ratio i.e. 1:40. It also implies that more teachers are appointed to provide good education. But in the case of high schools the pupil-teacher ratio increased from 37 in 1997-98 to 47 in 2004-05.

Literacy Rates

The central and state governments have been spending huge

amount for achieving total literacy in India. According to census the total literates in Anantapur district are 31, 83,814. Of them the males are 16, 35,996 and females are 15, 47,818. With the establishment of number of primary schools, upper primary and High Schools in rural and urban areas the literacy rate increased. As shown in Table 4 the literacy rate in Anantapur district increased from 42.7 per cent in 1991 to 56.0 per cent in 2001. Similarly the literacy rates among males and females rose from 49.0 and 36.0 to 68.0 and 42.0 respectively during the same period. The literacy rate among S.Cs and S.Ts also rose considerably from 26.7 and 26.7 to 45.3 and 31.8 per cent respectively. But as high as high 68 per cent of Scheduled Caste women and 78 per cent of Scheduled Tribe women are still illiterate.

Table-4: Literacy Levels in Anantapur District

Category	*1991 Population*	*Literacy Rate (%)*	*2001 Population*	*Literacy Rate (%)*
All				
Male	16,36,405	49.0	18,59,502	68.0
Female	15,47,409	36.0	17,79,802	42.0
Total	31,83,814	42.7	36,39,304	56.0
S.Cs				
Male	2,32,055	36.8	2,63,291	58.0
Female	2,19,755	13.8	2,51,605	32.0
Total	4,52,332	26.7	5,14,896	45.3
S.Ts				
Male	57,472	38.5	65,722	41.0
Female	53,735	14.1	61,439	22.0
Total	1,11,345	26.74	1,27,161	31.8

Source: District Educational Statistics, DPEP, Anantapur, 2005.

Features of Selected Schools

Table 5 shows the features of selected schools located in Hindupur mandal. It is observed that three schools became very old because these buildings were constructed between 1950 and 1960. All selected schools were constructed by Government of Andhra Pradesh. Expect the school at Muddireddpalli (Urban Area) all schools have pucca buildings. The area of each school building varies from 2750 sq.feet at Lakshmipuram (Urban) to 6000 sq. feet at G. Guddampali (Rural). While number of rooms in each school ranges from 5 to 8. It is quite unhappy to state that no selected primary school has toilet facility. But all schools have compound walls.

Table-5: General Information of Selected Schools

Area	*Location of School (Village)*	*Year of Establish-ment*	*Type of Building*	*Building Area sq.ft.*	*No. of rooms*	*General Toilet*	*Com-pound wall*
Rural	Kotipe	1975	Pucca	3000	07	N.A.	C
	G. Guddampalli	1976	Pucca	6000	08	N.A.	C
Semi Urban	S. Sadlapalli	1975	Pucca	3000	07	N.A.	C
	Singareddipalli	1956	Pucca	36000	06	N.A.	C
Urban	Muddireddipalli	1962	Semi pucca	3850	05	N.A.	C
	Lakshmipuram	1950	Pucca	2750	07	N.A.	C

Source: Records of selected school in Hindupur Mandal.

C = Constructed. N.A. = Not available.

Facilities

Table 6 shows the facilities available in selected schools. In all six schools the drinking water is not available in sufficient quantity. About four schools have bore water and the rest two have tap water facilities. Almost all the schools are within a distance of half k.m. from the village. The approach road was not laid in two villages. But the facility of play ground was available at all schools. The selected schools are within a radius of 11 k.m. from Hindupur town. It is observed the Library is not available at any school. But the Government of A.P. has been implementing the mid-day meal programme at all schools for reducing the dropout rates.

Table-6: Facilities available at selected Schools

Area/ village	*Drinking water*	*Distance from village (in k.m.*	*Approach road*	*Trans-port*	*Distance from Hindupur (in k.m.)*	*Mid day Meal*	*Play ground*
Rural							
Kotipe	Bore water	0.5	Not laid	N.A	9	A	A
G. Gudd-ampalli	Bore water	0.5	Not laid	N.A.	11	A	A
Semi Urban							
S. Sadlapalli	Tap water	Within village	Laid	N.A.	03	A	A
Singreddi-palli	Bore water	Within village	Laid	N.A.	04	A	A
Urban							
Muddireddi-palli	Bore water	0.5	Laid	N.A.	03	A	A
Lakshmi puram	Tap water	Within village	Laid	N.A.	0.5	A	A

Source: Records of selected schools in Hindupur Mandal.
A = Available, N.A. = Not available.

Strength of Students

It is observed that the admission progress is not so significant during 2000-2005 in selected schools. Because the parents admitted their children into English medium schools at urban and semi-urban areas. The total strength at Kotipe School increased from 147 in 2000-2001 to 167 in 2004-05 registering 13.6 per cent growth. Similarly the strength of students at G. Guddampalli also increased from 152 to 177 during the same period and registered a growth of 16.4 per cent. In semi-urban area there is no significant improvement in total strength. It is due to lack of facilities in semi-urban schools compared to those of private schools. However in urban area at Lakshipuram the students strength rose from 258 in 2000-01 to 284 in 2004-05 registering a growth of 10.07 per cent. In another school at Muddireddipalli the growth was estimated at 19.5 per cent during same period.

Reasons for Dropping Children Out of School

Table 7 shows the reasons for dropping children out of school. It is observed that out of 60 parents 29 dropped their children to assist their work, about 33 parents dropped their children due to poverty, and another reason expressed by 29 parents is that the children are not interested in education. The other important reason according to 36 parents is due to lack of sufficient facilities in primary schools. It is also observed that the reasons for dropping children are same in rural, semi-urban and urban areas.

Table-7: Reasons for Dropping Children out of School 2004-2005

Area/village	*No. of respondents expressed the reasons*			
	To assist the parents	*Due to poverty*	*Not in interested education*	*Other reasons*
Rural Kotipe	04	04	03	05
G. Guddampalli	07	06	06	07
Semi-urbanS. Sadlapalli	04	07	05	08
Singaraddipalli	03	05	03	06
UrbanMuddireddipalli	05	06	06	05
Lakshmipuram	06	05	06	05
Total	29	33	29	36

Source: Field data.

Suggestions

Since majority of the primary schools are not having the basic facilities there is dire need for providing infrastructure facilities in all schools. Despite several efforts the dropouts continue. This must be checked by implementing the existing programmes effectively and by encouraging the parents who lack motivation and capacity to send their children to school regularly. As the primary education is the base for higher education and achieving total literacy, its performance must be improved.

The retention at primary level and high enrollment rates at upper primary and high school level are the main concern. Specific policies are necessary to address the problem of disadvantaged groups. The pupils who are not interested in education must be encouraged. Public English medium schools must be started to attract students. At the same time the employment opportunities for educated youth must be improved. The teachers working in primary schools must dedicate their services to improve the standards of pupils. Financial allocations for education are to be increased to solve its problem and to improve the performance of primary education. Otherwise the performance of primary education may not be up to our expectations.

REFERENCES

1. Aruna, R. (1999), "Learn Thoroughly: Primary Schooling in Tamilnadu", *Economic and Political Weekly*, Vol. 34, No.18.
2. Chalam, K.S. (1998), "Education", in V. Hanumantha Rao *et. al.* (ed), *Andhra Pradesh at 50: A Data based Analysis*, Hyderabad: Data News Features.
3. Kaul, Rekha (2001), "Assessing Primary Education – Going Beyond the Classroom", *Economic and Political Weekly*, Vol. XXXVI, No.2, pp. 13-19, January.
4. Ratna Reddy, V. and R. Nageswara Rao (2003), "Primary Education: Causes and Constraints", in C.H. Hanumantha Rao and S. Mahendra Dev (ed), *Andhra Pradesh Development*, Centre for Economic and Social Studies, Hyderabad.
5. Shariff, A. and P.K. Gosh (2000), "Indian Education Scene and Public Expenditure Gap", *Economic and Political Weekly*, April 15, pp. 1396-1406.
6. Zacharaiah, Job (2005), "Universal Elementary Education", *Yojana*, Sept.

2

IMPACT OF SEX, CASTE AND TYPE OF SCHOOL ON "ADJUSTMENT" OF RESIDENTIAL SCHOOL STUDENTS

*R. Siva Prasad**

The present study intends:

(1) To find out the impact of sex on adjustment of residential school students.

(2) To find out the impact of caste on adjustment of residential school students.

(3) To find out the impact of type of school on adjustment of residential school students.

Hypotheses:

(1) There is no significant difference between boys and girls in respect of adjustment.

(2) There is no significant difference between different caste sub-groups in respect of adjustment.

(3) There is no significant difference between different types of schools in respect of adjustment.

* Asst. Professor, Institute of Advanced Studies in Education, Andhra University, Visakhapatnam, Andhra Pradesh

Methodology

Tools Used

In order to measure adjustment of students, an adjustment inventory has been developed for the use of students studying in residential schools. The final form, after experts rating and item analysis, consists of 40 items on home, social, educational and emotional areas.

Sample

The present sample consists of 877 students of A.P. Residential and A.P. Social Welfare Residential schools of Visakhapatnam, Vizianagaram and Srikakulam districts of Andhra Pradesh.

Statistical Techniques Used

In order to find out the significance of difference of means between various categories of sex, caste and types of schools, values of 't' are calculated.

Results and Discussions

(1) Impact of Type of School on Adjustment:

Type of Schools that are considered in the study are shown in Table-1.

Table 1: Type of Schools with Abbreviations

S.No.	*Type of School*	*Abbreviation*
1.	A.P. Residential Schools	A.P.R.S.
2.	A.P. Social Welfare Residential Schools	A.P.S.W.R.S.
3.	A.P. Residential Schools for General	A.P.R.S.(Ge)
4.	A.P. Residential Schools for Back Ward Castes	A.P.R.S. (B.C.)
5.	A.P. Residential Schools for Scheduled Tribes	A.P.R.S. (S.T)
6.	A.P. Residential Schools for Boys	A.P.R.S. (Boys)
7.	A.P. Residential Schools for Girls	A.P.R.S. (Girls)
8.	A.P. Social Welfare Residential Schools for Boys (Boys)	A.P.S.W.R.S
9.	A.P. Social Welfare Residential Schools for Girls. (Girls)	A.P.S.W.R.S

Table 2: Significance of 't' Between Different Types of Schools in Respect of Adjustment

S.No.	Type of School	A.M.	S.D	N	t
1.	A.P.R.S.	55.61	9.07	586	2.13*
	A.P.S.W.R.S.	54.24	8.71	291	
2.	A.P.R.S. (Ge)	57.47	8.52	300	0.68
	A.P.R.S. (BC)	56.84	7.41	108	
3.	A.P.R.S. (Ge)	57.47	8.52	300	6.77**
	A.P.R.S. (ST)	51.72	9.71	178	
4.	A.P.R.S. (B.C.)	56.84	7.41	108	4.71**
	A.P.R.S. (ST)	51.72	9.71	178	
5.	A.P.R.S. (Boys)	56.82	8.50	167	1.49
	A.P.R.S (Girls)	58.29	8.50	133	
6.	A.P.S.W.R.S. (Boys)	54.08	7.19	129	0.27
	A.P.S.W.R.S. (Girls)	54.36	9.77	162	
7.	A.P.R.S. (boys)	56.82	8.50	167	2.93**
	A.P.S.W.R.S. (boys)	54.08	7.19	129	
8.	A.P.R.S. (Girls)	58.29	8.51	133	3.64**
	A.P.S.W.R.S (Girls)	54.36	9.77	162	

* Significant at 0.05 levels.

** Significant at 0.01 levels.

A significant difference is found only when all types of A.P. Social Welfare Residential Schools and A.P. Residential Schools for Scheduled Tribes are compared with all types of A.P. Residential Schools. It is interesting to note that students belonging to all types of A.P. Social Welfare Residential Schools and A.P. Residential Schools for Scheduled tribes are less adjusted when compared to their counterparts in all types of A.P. residential schools. From the above results it is evident that there is impact of type of schools on adjustment of students.

Table 3: Values of 't' Between Different Types of Schools in in respect of Four areas of Adjustment

S.No.	*Type of School*	*Home*	*Social*	*Educational*	*Emotional*
1.	A.P.R.S. A.P.S.W.R.S.	3.00*	1.01	2.33*	3.11**
2.	A.P.R.S. (Ge) A.P.R.S. (BC)	1.38	0.14	1.70	0.68
3.	A.P.R.S. (Ge) A.P.R.S. (ST)	7.37**	0.35	3.11	6.32**
4.	A.P.R.S. (B.C.) A.P.R.S. (ST)	7.12**	0.16	0.97	7.21**
5.	A.P.R.S. (Boys) A.P.R.S (Girls)	2.08*	0.18	1.24	0.85
6.	A.P.S.W.R.S. (Boys) A.P.S.W.R.S. (Girls)	0.24	1.16	2.62**	2.54*
7.	A.P.R.S. (boys) A.P.S.W.R.S. (boys)	2.76**	1.48	0.54	2.16*
8.	A.P.R.S. (Girls) A.P.S.W.R.S (Girls)	4.32**	0.11	0.87	5.18**

* Significant at 0.05 levels.

** Significant at 0.01 levels.

The above results indicate that there is no significant difference between all the types of schools in respect of social adjustment. This shows that the type of school in which the student is studying, has nothing to do with social adjustment of the students. It is further found that, in respect of home and emotional adjustments there are significant differences among majority of the schools. This shows that the types of schools has impact on the home and social adjustments of students. In respect of educational adjustment, a significant difference is found between three out of eight categories of schools. From this it can be said that the type of school is rather indifferent to show any impact on educational adjustment of students.

Table 4: Values of Means of Different Types of Schools in Respect of All the Four Areas of Adjustment

S.No.	Type of School	Home	Social	Educational	Emotional
1.	A.P.R.S.	14.33*	14.23*	15.36	11.79
2.	A.P.S.W.R.S.	13.61	14.00	15.87*	10.85
3.	A.P.R.S. (Ge)	14.92*	14.27*	15.74*	12.62*
4.	A.P.R.S. (BC)	15.09*	14.22*	15.19	12.32*
5.	A.P.R.S. (ST)	12.69	14.16*	14.81	10.06
6.	A.P.R.S. (Girls)	15.35*	14.23*	15.99*	12.84
7.	A.P.S.W.R.S (Girls)	13.65	15.19*	16.28*	10.33
8.	A.P.R.S. (Boys)	14.58*	14.29*	15.55	12.44*
9.	A.P.S.W.R.S. (Boys)	13.56	13.76	15.36	11.48
10.	Total Sample	14.20	14.15	15.57	11.64

* Indicates greater than the total sample mean.

It is found that the present sample is superior in educational adjustment and inferior in emotional adjustment, when the total sample means for all the four areas of adjustment are compared. It is found that the ranking order, of all the four areas of adjustment from higher to least, is educational adjustment (15.57), home adjustment (14.20), social adjustment (14.15) and emotional adjustment (11.64). The range of scores for all the four areas of adjustment is 0 to 20 and hence the theoretical average is 10. It is interesting to note that the students of different types of schools are far above the theoretical mean in all the four areas of adjustment. This is an encouraging phenomena because all the students of residential schools taken for the present study display better adjustment, as the mean values of all types of schools are greater than theoretical mean.

Table 5: Signicance of 't' between Boys and Girls in Respect of Adjustment

Sex	*A.M.*	*S.D.*	*N*	*t*
Boys	54.66	8.70	582	2.31*
Girls	56.14	9.41	295	

* Significant at 0.05 level.

The value of 't' is significant and hence boys do differ significantly from girls in respect of their adjustment. This is in contradiction with the finding of Nomani, H.R. (1965), who found that there is no significant difference in the adjustment of males and females. This contradiction, perhaps, is due to the fact that Nomani (1965) studied adjustment of the Adivasi students only. But in the present investigation all types of caste sub-groups are taken into consideration.

Table 6: Significance of 't' between Boys and Girls in Respect of All Four Areas of Adjustment

Sex	*Home*	*Social*	*Educational*	*Emotional*
Boys	2.04*	0.38	4.27**	0.04
Girls				

* Significant at 0.05 level.

** Significant at 0.01 level.

It is found from the above table that there is significant difference between boys and girls in respect of their home and educational adjustments.

From the above results supremacy of girls over boys is observed on home, social and educational adjustments. The superiority of girls in home adjustment is confirmed by Tripathi, S.L. (1981), who found that girls were comparatively more adjusted to the home area. This high home and educational adjustment among girls may be due to an evident fact that they are by nature docile and submissive.

Table 7: Values of Means of Boys and Girls in Respect of all the the four areas of Adjustment

Sex	*Home*	*Social*	*Educational*	*Emotional*
Boys	13.93	14.12	15.21	11.47*
Girls	14.42*	14.21*	16.15*	11.46
Total sample	14.18	14.17	15.68	11.47

* Indicates greater than or equal to total sample.

(2) Impact of Caste on Adjustment

Table 8: Significance of 't' between the Different Castes of Students in respect of their Adjustment

S.No.	*Caste*	*A.M.*	*S.D.*	*N*	*t*
1.	Total O.Cs.	57.05	8.48	65	0.17
	Total B.Cs.	57.23	8.14	312	
2.	Total O.Cs.	57.05	8.48	65	2.09*
	Total S.Cs	54.50	9.02	317	
3.	Total O.Cs.	57.05	8.48	65	3.74**
	Total S.Ts	52.07	9.44	183	
4.	Total B.Cs.	57.23	8.14	312	3.98**
	Total S.Cs	54.50	9.02	317	
5.	Total B.Cs.	57.23	8.14	312	6.14**
	Total S.Ts	52.07	9.44	183	
6.	Total S.Cs	54.50	9.02	317	2.85**
	Total S.Ts	52.07	9.44	183	
7.	O.Cs. In A.P.R.S.	56.65	8.51	54	0.59
	O.Cs. in A.P.S.W.R.S.	58.40	8.65	10	
8.	B.Cs in A.P.R.S	57.86	8.38	183	0.29
	B.Cs in A.P.S.W.R.S	57.26	9.78	19	
9.	S.Cs. in A.P.R.S.	57.24	14.04	51	1.55
	S.Cs in A.P.S.W.R.S.	53.92	13.34	250	
10.	S.Ts. in A.P.R.S.	50.50	9.51	12	1.26
	S.Ts in A.P.S.W.R.S	54.08	8.08	12	

* Significant at 0.05 level.

** Significant at 0.01 level.

Significant inter-caste differences are found except between other castes and backward castes in regard to the adjustment. When means are compared, it is found that students of other castes and backward castes are better adjusted than their counterparts belonging to scheduled castes and scheduled tribes. This low adjustment among scheduled castes and scheduled tribes may be attributed to their low school-educational background. Singh, P. (1987) found that first generation learners in comparison to the subsequent generation learners are more worried about social and psychological relation. He further found that the first generation learners have more problems in comparison to subsequent generation learners in the areas related to adjustment to school work. In the present study students of scheduled castes and scheduled tribes mostly belong to first generation learners because in the selection procedure of A.P. social welfare residential schools preference is given to first generation learners. When the students belonging to same caste and studying different types of schools, it is found that they do not differ significantly.

It is interesting to observe that there are no significant inter-caste differences in social adjustment of students. As regards home adjustment there are significant inter-caste differences except between other castes and backward castes. Further inter-caste differences are found between backward castes and scheduled castes; and scheduled castes and scheduled tribes in respect of educational adjustment. There are significant inter-caste difference between all caste sub-groups except other castes, backward castes and scheduled castes in respect of emotional adjustment.

As regards students belonging to different caste sub-groups studying in various types of schools, no significant differences are noticed except between scheduled caste students of A.P. Residential Schools and A.P. Social Welfare residential schools in emotional adjustment. This indicates that type of school has no impact on home, social, educational and emotional adjustments of students belonging to different caste sub-groups.

Table 9: Values of 't' between the different Castes in respect of All the Four Areas of Adjustment

S.No.	Caste	Home	Social	Educational	Emotional
1.	Total O.Cs. Total B.Cs.	0.20	0.27	0.35	0.66
2.	Total B.Cs. Total S.Cs	3.99**	0.26	0.12	1.74
3.	Total O.Cs. Total S.Ts	5.50**	0.45	1.66	2.93**
4.	Total B.Cs. Total S.Ts	6.74**	0.004	0.81	4.08**
5.	Total B.Cs. Total S.Ts	8.56**	0.20	2.16*	5.60**
6.	Total S.Cs Total S.Ts	2.51*	0.19	2.82**	2.15*
7.	O.Cs. in A.P.R.S. O.Cs. in A.P.S.W.R.S.	0.03	1.97	0.47	0.68
8.	B.Cs in A.P.R.S B.Cs in A.P.S.W.R.S	0.98	0.25	1.43	0.31
9.	S.Cs. in A.P.R.S. S.Cs in A.P.S.W.R.S.	0.44	1.94	0.02	3.55**
10.	S.Ts. in A.P.R.S. S.Ts in A.P.S.W.R.S	1.62	0.27	0.59	0.81

* Significant at 0.05 level.

** Significant at 0.01 level.

It is interesting to observe that the educational adjustment is high in all the categories of caste sub-groups when compared to others areas of adjustment. Emotional adjustment is found to be low in all the caste-sub groups. From this it can be inferred that the A.P. residential schools and A.P. Social Welfare residential schools are successful in promoting educational adjustment. Any way, the main objective of these residential schools, to promote education among weaker sections of society, is accomplished. It is further affirmed when the total sample means of all the four areas of adjustment are observed, it is found that educational adjustment (15.51) is high, followed by home adjustment (14.19), social adjustment (14.18) and emotional adjustment (11.47).

Table 10: Means of Different Castes in Respect of All the Four Areas of Adjustment

S.No.	Caste	Home	Social	Educational	Emotional
1.	Total O.Cs.	15.03*	14.25*	15.72*	12.07*
2.	Total B.Cs.	15.23*	14.13	15.57*	12.44*
3.	Total S.Cs.	13.51	14.13	15.77*	11.11
4.	Total S.Ts.	12.74	14.19*	14.95	10.25
5.	O.Cs. in A.P.R.S.	15.33*	13.87	15.71*	02.11*
6.	O.Cs. in A.P.S.W.R.S.	14.53*	15.70*	16.20*	11.20
7.	B.Cs. in A.P.R.S.	15.27*	14.20*	15.74*	12.67*
8.	B.Cs. in A.P.S.W.R.S.	14.53*	14.00	16.79*	12.37*
9.	S.Cs. in A.P.R.S.	13.68	14.86*	15.82*	12.88*
10.	S.Cs. in A.P.S.W.R.S.	13.46	13.91	15.82*	10.74
11.	S.Ts. in A.P.R.S.	12.23	14.14	14.73	9.40
12.	S.Ts. in A.P.S.W.R.S.	13.92	14.42*	15.33	10.42
13.	Total sample	14.19	14.18	15.51	11.47

* Indicates greater than total sample mean.

Reddy (1978) and Sharma (1982) found that the socio-economic status has no effect on adjustment. Perhaps due to this reason that, in the present study, though the sample is drawn from different socioeconomic groups, it is found that the students have high educational adjustment.

REFERENCES

1. Allport, G.W. and B.M. Krammer (1946): "Some roots of prejudice", *J. Psychol.*, 22, 9-39.

2. Aruna, N.S. (1981): "A study of the factors influencing the achievement of standard VII students belonging to Scheduled Castes and Scheduled Tribes whose medium of instruction is Kannada", Ph.D. Edu., Mysore University.

3. Asha, C.B. (1978): "An Empirical study of the Adjustment Patterns of Creative children in Secondary schools". Ph.D. Psy. Kerala University.

4. Barel, B.N. (1969): "Some factors causing breakdown of social adaptability amongst students of Higher Secondary grade of West Bengal". Ph.D. Psy. Cal. University.

5. Beena Shah (1986): "Adjustment Inventory for school students (AISS)", Agra Psychological Research Cell, Tiwari Kothi, Belanganj, Agra.

6. Betty Minoer (1968): "Sociological background variable affecting school achievement" *The Journal of Educational Research,* Vol. 61, No. 8, April 1968.

7. Bhatnagar, R.P. (1968): "A study of some of the personality factors as predictors of academic achievement". C.I.E. students in Education and Psychology, Publication No. 63.

8. Bhatt, K.K. (1971): "Adjustment problems of the underachievers". University School of Psychology, Education and Psychology, Guj. University.

9. Dwyer, R.J. (1958): "A report on patterns of interaction in adesegregated schools". *J. Edu. Social,* 31, 253-156.

10. Gopinatha Rao, C. (1986): "Residential schools for weaker sections: A study A.S.C.I." *Journal of Management,* Vol. 15, No. 2, March, 1986.

11. Horowitz, E.L. (1944): "Race Attitudes". In O. Klineberg (Ed.) *Characteristics of the American Negro,* New York, Harper pp. 139-247.

12. Kailash Chand (1973): "A comparative study of group structure of Higher secondary school pupils in Grades ninth to Eleventh in Day Schools and Residential Schools". Ph.D., Edu., Agra University.

13. Kakkar, A. (1964): "Adjustment problems of Adolescents", Ph.D. Edu., All. University.

14. Mehrotra, S. (1986): "A study of the Relationship between Intelligence, Socioeconomic status, Anxiety, personality adjustment and academic achievement of High school students". Ph.D., Edu., Kan. University.

15. Nomanil, H.R. (1965): "Social-Psychological Study of Adjustment of the Adivasi Students", The Bihar Tribal Welfare Research Institute.

16. Panda, M. (1983): "The Relationship of Parental Life Style and Intellectual Achievement, Responsibility, Adjustment and cognitive performance among underprivileged children". Ph.D., Edn., Utkal University.

17. Pandey, P.S. (1981): "A study of socio-economic opportunity and Educational Achievement", Ph.D., Soc., Kashi University.

18. Reddy, I.V.R. (1978): "Academic Adjustment in relation to Scholastic Achievement of secondary School Pupils - A longitudinal Study". Ph.D. Psy., S.V. University.

19. Roy, A.K. (1969): "Development of a student Adjustment questionnaire (SAQ) and a study on the relationship of Adjustment to Academic Achievement". D. Phil. Psy. Cal. University.

20. Sharma, J.P. (1982): "A study of Scheduled Caste students in Patna University". Ph.D., Edn., Pat. University.

21. Singh, P. (1987): "A comparative Study of Achievement Adjustment, Attitudes and problems of First and Subsequent generation learners belonging Scheduled Castes at higher secondary level". Ph.D., Edu., Meerut University.

22. Tripathi, S.L. (1981): "Adjustment problems of Undergraduates of Varanasi Division". Ph.D., Edu., Gorakhpur, University.

3

TRENDS IN THE GROWTH OF PRIMARY EDUCATION IN VISAKHAPATNAM DISTRICT

A. Vamsi Krushna, A. Archana Bala** & R. Vijaya Krishna****

Knowledge is power. The earlier a person acquires the knowledge, the better would be his/her future life. Primary education constitutes a very important part of the entire structure of education because it is at this stage, the child starts going to a formal institution and formal education starts. And it is at this stage that the child empowerment starts to build up.

Article 45 of the Indian Constitution guarantees provision of free and compulsory education to all children up to the age of 14. Apart from being a Constitutional obligation, the provision of universal elementary education is crucial for spreading mass literacy, which is a basic requirement for economic development, modernization of the social structure and effective functioning of any democratic institution.

Although the policy intensions were articulated well, the experience with primary education reveals that there is a great failure both on enrollment and dropout fronts, which acted as leakages in the process of child empowerment. The educational

*, ** & *** Research Scholars, Dept. of Economics, Andhra University, Visakhapatnam.

policies could neither ensure cent per cent enrollment nor prevent the incidence of dropouts even at the basic level.

The social, cultural, religious, ethical and economic values play greater role than the constitutional and institutional factors in the realization of universal elementary education in India. It is the value attached by the masses to the primary education vis-à-vis their social, cultural, religious, ethical and economic values that persuade or dissuade the masses to go all out for universal primary education. The issues of school enrollment, continuation, dropout and re-enrollment including gender equality are highly linked to our social, cultural, religious, ethical and economic values.

District Primary Education Programme (DPEP)

The National Policy of Education (NPE), 1986 (as up dated in 1992) and the Programme of Action 1992 (POA) reaffirmed the national commitment of Universalisation of Elementary Education (UEE). Both U.E.E., N.P.E. resolved that free and compulsory education of satisfactory quality should be provided to all the children up to 14 years of age before we entered into the 21st century.

Educational Planning appears to be moving in the wrong direction. Until very recently, planning of universal elementary education was drawn from top to bottom, starting at the national and flowing down to the state level. But the right practice of planning is from bottom to the top. As the elementary education starts at the village/local level, its planning should also start at the village/local level. Hence the local area planning is emphasized. The district plan shall be only a summation of the village / local plans.

DPEP Phase-I

The District Primary Education Programme with the assistance of ODA was first implemented in 5 districts of Andhra Pradesh, viz., (1) Vizianagaram (2) Warangal (3) Kurnool (4) Nellore (5) Karimnagar. These districts are selected under Phase I as girls literacy rate was found to be very less in these districts.

DPEP Phase-II

The DPEP-II is extended to 14 more districts of Andhra Pradesh where the enrollment is found to be very poor and the gender equity was also found to be against the girl child. This phase is being financed by the World Bank. Visakhapatnam is one of the 14 districts selected under DPEP Phase-II in Andhra Pradesh. This programme was started during the academic year 1998-99 and it will be in operation for a period of 5 years. The main objectives of DPEP are: (1) Universal access; (2) Universal enrollment; (3) Universal retention of children up to 14 years of age; and (4) Substantial improvement in quality of education to enable all children to achieve essential levels of learning.

Objectives

The basic objective of this paper is to examine the process of child empowerment through elementary education. The other objectives are:

(a) To examine the current status of primary and upper primary education in Visakhapatnam District,

(b) To examine the trends in the growth of primary and upper primary education in Visakhapatnam District from 1986-87 to 2007-2008, and

(c) To identify the changing value perspectives that caused variations in the growth patterns of primary and upper primary education in Visakhapatnam District, with special reference to the DPEP.

The Data

The secondary data relating to the number of schools, enrollment, corresponding school age population in primary and upper primary schools and the number of teachers working in primary schools for about one and a half decade period from 1986-87 to 2007-2008 were obtained from the offices of the Commissioner and Director of School Education, Hyderabad and the District Educational Officer, Visakhapatnam. It was however found that there are some discrepancies in the data supplied by these offices particularly with respect to the primary education. Suitable adjustments were made where ever feasible. There is a difference between enrollment in primary schools and enrollment at primary stage. Therefore, we have taken the enrollment of the primary schools as a proxy to enrollment in primary stage. Similar is the case with upper primary schools. The difference is to be kept in mind while interpreting the trends in the growth of primary education in Visakhapatnam District. The data with respect to the number of schools, number of children enrollment, number of teachers employed and student-teacher ratio are presented separately for analytical purpose.

Visakhapatnam District is located at the northeastern corner of Andhra Pradesh. There are 43 mandals in Visakhapatnam District. It has got a rich and well-diversified socio-cultural heritage. Visakhapatnam city is well-known for its socio-cultural and educational advancement all over the country and also in some parts of the world. But the hinterland is far backward and neglected. Though a highly popular and internationally famous Andhra University is located in this district head quarters i.e. Visakhapatnam city, until very recently the rural folk of this district never thought of sending their children to the university education. Instead, people from all over the country and even from other parts of the world had taken advantage of this great facility. The basic reason was the low value score attached by the rural folk of this district towards education. Only over the last 10 to 12 years, the rural folk of this district had realized their past mistake and are now trying to rectify. Over this one and a half decade period there is a great surge in elementary education in this district both qualitatively and quantitatively.

The Results

A. Current Status of Primary and Upper Primary Education

The population of the district is 37.89 lakhs as per 2001 census and this constitutes 5.0 per cent of the population of the state. There are 19.81 lakhs literates forming 59.45 per cent of total population of the district. Among literates, male literates constitute 68.84 per cent while female literates constitute 49.99 per cent as per the 2001 census.

Table 1: Growth of Primary Education in Visakhapatnam District during 1986-87 to 2007-08

Year	*School age Population (6-11 yrs)*	*Index*	*No. of Schools*	*Index*	*No. of children enrolled (6-11Yrs)*	*Index*	*Rate of enrolle-ment to the correspon-ding age group (%)*	*No. of children per school*
Before DPEP		1986-87=100						
1986-87	384510	100	1888	100	285024	100	74.13	151
1987-88	385283	100	2275	121	303129	106	78.68	133
1988-89	386658	101	2290	121	336279	118	86.97	147
1989-90	386835	101	2315	123	283369	99	73.25	122
1990-91	387613	101	2322	123	289628	102	74.72	125
1991-92	388393	101	2328	123	292689	103	75.36	126
1992-93	389174	101	2308	122	249465	88	64.10	108
1993-94	389957	101	2315	123	250666	88	64.28	108
1994-95	390742	102	2321	123	252025	88	64.50	109
1995-96	391528	102	2540	135	258456	91	66.01	102
1996-97	494269	129	2362	125	259849	91	52.57	110
1997-98	506426	132	2466	131	276355	97	54.57	112
After DPEP		1997-98=100						
1998-99	518882	102	2767	112	299907	109	57.80	108
1999-00	531632	105	2980	121	294048	106	55.31	99
2000-01	543792	107	3024	123	293796	106	54.03	97
2001-02	554421	109	3345	136	324740	118	58.57	97
2002-03	518738	102	3550	144	280342	101	54.04	79
2003-04	214104	42	3492	142	263891	95	123.25	76
2004-05	248534	49	3087	125	233606	85	93.99	76
2005-06	404213	80	3080	125	223243	81	55.23	72
2006-07	423285	84	3170	129	227523	82	53.75	72
2007-08	415714	82	3183	129	216000	78	51.96	68
Growth Rates								
Before DPEP		1.9		1.4		-1.7		
After DPEP		-5.0		0.9		-4.3		
Total	0.1		2.4		-1.0			

Source: Commissioner and Director of School Education, Hyderabad & District Educational Officer, Visakhapatnam.

B. Growth of Primary Education

In Table 1, details relating to the number and growth of schools and the enrollment into primary education during the period 1986-87 to 2007-2008 are provided. The rate of enrollment to the corresponding age group and the number of children per school are also presented. There were, 1888 primary schools in the district during 1986-87. The number has increased to 3183 by 2007-2008, an increase of 68.59 per cent[1]. The annual growth of the schools and the number of children in 6-11 year age group was estimated with the help of index numbers. It is observed that the growth in the number of schools is higher when compared to the growth of children of school going age (6-11 years) throughout the period under study.

The total enrollment in primary schools in the year 1986-87 was 2.85 lakhs. There were wide fluctuations in enrollment in the following years up to 1991-1992. But afterwards enrollment increased to 3.24 lakhs in 2001-2002 and then declined gradually and stood at 2.16 lakhs in 2007-08.

The growth of enrollment and the achievement in universalisation of elementary education in the district can be known only in terms of school enrollment with respect to the corresponding age group. Therefore, we have estimated the proportion of school going children to the school going age group. It is interesting to find that the district has an enrollment rate of 74.13 per cent in 1986-87 and this proportion has increased to 86.98 per cent in 1988-89 then it has decreased to 73.25 per cent in the next year i.e., 1989-90, reached to 75.36 per cent in 1991-92. Thereafter, there has been a decline in the enrollment rate. In the year 2007-2008 it stood at 51.96 per cent.[2]

The figures in Table 1 suggest that the district still has a backlog of more than 25 per cent towards universalization of elementary education. A peculiar trend that may be noted is that the number of students in each school has been decreasing substantially during the period of the study because of decreasing number of enrolled children and increasing number of schools due to various schemes like Andhra Pradesh Primary Education

Table 2: Growth of Upper Primary Education in Visakhapatnam District during 1986-87 to 2007-08

Year	School age Population (11-13 yrs)	Index	No. of Schools	Index	No. of children enrolled (11-13Yrs)	Index	Rate of enrollement to the correspon-ding age group (%)	No. of children per school
Before DPEP	1986-87 = 100							
1986-87	175225	100	154	100	76395	100	43.60	496
1987-88	176647	111	169	110	76889	101	43.53	455
1988-89	178081	102	182	118	77978	102	43.79	428
1989-90	179527	102	193	125	79634	104	44.36	413
1990-91	180984	103	202	131	80968	106	44.74	401
1991-92	182453	104	204	132	80995	106	44.39	397
1992-93	183934	105	203	132	72154	94	39.23	355
1993-94	185427	106	210	136	73327	96	39.54	349
1994-95	186932	107	207	134	69490	91	37.17	336
1995-96	188449	108	211	137	73158	96	38.82	347
1996-97	188026	107	225	146	75598	99	40.21	336
1997-98	192650	110	245	159	79629	104	41.33	325
After DPEP			1997-98 = 100					
1998-99	197388	102	292	119	91420	115	46.31	313
1999-00	202247	105	286	117	87568	110	43.30	306
2000-01	207381	108	305	124	95549	120	46.07	313
2001-02	210767	109	475	194	92052	116	43.67	194
2002-03	228897	119	485	198	117769	148	51.45	243
2003-04	209354	109	534	218	114129	143	54.51	214
2004-05	273490	142	611	249	117744	148	43.05	193
2005-06	245529	127	648	264	121121	152	49.33	187
2006-07	167693	87	717	293	129440	163	77.19	181
2007-08	182131	95	734	300	129337	162	71.01	176
Growth Rates								
Before DPEP		0.8		3.2		0.1		
After DPEP		0.1		11.7		4.7		
Total		1.0		7.5		2.7		

Source: Commissioner and Director of School Education, Hyderabad & District Educational Officer, Visakhapatnam

Project (APPEP), Operation Black Board (OBB), DPEP, etc., in addition to the mushroom growth of private unregistered convents in the district.

C. Growth of Upper Primary Education

From the Table 2, it may be observed that there were only 154 upper primary schools in 1986-87 and this number increased to 734 by 2007-2008.

The rate of enrollment in upper primary schools in terms of rate of enrollment to the corresponding age group has shown a very discouraging trend recording less than 45 per cent[3]. In 1986-87 the rate of enrollment for the corresponding age group was 43.60 per cent. It is almost all stagnant up to 1991-92. Later it decreased to 39.23 per cent in 1992-93. Then it increased to an all time high of 77.19 per cent in 2006-2007. In the next year it declined and finally stood at 71.01 per cent in 2007-08.

D. Pupil-Teacher Ratio in Primary Education

The pupil teacher ratio shows the quality of education. Here, we examined the number of teachers employed in the primary schools in the district and the rate of growth of number of teachers during the period under study. The data are presented in Table 3. It is observed that there were 4,026 teachers employed in primary schools in 1986-87, of which 1,312 were women, constituting 32.59 per cent of the total. The number increased to 4,440 in 1988-89 and decreased to 4,187 in the immediate next year. Then the number increased to 4,619 in 1991-92. Then the number declined to 4,293 in 1994-95. Further the number rapidly increased to 7,552 in 1999-2000 and decreased to 6616 and increased to 7575 in 2001-2002 in the immediate next year and thereafter it declined and ultimately stood at 6491 in 2007-08.

The number of women teachers reached on all time high in 2001-2002 (3105) and it constituted 41 per cent of the total teachers, indicating that women teaching community has been on the increase all through and thereafter it has witnessed fluctuations and finally stood at 2997 in 2007-08.

Table 3: No. of Teachers Appointed in the Primary Schools of Visakhapatnam District during 1986-87 to 2007-08

Year	*Men*	*percentage*	*Index*	*Women*	*percentage*	*Index*	*Total*	*Percentage*	*Index*	*Pupil teacher ratio*
Before DPEP			1986-87 = 100							
1986-87	2714	67.41	100	1312	32.59	100	4026	100	100	70.80
1987-88	3078	70.92	113	1262	29.08	96	4340	100	108	69.85
1988-89	3164	71.26	117	1276	28.74	97	4440	100	110	75.74
1989-90	2926	69.88	108	1261	30.12	96	4187	100	104	67.68
1990-91	3120	68.45	115	1438	31.55	110	4558	100	113	63.54
1991-92	3164	68.50	117	1455	31.5	111	4619	100	115	63.37
1992-93	2910	65.61	107	1525	34.39	116	4435	100	110	56.25
1993-94	2911	65.64	107	1524	34.36	116	4435	100	110	56.52
1994-95	2760	64.29	102	1533	35.71	117	4293	100	107	58.71
1995-96	3108	63.81	114	1763	36.19	134	4871	100	121	53.06
1996-97	3044	63.39	112	1758	36.61	134	4802	100	119	54.11
1997-98	3379	61.40	124	2124	38.6	162	5503	100	137	50.22
After DPEP		1997-98 = 100								
1998-99	4161	60.80	123	2683	39.2	126	6844	100	124	43.82
1999-00	4709	62.35	139	2843	37.65	134	7552	100	137	38.94
2000-01	3999	60.44	118	2617	39.56	123	6616	100	120	44.41
2001-02	4470	59.00	132	3105	41.00	146	7575	100	138	42.87
2002-03	3804	56.09	113	2978	43.91	140	6782	10	123	41.34
2003-04	3766	55.03	111	3078	44.97	145	6844	100	124	38.56
2004-05	3481	54.50	103	2906	45.50	137	6387	100	116	36.58
2005-06	3365	52.70	100	3020	47.30	142	6385	100	116	34.96
2006-07	3629	54.53	107	3026	45.47	142	6655	100	121	34.19
2007-08	3494	53.83	103	2997	46.17	141	6491	100	118	33.28
Growth Rates										
Before DPEP		0.5			4.1			1.7		
After DPEP		-3.0			1.2			-1.2		
Total		1.4			5.2			2.92		

Source: Commissioner and Director of School Education, Hyderabad & District Educational Officer, Visakhapatnam

The trends in the growth of teachers show a peculiar feature with irregular ups and downs from 1986-87 to 1994-95. Since then one notices an increasing trend. The index of growth of male teachers increased to 117 in 1988-89, then it decreased to 108 in 1989-90. It increased in 1990-91 and 1991-92. Later it went down to 100 in 2005-06. This is the lowest level for the period of our study. In 2007-08 it stood at 103. However, there is some positive change in the case of female teachers. Their index has been rising almost continuously but for the set back during 1987-88 to 1989-90. Then it has increased gradually and ultimately it reached to 162 by 1997-98 and all time high for the period under study. Finally, it stood at 141 by 2007-08. The index of female teachers is higher than that of the male teachers in general. This may be due to implementation of 33.33 per cent reservation policies of the government in favour of women.

During the period under study, the increase in the number of teachers was around 3600. As the enrollment in primary schools showed a decreasing trend, it resulted in a favourable change in pupil-teacher ratio. It is observed that there were 70.79 pupils per teacher in 1986-87 and it was declining continuously except in three years i.e., 1988-89, 1994-95 and 1996-97. It reached to 33.28 pupils per teacher by 2007-2008. This figure is close to the pupil teacher ratio of 40 recommended by the government for aided schools. It is desirable that the present ratio is brought down further. Finally it gradually decreased and reached to 33.28 by the year 2007-08.

E. Pupil-Teacher Ratio in Upper Primary Education

The data relating to men, women and total teachers appointed in upper primary education and also teacher pupil ratio in Visakhapatnam District during the period 1986-87 to 2007-08 are presented in Table – 4.

The index of male teachers appointed has steadily increased up to 1992-93 and stood at 114. By the next year it has declined to 98. Afterwards, again it increased gradually to 150 by the year 1997-98. But in the next two years it has declined again and stood in 115 by 1999-2000. From 2000-01 onwards, it started

Table 4: No. of Teachers Appointed in Upper Primary Schools of Visakhapatnam District during 1986-87 to 2007-08

Year	*Men*	*Percen-tage*	*Index*	*Women*	*Percen-tage*	*Index*	*Total*	*Percen-tage*	*Index*	*Pupil teacher ratio*
Before DPEP		1986-87 = 100								
1986-87	664	57.24	100	496	42.76	100	1160	100	100	65.86
1987-88	661	57.33	100	492	42.67	99	1153	100	99	66.69
1988-89	673	58.32	101	481	41.68	97	1154	100	99	67.57
1989-90	673	58.32	101	481	41.68	97	1154	100	99	69.01
1990-91	760	60.70	114	492	39.30	99	1252	100	108	64.67
1991-92	754	60.86	114	485	39.14	98	1239	100	107	65.37
1992-93	759	60.91	114	487	39.09	98	1246	100	107	57.91
1993-94	650	57.07	98	489	42.93	99	1139	100	98	64.38
1994-95	698	58.56	105	494	41.44	100	1192	100	103	58.30
1995-96	818	58.55	123	579	41.45	117	1397	100	120	52.37
1996-97	867	58.54	131	614	41.46	124	1481	100	128	51.05
1997-98	997	58.51	150	707	41.49	143	1704	100	147	46.73
After DPEP		1997-98 = 100								
1998-99	1262	58.53	127	894	41.47	126	2156	100	127	42.40
1999-00	1150	58.52	115	815	41.48	115	1965	100	115	44.56
2000-01	1272	58.54	128	901	41.46	127	2173	100	128	43.97
2001-02	1280	49.21	128	1321	50.79	187	2601	100	153	35.39
2002-03	1609	51.46	161	1518	48.54	215	3127	100	184	37.66
2003-04	1617	51.84	162	1502	48.16	212	3119	100	183	36.59
2004-05	1811	53.50	182	1574	46.50	223	3385	100	199	34.78
2005-06	1892	54.68	190	1568	45.32	222	3460	100	203	35.01
2006-07	2046	52.47	205	1853	47.53	262	3899	100	229	33.20
2007-08	2126	52.03	213	1960	47.97	277	4086	100	240	31.65
Growth Rates										
Before DPEP		2.8			2.5			2.6		
After DPEP		7.1			9.7			8.2		
Total		6.2			7.6			6.8		

Source: Commissioner and Director of School Education, Hyderabad & District Educational Officer, Visakhapatnam.

raising and continuously moved in that way up to 2007-08 and stood at 213, which is all time high in male teachers appointed.

The index of women teachers appointed started declining from 100 in 1986-87 to 97 by 1989-90. In the next year it increased to 99, but immediately it decreased in the next two years and stood at 98 by 192-93. From 1993-94 onwards up to 1997-98 the index gradually increased to 143. From 1998-99 to 2007-08 the index has shown fluctuations and finally it stood at 277 in 2007-08, which is all time high as in men teachers index.

Regarding the total teachers appointed the index has steadily declined from 100 in 1986-87 to 99 in 1989-90. In 1990-91 it increased to 108, followed by reducing trend up to 1993-94. From 1994-95 onwards up to 1997-98 it increased from 103 to 147. Then, again the index has shown decreasing in the next two years. Further, it increased from 128 in 2000-01 to 184 in 2002-03. Except in the next year in which the index decreased, it increasing during the remaining period, i.e., from 2004-05 to 2007-08. Like in men and women teachers, the last year index is all time high.

The quality indicator of education, i.e., pupil teacher ratio was also examined. The teacher pupil ratio increased from 65.86 in 1986-87 to 69.01 in 1989-90. Up to 1993-94 it has fluctuated, but from 1994-95 to 1998-99 it gradually decreased from 58.30 to 42.40. From 1999-2000 onwards up to 2005-06 the ratio shows ups and downs frequently. In the last two years it decreased and ended as 31.65 in 2007-08, which is the best year for this indicator.

Impact of DPEP

To study the impact of DPEP in the district, we have adopted a 'before and after' approach. Thus data on several variables are provided for the period prior to the introduction of DPEP (in 1998-99) and since, considering the annual growth rate of schools, we find that for the pre DPEP period (1986-87 to 1997-98), it was 1.4 per cent and for the post DPEP period (1998-99 to 2007-08), it was 0.9 per cent. Though the programme has a positive impact on the number of schools set up in the district, but it is not significant (Table-1).

In respect of enrollment of children (6-11) the DPEP has had a negative impact. The pre DPEP period witnessed a negative growth rate of 1.7 per cent. During the post DPEP period it increased to -4.3 per cent (Table-1).

The positive effect of DPEP noticed in respect of primary education could also be noticed in case of upper primary education. Thus, the annual growth rates of upper primary schools were 11.7 per cent and 3.2 per cent respectively for the post and pre DPEP periods. Also, the growth rate of enrollment of children between 11 and 13 years of age was better at 4.7 per cent in the post DPEP phase compared to 0.1 per cent in the pre DPEP phase.

Conclusion

The number of children per school has been decreasing substantially at primary level because of the increasing number of schools boosted by various incentives of the government of Andhra Pradesh. The mushroom growth of the unregistered convents is another reason for this tremendous growth of schools. The notion that private schools impart better education is gaining ground and this explains the large increase in the number of private schools. However, the rate of enrollment of children in the age group of 11-13 years (at upper primary level) has been decreasing which indicate heavy dropouts at the primary level. This suggests that a large section of population is still not giving as much value for upper primary education as they are giving to the primary education. This resulted in the lower per school enrollment that made the upper primary education economically unviable for the private management. The pupil teacher ratio though declined from 70.79 in 1986-87 to 42.87 by 2001-2002 is still high. This resulted in poor quality of education. Further the pupil teacher ratio declined to 33.28 by the year 2007-08. Even the favourable pupil teacher ratio is not attracting the masses to send their children for upper primary education and above. The DPEP initiated by the government has had a positive effect on the growth rate of schools and enrollment. The programme thereafter deserves to be paid even greater attention if an intension is to draw the child to the school and to retain him/her there.

NOTES

1 It may be noted that there was a great spurt in the number of schools established in the year 1995-96 (from 2321 to 2540) though most of them were closed the very next year (the number came down from 2540 to 2362) i.e. 1996-97. This was due to the abortive drive by the then project officer I.T.D.A. which was not approved and funded by the government a year later.

2 These variations shall not be taken seriously. Over the period many primary schools had become upper primary schools and even high schools. Similarly, many upper primary schools had become high schools. And the number of children in the primary sections of the upgraded primary schools and upper primary schools are not included in this data.

3 In fact for 4 years i.e., from 1992-93 to 1995-96 this proportion was as low as 40 per cent.

REFERENCES

1. Aggarwal, J.C. (1982): *Development and Planning of Modern Education with Special Reference to India,* Vikas Publishing House Pvt. Ltd., New Delhi.

2. Fordham, Paul (1992): *Education for All – An Expanded Vision,* UNESCO.

3. Grewal, J.S. (1998): *Early Childhood Education,* H.P. Bhargava Book House, Agra.

4. Lokanadha Reddy, G (2000): *Education of Children with Special Needs,* H.P. Bhargava Book House, Agra.

5. Singh and Surdarshan (1996): *Primary Education,* H.P. Bhargava Book House, Agra.

6. Tilak, J.B.G. (1995): Elementary Education in India – Problems and Perspective, *Margin,* Vol.27, July-September, pp.387-407.

4

URBAN-RURAL DISPARITIES IN LITERACY RATES IN INDIA: SOME DIMENSIONS

D. Pulla Rao, D. Francis** & P. Raj Kumar****

Introduction

Literacy is an important element of transformation and social, economic and political development. India today, in its critical stage of demographic evolution, badly stands in need of an accelerated pace of literacy transition which alone can serve the cause of continuing the menace of growing population which poses a serious danger to the progress of the country. A thrust on rural literacy assumes special significance in the context of India where more than 70 per cent of the India's population lives in rural areas. The number of rural illiterates in India is more than the total combined population of Japan, United Kingdom, Canada and Australia. India has undoubtedly recorded a phenomenal educational development since Independence. Urban literacy, has, no doubt, improved significantly. However, the malaise still persists. Rural areas characterized by a literate

* Professor, Dept. of Economics, Andhra University, Visakhapatnam.

** Teaching Associate, Dept. of Economics, Dr. B.R. Ambedkar University, Etcherla, Srikakulam, (A.P.)

*** Research Scholar, Dept. of Economics, Andhra University, Visakhapatnam.

majority continue to be primarily concentrated only in north east, north west and southern coastal areas while vast rural areas in the rest of the country have yet to free themselves from the curse of low rural literacy resulting in lower general literacy. In rural areas more than two-fifths of the population is still illiterate. Urban-rural literate ratio still calls for more vigorous efforts especially among the rural female population.

Definition of Literacy

The definition of literacy varies from country to country depending upon its existing social and educational patterns and upon different needs of urban and rural life. Literacy has been commonly accepted as a skill through which an individual possesses mastery over symbols in written form or able to code or decode written messages that is knowledge and acquire ability to read and write. However, literacy goes much beyond this accepted definition. The International Liaison Committee for Literacy has explained, "Literacy is not the simple reading of a word or set of associated symbols of sounds, but an act of critical understanding of any situation in the World" (UNESCO 1972).

United Nations Development Programme defines literates as those who can with understanding; both read and write, a short, simple statement related to their everyday life. According to this definition, the least developed countries of the world had an average adult literacy rate (i.e. the percentage of people aged 15 and above) of 53.3 per cent in 2001 (U.N. 2003). The developed and less developed countries presented a contrast with regard to levels of literacy. Although non-availability of comparable specific data on literacy of various countries restricts our analysis in this regard yet it is possible to state with reasonable confidence that while the developed countries are fortunate in having universal adult literacy, in case of the less and least developed countries the corresponding figures are depressingly low. Developed countries like U.S.A., Canada, Japan, Australia etc. achieved almost universal literacy and education with a negligible proportion of illiterates. Developing countries, on the threshold of development, exhibited an adult literacy rate of 74.5 percent (U.N. 2003).

The most recent Indian census of 2001, however a registered a literacy rate of 65.20 per cent which varies considerably from the above mentioned U.N. figures. This is so because the 2001 India census defines literate as "a person aged seven and above who can both read and write with understanding in any language". A person, who can only read but cannot write, is not deemed to be literate. It is not necessary that to be treated as literate, a person should have received any formal education or passed any minimum educational standard. Literacy could also have been achieved through adult classes or through any non-formal educational system.

Trends of Literacy in India

All India average of percentage of literacy in the country was 5.36 per cent in 1901. The literacy ratio of male was 9.80 per cent and female less than one (0.60). In 1931 the average literacy rate was 9.51. During 30 years of period there was no more change in this rate. The drastic change started after 1941.

Table 1: Literacy in India (1901-2001)

Year	*Age Group*	*In Million*			*In Percentage*		
		Population	*Illiterate*	*Literate*	*Person*	*Male*	*Female*
1901	All	235.1	225.5	12.6	5.36	9.8	0.6
1911	All	248.2	233.5	14.7	5.92	10.6	1
1921	All	246.7	229	17.7	7.17	12.2	1.8
1931	All	273.4	247.4	26	9.51	15.6	2.9
1941	All	312	261.8	50.2	16.09	25	7.3
1951	5 and above	316.1	300	60.19	19.04	27.2	8.9
1961	5 and above	372.84	267.3	105.52	28.3	40.4	15.3
1971	5 and above	468.6	307.1	161.41	34.45	45.95	22
1981	7 and above	581.78	340.7	241.03	41.43	56.5	29.8
1991	7 and above	688.16	328.8	359.28	52.21	64.1	39.3
2001	7 and above	869.15	302.44	566.71	65.2	75.8	54.2

Sources: Census India, Various Issues.

In the period from 1901 to 1931, the spread of literacy in India was almost stagnant. In 30 years, it is increased from 5.36 per cent to 9.51 per cent. After 1931, there was steady growth in the literacy percentage. In the period between 1931 and 2001, the literacy expansion was almost seven times i.e. from 9.51 per cent to 65.20 per cent. This positive trends can be seen both in, case of male as well as female literacy in the Table -1.

Urban-Rural Literacy Rates in India

After independence, India has recorded a significant development in the field of literacy and education. Total eradication of illiteracy is an elusive goal in India. The overall literacy rate has shown a steady increase in every successive decade from 1951 to 2001 has rose from 18.33 per cent in 1951 to 65.38 per cent in 2001. Rural literacy in India increased from 12.10 per cent in 1951 to 59.40 per cent in 2001 (Table-2). A comparison of increase in overall and rural literacy rates during the second half of the 20th century is quite significant. Both have shown a steady increase in every successive decade. The overall and rural literacy rates in 1951 were 18.33 and 12.10 respectively. In 2001 they stood at 65.38 and 59.40 respectively. The urban character of the former British administration was fairly responsible for creating a wide gap between urban and rural literacy. The ratio between urban and rural literates which was 2.86 : 1.00 in 1951 has got reduced to 1.35 : 1.00 in 2001. The contrasts have been sharper in urban-rural female literate ratio than urban rural male literate ratio from 1951 to 2001. Urban-rural female literate ratio has experienced continuous decline since 1951 and it has come down from 4.58 : 1.00 in 1951 to 1.57 : 1.00 in 2001. The urban-rural gap in literacy is attributed to appalling poverty in rural areas, even when education is free to all children up to 14 years in India.

Table - 2: Urban-Rural Literacy Rates and Ratios in India: 1951- 2001

Year	*Males*	*Urban Rural Male Literate Ratio*	*Females*	*Urban Rural Female Literate Ratio*	*Persons*	*Urban Rural Literate Ratio*
1951		2.40:1.00		4.58:1.00		2.86:1.00
Rural	19.02		4.87		12.10	
Urban	45.60		22.33		34.59	
Total	27.16		8.86		18.33	
1961		1.92:1.00		4.01:1.00		2.42:1.00
Rural	34.30		10.10		22.50	
Urban	66.00		40.50		54.40	
Total	40.40		15.35		28.30	
1971		1.44:1.00		3.15:1.00		2.16:1.00
Rural	48.60		15.50		27.90	
Urban	69.80		48.80		60.20	
Total	45.96		21.97		34.45	
1981		1.55:1.00		2.59:1.00		1.87:1.00
Rural	49.60		21.70		36.00	
Urban	76.70		56.30		67.20	
Total	56.38		29.76		43.57	
1991		1.40:1.00		2.09:1.00		1.64:1.00
Rural	57.90		30.60		44.70	
Urban	81.10		64.00		73.10	
Total	64.13		39.29		52.21	
2001		1.21:1.00		1.57:1.00		1.35:1.00
Rural	71.40		46.70		59.40	
Urban	86.70		73.20		80.30	
Total	75.85		54.16		65.38	

Source: Census of India, 2001.

State-wise Urban-Rural Disparities in Literacy Rates in India

The average literacy rate of our country was 65.20 per cent in 2001. The literacy rate among male and female was 76 and 54 per cent respectively. But in Table -3 there are many disparities among the states. On the one side the Kerala has the highest literacy rate of 90.92 per cent followed by Maharashtra (77.27%), Himachal Pradesh (75.915%), Tamil Nadu (73.47%), Punjab (69.75%), west Bengal (69.22%), Karnataka (67.04%), and Gujarat was (66.43%). Rests of the states have literacy levels below the national average. The lowest literacy level is in Bihar (47.53 %) followed by Utter Pradesh (57.36%), Rajasthan (61.03%), Andhra Pradesh (61.11 %), Madhya Pradesh (64.08%) and Assam (64.28%).

Table 3: State-wise Urban - Rural Literacy Ratios of Male and Female In India: 2001 Census

Census-2001	*Total*	*Male*	*Female*	*Rural*	*Urban*
Andhra Pradesh	61	71	51	55	76
Assam	64	72	56	61	86
Bihar	48	60	34	44	73
Gujarat	70	81	59	59	79
Haryana	69	79	56	69	80
Himachal Pradesh	77	86	68	74	90
Karnataka	67	76	57	60	81
Kerala	91	94	88	90	93
Madhya Pradesh	64	77	50	58	80
Maharashtra	77	86	68	71	86
Orissa	64	76	51	60	81
Punjab	70	76	64	65	79
Rajasthan	61	76	44	56	77
Tamil Nadu	73	82	65	67	82
Uttar Pradesh	57	70	43	54	71
West Bengal	69	78	60	64	82
All India	65	76	54	59	80

Source: Census of India, 2001.

The national average of Literacy in urban areas was 80.06 per cent in 2001, the highest rate being in Kerala (93.38%) followed by Himachal Pradesh (89.63%), Assam (85.95%). Remaining other states had literacy rate below the national average.

The national average of literacy in rural areas in 2001 was 59.21 per cent, the highest literacy being in Kerala (90.05%) followed by Himachal Pradesh (74.38 %), Maharashtra (70.84%), Haryana (68.82%), Tamil Nadu (66.66%), Punjab (65.16%), West Bengal (64.06%), Assam (60.92%) and Orissa (60.44%). The lowest literacy rates in rural India were in Bihar (44.42%), Uttar Pradesh (53.68%), Rajasthan (55.92%), Madhya Pradesh (58.10%) and Gujarat (58.53%).

Progress of Scheduled Caste and Scheduled Tribe Literacy in Urban and Rural India

Urban-rural disparity has been decreasing significantly among both the scheduled castes and scheduled tribes since 1961. The disparity has been decreasing in both males and females in both the social groups. Among scheduled tribe population the urban-rural differential in female population has decreased most impressively. The urban-rural disparity among scheduled tribe females has decreased from 4.64: 1.00 in 1961 to 1.84: 1.00 in 2001 (Table - 4). The decrease of the disparity is a positive sign. This situation may be due to so many policies and programmes implemented by the Government of India after Independence to improve the literacy and enrollment of scheduled tribe population through concessions and reservations and awareness campaigns to improve the literacy of scheduled tribe population especially for the improvement of literacy among scheduled tribe females. It is most encouraging to find that in more recent times, the females from the rural poor have been awakened through public awareness campaigns and the disparity has reduced significantly.

Though a number of strategies have been used in India to meet the educational needs of the tribal students, yet they are inadequate. Therefore, there is a need to take effective measures on the following lines.

Table - 4: Literacy Rates of Scheduled Caste and Scheduled Tribe Population by Sex and Residence in India: 1961 -2001

State / Union Territory	*Scheduled Caste Population*			*Urban rural SC literate*	*Scheduled Tribe Population*			*Urban rural ST Literate*
	Total	*Rural*	*Urban*		*Total*	*Rural*	*Urban*	
1961	10.27	8.89	21.81	2.45:1.00	8.53	8.16	22.41	2.75:1.00
1971	14.67	12.77	28.65	2.24:1.00	11.30	10.68	28.84	2.70:1.00
1981	21.38	18.48	36.60	1.98:1.00	16.35	14.92	37.93	2.54:1.00
1991	37.41	33.25	55.11	1.66:1.00	29.60	27.38	56.60	2.07:1.00
2001	54.69	51.16	68.12	1.33:1.00	47.10	45.02	69.09	1.53:1.00
Males								
1961	16.96	15.06	32.21	2.14:1.00	13.83	13.37	30.43	2.27:1.00
1971	22.36	20.04	38.93	1.94:1.00	17.63	16.92	37.09	2.19:1.00
1981	31.12	27.91	47.54	1.70:1.00	24.52	22.94	47.60	2.07:1.00
1991	49.91	45.95	66.06	1.45:1.00	40.65	38.45	66.56	1.73:1.00
2001	66.64	63.66	77.93	1.22:1.00	59.17	57.39	77.77	1.35:1.00
Females								
1961	3.29	2.52	10.04	3.98:1.00	3.16	2.90	13.45	4.64:1.00
1971	6.44	5.06	16.99	3.36:1.00	4.85	4.36	19.64	4.50:1.00
1981	10.93	8.45	24.34	2.88:1.00	8.04	6.81	27.32	4.01:1.00
1991	23.76	19.45	42.29	2.17:1.00	18.19	16.02	45.66	2.85:1.00
2001	41.90	37.84	57.49	1.52:1.00	34.76	32.44	59.87	1.84:1.00

Source: Censuses of India for various years.

1. Provision of more schooling facilities, particularly model schools.
2. Undertake teacher training and orientation about tribal needs and educational programmes.
3. Re-orienting curriculum, content and medium of instruction suited to the tribal children.
4. Provision of teaching/learning materials.
5. Innovative methods to be developed for supervision of schools.
6. Micro planning and effective implementation.

Table 5: Percentage of Literate Persons Aged 7 Years and Above in Rural and Urban Areas by Social Group based on 55th Rounds

State	*ST*		*SC*		*OBC*		*Others*		*All*	
	Rural	*Urban*	*Rural*	*Urban*	*Rural*	*Urban*	*Rural*	*Urban*	*Rural*	*Urban*
Andhra Pradesh	26.1	57.5	39.4	67.3	42.5	68.8	62.3	82.2	45.8	74.5
Assam	71.6	85.3	69.7	69.2	72.9	80.1	66.7	89.7	69.0	86.1
Bihar	34.4	69.7	25.7	47.5	42.4	63.6	59.2	84.0	41.8	69.6
Gujarat	50.3	66.8	55.5	71.2	55.8	76.7	75.0	91.2	62.0	84.1
Haryana	48.3	93.7	50.7	53.4	58.1	75.5	67.7	84.6	61.2	76.6
Himachal Pradesh	73.1	85.4	67.7	81.2	81.1	78.9	74.2	93.3	73.4	90.2
Karnataka	41.3	53.9	44.3	65.6	56.6	79.6	65.2	88.9	55.9	82.1
Kerala	80.2	97.5	79.1	87.9	88.3	92.3	94.1	96.4	89.4	93.7
Madhya Pradesh	32.4	59.8	46.0	64.0	55.6	73.5	67.8	87.9	49.8	77.5
Maharashtra	49.9	79.4	63.5	80.1	69.0	83.0	72.2	88.3	66.5	86.0
Orissa	33.1	55.2	47.8	53.2	61.6	79.4	73.9	85.8	53.8	75.5
Punjab	69.2	75.5	51.9	60.1	63.5	80.3	70.4	87.2	62.5	78.9
Rajasthan	38.4	69.1	36.7	56.0	46.3	70.0	57.8	84.4	46.5	75.1
Tamil Nadu	50.8	95.7	55.9	74.1	66.3	84.0	81.7	92.9	63.8	84.5
Uttar Pradesh	47.7	78.5	40.7	58.1	47.6	59.3	64.9	79.7	51.1	70.1
West Bengal	41.6	63.2	57.1	67.4	74.6	81.2	64.7	86.2	61.7	82.2
All India	42.2	70.0	46.6	66.2	54.8	75.3	67.7	86.5	56.0	79.8

Source: NSSO Report No. 473: Literacy and Levels of Education in India 1999-2000.

State-wise Urban -Rural Disparities in Literacy Rates among Social Groups in India

Table-5 presents distributions of persons aged 7 years and above by major social groups. The pattern of variation in the literacy rate was almost the same in rural as well as urban areas. However, in rural India, the literacy rate was the lowest for persons belonging to STs (42%) followed by persons belonging to SCs (47%). But in urban India, the literacy rate was the lowest for SC groups (66%) followed by ST Groups (70%). In both the sectors the literacy rate was the highest for persons belonging to group 'others' (Upper Castes).

The urban-rural bias can be seen in the literacy as is reflected in Table- 5. The urban literacy stood at 70 per cent where as it was just 42.2 per cent in rural area. The gap is explicit more in state like Tamil Nadu where in urban literacy stood at 95.7, which is far higher than just 50.8 per cent for rural Tamil Nadu.

State-wise Urban -Rural Disparities in Literacy Rates among Religions Groups in India

The distribution of persons aged 7 years and above by each sector and religions are shown in Table - 6. It is noticed that the literacy rate was lower in rural India for 'Islam' compared to other religions. Literacy rate for all the religious groups, as revealed again for the first time in 2001 Census, were very encouraging, shattering many myths earlier when such a data set was not available for the country as a whole. The literacy among Hindus (65.1%) was slightly better than the national average (64.8%) for all religious groups combined. Among Muslims the literacy rate is 59.1 per cent, below the national average. The highest literacy rate is recorded among the Jains (94.1%), followed by Christians (80.3%), Buddhists (72.7%) and Sikhs (69.4%). Against the exiting popular perception, the female literacy rate among different religious groups does not show wide variations. Among the Muslims, for instance, the literacy rate among the females was stagnant 50.1 per cent, below the national average of 53.7 per cent. Slightly better is the females' literacy rate among the Hindus (53.2%), again below the national average.

The highest literacy rate among the females was recorded among the Jains (90.6%), like their male counterparts. Female literacy rate among Christians was 76.2 per cent, followed by Sikhs (63.1%) (Census, 2001).

The 55th round NSSO report reveal the difference in literacy indifferent religions communities. The literacy rate in Christians is the highest both in Rural as well as urban areas. Hindus stand at the second place where as Muslim occupy the third place with 52 and 70 per cent literacy respectively in rural as well as urban areas (Table-6).

Table 6: Percentage of Literate Persons Aged 7 years and Above in by Religions Group based on 55th Round

State	*Hinduism*		*Islam*		*Christianity*		*Others*		*All*	
	Rural	*Urban*	*Rural*	*Urban*	*Rural*	*Urban*	*Rural*	*Urban*	*Rural*	*Urban*
Andhra Pradesh	45.4	75.0	51.0	70.7	51.5	78.9	55.5	96.1	45.8	74.5
Assam	74.5	87.0	59.4	79.7	53.5	80.5	85.7	-	69.0	86.1
Bihar	42.6	70.7	36.1	61.1	44.7	83.5	41.3	96.0	41.8	69.6
Gujarat	61.8	83.7	69.1	82.7	62.5	94.2	-	-	62.0	84.1
Haryana	61.7	76.9	31.0	54.5	-	-	-	-	61.2	76.6
Himachal Pradesh	73.7	90.2	56.9	73.6	-	-	83.2	-	73.4	90.2
Karnataka	55.3	82.9	63.2	77.1	68.0	95.5	52.0	73.4	55.9	82.1
Kerala	88.4	94.2	87.2	91.0	95.1	95.8	-	-	89.4	93.7
Madhya Pradesh	49.1	77.5	60.3	73.6	66.5	89.1	-	61.3	49.8	77.5
Maharashtra	66.2	87.3	67.1	79.9	61.4	95.3	76.4	86.6	66.5	86.0
Orissa	53.7	76.6	67.1	56.7	48.5	63.7	62.6	-	53.8	75.5
Punjab	68.4	79.2	62.9	65.4	44.2	77.7	84.7	-	62.5	78.9
Rajasthan	46.7	76.0	38.4	64.9	-	100.00	47.8	92.6	46.5	75.1
Tamil Nadu	61.7	84.3	84.1	81.6	83.6	91.2	-	90.6	63.8	84.5
Uttar Pradesh	52.9	76.8	38.9	52.6	66.4	100.00	37.6	59.7	51.1	70.1
West Bengal	65.5	84.3	53.7	66.6	79.6	91.8	57.7	87.3	61.7	82.2
All India	55.7	81.1	52.1	69.8	73.7	91.1	54.2	87.1	56.0	79.8

Source: NSSO Report No. 473: Literacy and Levels of Education in India 1999-2000.

Conclusion

In India more than 70 per cent of the population is living in rural areas. The number of rural illiterates is more than the urban illiterates. There is no doubt that in India, there is a phenomenal development in education after independence. The population of literates in India increased from 12.6 millions in 1901 to 566.71 millions in 2001. The rural literacy in India increased from 12.10 per cent in 1951 to 59.40 per cent in 2001. The ratio between urban and rural literates which was 2.86 : 1.00 in 1951 was reduced to 1.35 : 1.00 in 2001. Kerala has the highest overall literacy rate of 90.92 per cent whereas the lowest literacy level is in Bihar (47.53%) as per 2001 census. The disparity of literacy rate has been decreasing in both males and females in both SCs and STs. In both urban and rural areas, the literacy rate was the highest for persons belonging to the 'Others' group (i.e. Other than SC, ST, and OBC). The literacy rate was lower in rural India for 'Islam' compared to other religions. The literacy rate in Christians is the highest in rural as well as urban areas.

We conclude that urban-rural literate ratio still calls for more vigorous efforts especially among the rural female population. Much still remains to be done. Rural women need to wake up and actively participate in the movement for universalisation of literacy. Special effort needs to be paid to promote rural literacy among various groups comprising SCs and STs especially among the female components of these groups.

REFERENCES

1. Krishna G. and Shyam, M. (1978): "Regional Aspects of Urban and Rural Differential in India, 1971", *The Journal of Development Areas*, Vol .13, No.1, pp.11-21.

2. Krishna, G. and Shyam, M. (1973): "Spatial Perspective on Progress of Female Literacy in India: 1901-71" *Pacific Viewpoint*, Vol.13, pp.22-36.

3. Mehta, Arun C. (2006): Elementary Education in India, Analytical Report 2004-2005, Published by National Institute of Education Planning and Administration and Ministry of Human Resource Development, GOI.

4. Singh, Nina. (1998): "Female Literacy in India: The Emerging Trends," *Population Geography*, vol.20.Nos.1&2, June-Dec.1998, pp. 23-26.

5. UNESCO. (1990): *Final Report of World Conference on Education for All: Meeting Basic Learning Needs*, 5-9 March, 1990, Thailand.

6. United Nations. (2005): *Economic and Social Survey of Asia and the Pacific 2005*, Economic and Social Commission for Asia and The Pacific, New York, 2005, pp.220.

7. United Nations Development Programme (2003). *Human Development Report*, 2003, Oxford University Press, New York.

8. United Nations Development Programme. (2004): *World Development Report*, 2004, Oxford University Press, Oxford.

9. UNDP. (2004): "Human Development Report 2004", Cultural Liberty in Today's Diverse World, New York: Oxford University Press.

5

EDUCATIONAL DROPOUT OF CHILDREN AT PRIMARY STAGE IN EAST GODAVARI DISTRICT OF ANDHRA PRADESH

D. Narayana Rao, V. Seshagiri Rao** & P. Arun Kumar****

Primary education is considered as highly essential for eradication of poverty, fostering economic progress, managing the growth of population and creating a clean and healthy environment. Realizing the need of primary education, the Baroda ruler Late Maharaja Sayaji Rao Gaikwad introduced compulsory primary education in his state. Inspired by the efforts of the Baroda ruler, Gopala Krishna Gokhale submitted a proposal to the Imperial Legislature to make primary education free and compulsory throughout India. But, he did not succeed in his efforts at that time. In 1945, Mahatma Gandhi in his letter to Pandit Jawaharlal Nehru, pleaded for making the villages to be the focal point of free India's political, structural, economic and developmental policies. But Nehru wrote back to him by describing that Indian villages are intellectually and culturally backward from where no progress could be made. In a way, Pandit Jawaharlal Nehru

* Lecturer, Govt. Degree College, Narsipatnam, Visakhapatnam, A.P.

** Associate Professor, Dept. of Economics, Andhra University, Visakhapatnam, A.P.

*** Professor, Dept. of Politics & Public Administration, Andhra University Campus, Kakinada, East Godavari District, A.P.

was right as the villages were languishing under illiteracy and ignorance. Founding fathers of the constitution realizing the need for primary education set a time frame to provide "free and compulsory education" to all the children up to the age of 14 by 1960. However, this was not achieved even after 56 years of independence though the target dates were revised several times, 1970, 1976, 1990, 1995 and 2000. Now the government's target is, that all children should complete five years of primary schooling by 2007, and eight years of elementary schooling by 2010.

Although, the policy intentions were well articulated, there was no comprehensive operational plan. Though efforts are being taken to improve the status of primary education in India, the child in the classroom is not focused fully. Unless the child is focused as the centre of classroom activity dropouts and stagnation will continue to exist. An analysis of data on primary education reveals that there is failure both on enrollment and on dropout fronts. The educational policies could neither ensure cent per cent enrollment nor prevent the incidence of dropouts. Among the failures in the achievement of compulsory primary education the turn dominant factors appear to be the dropouts and repeaters. Some pupils, leave the system at different points without completing primary stage and it is designated as dropouts or push outs while some pupils repeat the same grade and it is called stagnation or repeaters, while the concept of stagnation is simple and straight forward, the dropout phenomenon creates certain conceptual problems.

The National Policy on Education (NPE), 1986 and the programme of Action, 1992 reiterated the commitment or retaining the children in schools at least up to class VIII. The question of dropouts may represent the insufficiency of the Educational System and this leads to the wastage of the scarce resources in a developing country like India. We consider enrollment as the indicator for various levels or stages as well as various classes. The target is still to enroll all children of 6 years age in class I and ensure their continuance till they get through class V. However, this issue has to be more thoroughly enquired in to as the reasons for dropout are varied and diverse across the length and breadth of the vast country like India which exhibits varied and diverse socio-cultural backgrounds. Keeping this objective in mind, an attempt is made in this paper to examine the status of dropouts and also the causes for dropouts at primary education in East Godavari District of Andhra Pradesh.

Main Objectives

There are three major objectives as stated below:

1) To study the dropout rates at primary level in East Godavari District during the period 1997-98 to 2001-02 and to find out the causes for dropouts in the district.
2) To examine whether the socio-economic factors have any impact on the dropouts, and
3) To examine the regional heterogeneity in dropouts.

Methodology

East Godavari District is purposefully selected since it happens to be the author's native district about which he got a fairly comprehensive understanding of its socio-economic backdrop.

For administrative convenience, this district divided in to 59 mandals (including 2 urban mandals) and 5revenue divisions. The analysis is coming out both mandal wise and revenue division wise. The quantitative data are obtained from the records of the District Educational Officer, Kakinada. And the primary information on the causes for dropouts is obtained from about 200 primary school teachers spread over in 20 mandals of which 5 mandals are from the tribal area.

Dropout Rate

Dropout rates are taken as 100 minus the ratio of enrollment in class V in the year 't' to the enrollment in Class I in the base year i.e., (t-4) for primary level. In calculating the dropout rate in mandal wise the standard formula has been used, i.e., Dropout rate for Class I to (1+n) in the year t to (t+n)

$$\text{Dropout rate} = 100 - \frac{\text{Enrollment in class (1+n) in the year (t+n)}}{\text{Enrollment in class 1 to year t}}$$

For the calculation of Crude Dropout Rates (CDR) the following formula is used.

Dropout rate, class I as base year.

$$\text{Dropout rate} = 1- \frac{Et^{c+1}}{Et^{1}} \acute{}100$$

Here Et^{c+1} is enrollment in class C+1 in year t and Et^{1} is enrollment in class '1' in the year 't'.

The analysis has been carried out for primary classes, i.e., I to V during the period 1997-1998 to 2001-2002.

Table -1 shows the data in mandal wise dropout rates in East Godavari District. Among boys, the highest dropout rate was recorded in Gangavaram mandal with 86.49 per cent followed by Y. Ramavaram mandal with 84.30 per cent, while the lowest dropout rate was recorded in Mamidikuduru mandal with 22.06 per cent. In total about 61 per cent mandals are in the range of 45 per cent to 65 per cent. As many as 15 mandals (25.42 per cent) are in the range of 25 to 45. Eight mandals (including Gangavaram and Y. Ramavaram), i.e., Maredumilli, Rampachodavaram, Devipatnam, Addategala, Rajavommangi and Thondangi mandals are in the range of 65 per cent and above. The eight mandals except Thondangi mandal are tribal mandals. Thondangi mandal is a remote, upland and rural mandal.

This clearly indicates, how the socio-economic factors influence the dropout rates. Another tribal mandal i.e., Gangavaram is represented by the highest dropout rate. It is interesting to note that rural based, Mamidikuduru mandal has recorded the lowest dropout rate. Geographic factors, economic status and literacy levels of the population must have accounted for the situation in Mamidikuduru mandal which need thorough enquiring on those times.

The highest dropout rate is recorded in Maredumilli mandal among girls with slightly more than 88 per cent and lowest dropout rate is in Mamidikuduru mandal with only 20.91 per cent. About 44 per cent of mandals are in the range of 25 to 45 per cent dropout rates. Nearly 39 per cent of mandals are in the range of 45 to 65 per cent dropout rate. Only four mandals Addategala, Rajavommangi tribal mandals, Thondagi and Kirlampudi, rural mandals are in the range of 65 to 75 per cent of dropout rate. The five mandals Gangavaram, Y. Ramavaram, Devipatnam, Rampachodavaram including the highest dropout rate mandal Maredumilli are in the range of 75 and above per cent dropout rate. These five tribal mandals clearly show that the socio-economic and geographic factors are influencing the dropout rates in the area.

Table-1: Mandal-wise Dropout Rates at Primary Level of East Godavari District during 1997-98 to 2001-2002

S.No.	*Name of the Mandal*	*Boys*	*Girls*	*Total*
1	*2*	*3*	*4*	*5*
1	Maredumilli	78.90	88.02	83.04
2	Y. Ramavaram	84.30	84.14	84.23
3	Addategala	70.83	73.75	73.28
4	Rajavommangi	65.62	70.90	68.09
5	Kotananduru	56.46	59.27	57.80
6	Tuni	32.38	38.03	35.18
7	Thondangi	65.86	65.96	65.91
8	Gollaprolu	64.10	63.34	63.72
9	Sankavaram	61.36	57.50	59.44
10	Prathipadu	51.68	50.52	51.09
11	Yeleswaram	46.39	51.13	48.86
12	Gangavaram	86.49	84.29	85.40
13	Rampachodavaram	76.84	78.06	77.43
14	Devipatnam	76.15	79.28	77.80
15	Seethanagaram	55.92	55.20	55.56
16	Korukonda	57.35	56.45	56.89

(contd.)

1	2	3	4	5
17	Gokavaram	60.90	55.63	58.27
18	Jaggampeta	64.10	62.71	63.40
19	Kirlampudi	63.98	67.32	65.73
20	Peddapuram	51.60	43.04	47.10
21	Pithapuram	57.58	57.19	57.38
22	U.Kothapilli	57.53	58.41	57.99
23	Kakinada®	50.04	47.70	48.85
24	Kakinada(U)	56.37	49.38	52.69
25	Samalkota	47.10	49.51	48.35
26	Rangampeta	53.45	50.49	51.87
27	Gandepalli	51.34	49.67	50.44
28	Rajanagaram	58.11	53.39	55.61
29	Rajahmundry®	45.29	43.76	44.54
30	Rajahmundry(U)	49.57	48.23	48.92
31	Kadiam	47.12	43.77	45.39
32	Mandapeta	46.61	38.35	42.53
33	Anaparthi	37.78	38.86	38.32
34	Biccaavolu	45.54	37.84	41.57
35	Pedapudi	50.44	44.66	47.45
36	Karapa	36.92	42.68	39.82
37	Tallarevu	47.41	41.12	44.06
38	Kajuluru	47.97	44.18	46.04
39	Ramachandrapuram	45.67	44.03	44.86
40	Rayavaram	48.46	43.49	45.90
41	Kapileswarapuram	45.27	38.01	41.62
42	Alamuru	45.79	43.23	44.50
43	Atreyapuram	44.62	51.72	48.31
44	Ravulapalem	39.55	37.97	38.75
45	Pamarru	42.01	41.64	41.82
46	Kothapeta	42.83	41.81	42.32
47	P. Gannavaram	42.11	41.56	41.84
48	Ambajipeta	46.23	47.18	46.71
49	Ainavilli	48.40	49.52	49.40

1	2	3	4	5
50	Mummidivaram	38.39	36.77	37.57
51	I. Polavaram	47.63	43.87	45.72
52	Katrenikona	48.69	47.91	48.33
53	Uppalaguptam	38.29	43.65	40.95
54	Amalapuram	27.87	28.52	28.20
55	Allavaram	47.77	48.54	48.14
56	Mamidikuduru	22.06	20.91	21.49
57	Razole	42.39	41.06	41.70
58	Malikipuram	43.18	42.16	42.67
59	Sakhinetipalli	29.10	36.45	32.84

Source: District Educational Officer, East Godavari, Kakinada.

From the above data one can easily see that the Gangavaram mandal reported the highest dropout rates for boys, and in total whereas in the case of girls the highest dropout rate could be seen in Maredumilli mandal. In the case of Gangavaram mandal the dropout rates are 86.49 per cent (for boys), 84.29 per cent (for girls) and 85.40 per cent (for total). On the average, above 85 per cent dropout rate is recorded in this tribal mandal. And in the same way the lowest dropout rates are recorded in the Mamidikuduru mandal, viz., 22.06 per cent (for Boys), 20.91 per cent (for girls) and 21.49 per cent (for total).

From the Table –1 it could be seen that more than 80 per cent of dropout rate is recorded in three mandals, i.e., Gangavaram, Y. Ramavaram and Maredumilli. The data describes that out of 100 children who took admission in Class I in the year 1997-98 more than 80 children dropped out without reaching Class V by 2001-02. At the same time another set of three mandals Devipatnam, Rampachodavaram and Addategala report more than 70 per cent dropout rate. The figures for other mandals do not present a different picture. There is a strong evidence of very high rate of dropouts contributing to high level of wastage at primary/elementary stage of education in East Godavari District.

It is clear that only 15 per cent of the enrolled children complete primary education in Gangavaram mandal, and 16 to

17 per cent in Y. Ramavaram and Maredumilli mandals. It means that the objective of the Universalization of Elementary/Primary Education has not been reached even one fifth of the target set for the year 1995, as per the NPE 1986 even in 2001-02. It is clear that the enrollment of children is not the only criterion for achievement of universalisation of elementary education (UEE) but also it is a great task to retain the student up to V class. It is also clear that, despite a high coverage of enrollment in class I the target of achieving UEE does not seem to be possible in the near future in the wake of high dropout rates as seen in East Godavari District.

While calculating Crude Dropout Rates (CDR) in some instances, negative signs have been observed indicating that intake of children has been higher than the base year figures. The phenomenon is quite possibly due to either failures of the children in the higher class, or direct admission of quite a few children in the higher classes (class II or above). However, there is no detention of students in the primary schools, once a child gets admitted in class I he will taken the common examination only at the end of Class VII. A student's promotion is based on his attendance only. The detention system is followed only in Private Un-aided Schools. In the case of Private Un-aided Schools a child gets promotion only on his performance at the year-end examinations. Similarly, direct admission of children in Class II or above is possible only in private un-aided schools. The important limitation of our data is that we do not have dropout figures for Govt./Private Aided/Private Un-aided schools separately.

Table-2 presents the highest and the lowest crude dropout rate for boys and girls for I-II classes for 1997-98 to 2001-02. The highest dropout rates among boys were recorded in Maredumilli mandal with 62 per cent in 1997-98, 55 per cent in 1998-99, 57 per cent in 1999-2000 continuously and again 51 per cent in 2001-2002. In 2000-2001 the highest dropout rate was recorded in Gangavaram mandal with 51 per cent. Maredumilli and Gangavarm are tribal mandals. To conclude, the highest dropout rate was recorded in Maredumilli mandal for boys in I-II classes for the entire period. The lowest crude dropout rate for boys

0.64 per cent was recorded in Uppalaguptam mandal during the total period with only 1.39 per cent crude dropout rate. Sakhinetipalli comes next to Uppalaguptam mandal.

As regards girls, the highest Crude Dropout Rate (CDR) was recorded again in Maredumilli mandal during 1999-200. Maredumilli and Y. Ramavaram are tribal mandals. The lowest Crude Dropout Rate for girls was recorded in Kadiam mandal in 1999-2000, 7 per cent in Mandapeta mandal (2001-02), 6 per cent in Mamidikuduru mandal (1997-98), 4 per cent in Sakhinetipalli mandal (2000-01), 0.21 per cent in Kakinada (urban) (1998-99). It is gratifying to note that Kadiam is the only mandal, which exhibited a nil crude dropout rate over time.

Table-2: Highest and Lowest Dropout Rates of Boys and Girls in Class I -II during 1997-98 and 2001-02

Year	*Boys*		*Girls*	
	Highest	*Lowest*	*Highest*	*Lowest*
1997-98	61.66 (Maredumilli)	6.65 (Kakinada(U))	58.60 (Y.Ramavaram)	6.16 (Mamidikuduru)
1998-99	55.18 (Maredumilli)	1.39 (Sakhinetipalli)	58.33 (Maredumilli)	0.21 (Kakinada(U)
1999-2000	57.17 (Maredumilli)	0.64 (Uppalaguptam)	73.41 (Maredumilli)	0.00 (Kadiam)
2000-2001	51.44 (Gangavaram)	3.15 (Mamidikuduru)	49.13 (Y.Ramavaram)	4.04 (Sakhinetipalli)
2001-2002	51.35 (Maredumilli)	5.11 (Rajahmundry (U))	48.49 (Maredumilli)	6.68 (Mandapeta)

Source: District Education Officer, East Godavari District, Kakinada.

In Table-3 the highest and lowest Crude Dropout Rates for boys and girls for I–III classes for 1997-98 to 2001-02 are presented. During the period the highest crude dropout rate is recorded as 80 per cent in 1998-99 and 75 per cent in 1999-2000 in Maredumilli mandal, 80 per cent in 1997-98, 79 per cent in 2000-01 in Y. Ramavaram mandal and 68 per cent in 2001-02 in Gangavaram mandal for boys. All these mandals fell in the tribal belt. The lowest CDR 1.14 per cent (1999-2000) and 5.57

per cent (2000-2001) are recorded continuously in Tallarevu mandal, which is a rural, plain and coastal mandal. In the case of girls the highest CDR of 84 per cent (1997-98), 82 per cent (1999-2000) and 2000-01 were recorded in Y Ramavaram mandal, which is a tribal mandal. This clearly shows the tribal background is the most responsible factor for the highest CDR for Classes I-III. And the lowest CDR was reported in Sakhinetipalli mandal with 4 per cent (2000-01) and zero per cent (1999-2000) was recorded in Anaparthi mandal, Mamidikuduru mandal reported very low CDRs twice with 8.11 per cent (1998-99), 10.22 per cent (1997-98). These three are plain and rural mandals.

Table 3: Highest and Lowest Dropout Rates of Boys and Girls in Class I–III during 1997-98 and 2001-02

Year	*Boys*		*Girls*	
	Highest	*Lowest*	*Highest*	*Lowest*
1997-98	79.52 (Y.Ramavaram)	16.76 (Kakinada (U)	84.47 (Y.Ramavaram)	10.22 (Mamidikuduru)
1998-99	79.92 (Maredumilli)	9.56 (Mamidikuduru)	79.57 (Maredumilli)	8.11 (Mamidikuduru)
1999-2000	74.95 (Maredumilli)	1.14 (Tallarevu)	82.12 (Y.Ramavaram)	0.00 (Anaparthi)
2000-2001	78.50 (Y.Ramavaram)	5.57 (Tallarevu)	81.94 (Y.Ramavaram)	3.92 (Sakhinetipalli)
2001-2002	68.43 (Gangavaram)	12.14 (P. Gannavaram)	66.94 (Gangavaram)	18.19 (P.Gannavaram)

Source: District Education Officer, East Godavari District, Kakinada

Table-4 presents the highest and the lowest CDRs of both boys and girls for I-IV classes. The highest CDR during this period for boys was recorded in Y. Ramavaram mandal with 85 per cent (1997-98). The lowest CDR was recorded in Anaparthi, P. Gannavaram and Mamidikuduru mandals. Among the girls the highest CDR 90 per cent was reported by Maredumilli mandal. The lowest CDR 12.2 per cent was recorded in Mamidikuduru mandal during the study period.

Table-4: Highest and Lowest Dropout Rates of Boys and Girls in Class I – IV during 1997-98 and 2001-02

Year	*Boys*		*Girls*	
	Highest	*Lowest*	*Highest*	*Lowest*
1997-98	84.90 (Y.Ramavaram)	12.82 (Anaparthi)	87.48 (Y.Ramavaram)	18.59 (Anaparthi)
1998-99	83.93 (Maredumilli)	8.38 (Anaparthi)	82.28 (Y.Ramavaram)	14.89 (Anaparthi)
1999-2000	82.58 (Maredumilli)	13.29 (Anaparthi)	89.33 (Maredumilli)	14.96 (Mamidikuduru)
2000-2001	83.81 (Gangavaram)	11.01 (Mamidikuduru)	88.16 (Y.Ramavaram)	12.22 (Mamidikuduru)
2001-2002	77.14 (Gangavaram)	8.53 (P.Gannavaram)	79.17 (Gangavaram)	16.92 (P.Gannavaram)

Source: District Education Officer, East Godavari District, Kakinada

Table-5: Highest and Lowest Dropout Rates of Boys and Girls in Class I-V during 1997-98 and 2001-02

Year	*Boys*		*Girls*	
	Highest	*Lowest*	*Highest*	*Lowest*
1997-98	85.40 (Maredumilli)	31.46 (Rajahmundry (U)	89.32 (Y.Ramavaram)	25.23 (Kapileswa-rapuram)
1998-99	85.17 (Y. Ramavaram)	16.37 (Anaparthi)	84.22 (Y.Ramavaram)	21.13 (Anaparthi)
1999-2000	87.84 (Maredumilli)	12.87 (Anaparthi)	88.95 (Maredumilli)	16.35 (Mamidikuduru)
2000-2001	85.78 (Maredumilli)	14.55 (Mamidikuduru)	87.66 (Maredumilli)	20.98 (Rajahmundry (U)
2001-2002	86.43 (Gangavaram)	17.57 (P.Gannavaram)	87.17 (Maredumilli)	21.40 (Rajahmundry (U)

Source: District Education Officer, East Godavari District, Kakinada

According to table-5 the highest CDRs are repeated thrice in Maredumilli mandal and the lowest CDR in Anaparthi mandal (13 per cent) among boys. Among Girls the highest CDR is reported in Y. Ramavarm and the lowest CDR in Mamidikuduru mandal. Almost all tribal mandals have shown the highest CDR and socially, economically, culturally developed mandals and urban mandals have shown the lowest CDR both for boys and girls during the study period for I-V classes.

To sum up all the tribal mandals have shown the highest CDRs. The lowest CDRs are reported in those mandals which are socially, culturally and economically better placed though rural in nature basically. This has a positive effect in reducing CDRs among both boys and girls.

Causes for Dropouts

The preceding analysis shows the existence of high dropout rates in the primary schools in East Godavari Disrict. In Order to understand the causes for dropouts and non-enrollment of children and also to identify the socio-economic barriers at the primary education, opinions from the teachers in a majority of mandals in the district were elicited on the causes for dropout rates. Since local teachers possess greater knowledge about the school children, parents and also about the local problems, the information from the teachers is found to be more appropriate and fruitful. The opinions of the primary school teachers are as follows.

1) Poor economic condition of the family.
2) Poor educational background of the parents.
3) Excessive involvement of children in domestic work.
4) Negligence of parents in educating their children.
5) Caste factors.
6) Frequent shifting of the families, for seasonal work, from one place to other place for seeking livelihood.
7) Due to ill-health, some of the students dropout from the schools.
8) Hostel accommodation is also identified as a factor that contributes for school dropouts.

9) Child marriages and social customs are also influenced the dropout rate especially in tribal mandals.

Conclusion

Universalization of primary education means enrolling cent per cent of school going children of 6 years age in Class I and ensuring their continuance till they complete their primary education, i.e., class V. An analysis is carried out in this paper on the problem of dropouts in primary education in East Godavari District in Andhra Pradesh, which has been suffering from high dropout rates. The results of the study show that the dropout rates differed between boys and girls. About 86 per cent of boys in Gangavaram mandal and 88 per cent of girls in Maredumilli mandal dropped out. In the case of girls the dropout rate is relatively higher than that of boys for reasons like social customs and traditions. High dropout rates are among weaker sections of the society like scheduled castes, scheduled tribes and backward classes. Almost all the tribal mandals except Rajavommangi, have shown very high dropout rates, i.e., more than 70 per cent.

The lowest dropout rate (about 22 per cent) is recorded in Mamidikuduru mandal both for boys and girls. In the case of girls the dropout rate is relatively lower than that of boys due to greater social awareness and higher economical status of the people. Though Mamidikuduru has a rural background of mandal in Konaseema area, the educational and social awareness and economical status of the people has influenced the dropout rates by showing a lower rate. As a whole, the highest dropout rate is recorded in a tribal mandal, i.e., Gangavarm mandal with 85 per cent and the lowest is recorded in Mamidikuduru mandal with 21 per cent. The results show that tribal mandals are not equipped themselves to realize the target. Except few mandals, the coverage of the concept of Universalization of Elementary Education has not even touched a one-fifth of the target. On the other hand, crude dropout rates calculated exhibit the same phenomenon. The dropout rates are lower in semi urban, educational and social awareness mandals and higher in tribal and backward mandals.

Opinions from the teachers indicated that the literacy levels of parents and poor economic conditions of the families as the two basic factors responsible for dropouts at the primary school level. The dropout rates are higher in tribal mandals compared to the non tribal mandals. Excessive involvement of children in domestic work, negligence of parents towards education of their children, social customs, shifting of families from one place to the other and early marriages of girl children are the other causes for the higher dropout rates. Realization of universalization of primary/elementary education will be fulfilled if all the above said hurdles are purposefully removed.

REFERENCES

1. Ambasht, N.K. (1994): "Universalization of elementary education, constitutional right to Education", *Journal of Indian Education,* March.
2. Brimer, M.A. and Pauli, C. (1971): *Wastage in Education – A world problem,* UNESCO.
3. Chalam, K.S. (1988): *Education and Weaker Sections,* Inter India Publications, New Delhi.
4. Chauhan, C.P.S. (2004): *Modern Indian Education, Policies, Progress and Problems.* Kanishka Publishers, New Delhi.
5. Chickermane, D.V. (1962): "A study of wastage in primary education", *Education and Psychology Review,* Vol.II, January.
6. East Godavari Disrict handbooks for various years: Disrict Planning Officer, Kakinada.
7. Pulla Rao, D. (1998): *Economics of Primary Education,* Rawat Publications, Jaipur.
8. Rajaiah, B. (1987): *Economics of Education,* Mittal Publications, New Delhi.
9. Rajput, J.S. (1993): "A problem of dropouts", *The Hindustan Times,* New Delhi, July 10.
10. Sharma, R.C. and C.L. Sapra (1969): *Wastage and Stagnation in Primary and Middle Schools in India,* NCERT, New Delhi.

6

STATUS OF PRIMARY EDUCATION IN VIZIANAGARAM DISTRICT OF ANDHRA PRADESH

Mohammed Khasim Shaik, D. Francis & D. Pulla Rao***

Education plays a vital role in the process of development of human resources. For an overall development of economy, development of education in general and universalisation of elementary education in particular are given very high priority in India and other developing countries of the World. Primary education occupies an important position in the entire structure of education. Therefore, a high priority has been given to invest in education. This is, perhaps the reason that Article 45 of the Indian Constitution guarantees provision of free and compulsory education to all children up to the age of 14 or 7 years of schooling.

Vizianagaram district is one of the North-Eastern Coastal districts of Andhra Pradesh. The population of the district is about 22.49 lakhs as per 2001 census and this constitutes 2.95 per cent of total population of the State. There are about 9.97 lakh literates forming 44.33 per cent of total population of the

* Research Scholar, Dept. of Economics, Andhra University, Visakhapatnam.

** Teaching Associate, Dept. of Economics, Dr. B.R. Ambedkar University, Etcherla, Srikakulam, Andhra Pradesh.

*** Professor, Dept. of Economics, Andhra University, Visakhapatnam.

district. Among literates, male literates constitute 60.68 per cent while female literates form 39.32 per cent as per 2001 census.

Status of Primary Education

The growth in the number of schools and the enrolment into primary education in Vizianagaram district during the period 1996-97 to 2005-06 are provided in Table-1. The rate of enrolment of the corresponding age group and the number of children per school are also presented in the table. There were 2,124 primary schools in the district in 1996-97 and the number of schools has increased to 2,379 by 2005-06; during this period the growth rate is 10.72 per cent. The growth of the institutions year wise is also calculated with the help of Index Numbers by taking 1996-97 as the base year.

The total enrolment in absolute numbers at primary education in the year 1996-97 was 2.60 lakhs, it increased to 2.70 lakhs in 1997-98 and it increased to 2.77 lakhs in 1998-99 and decreased to 2.01 lakhs in 2002-03 and further also gradually decreased and stood at 1.64 lakhs by 2005-06.

Since 1999-2000 the number of children enrolled in schools has come down to 1.64 lakhs in 2005-06. It is found from the data that the enrolments are uneven and recorded negative growth during the period of study. Further it is found from the data that school age population also came down from 3.03 lakhs in 1996-97 to 1.97 lakhs in 2005-06.

Growth of enrolment and the achievement in the universalisation of primary education in the country or in the State or in the district can be found out only in terms of the achievement with respect to the corresponding age groups, as data on enrolment alone do not convey any meaningful inferences. Therefore, we have also estimated the proportion of school going children enrolled into the primary schools to find out how many of them are still left out. It is interesting to find that the district had an enrolment rate 86.04 per cent in 1996-97 and the proportion has increased to 88.83 per cent by 1998-99. But it declined to 77.16 in 1999-2000. Later, for the two consecutive years the rate of enrolment has been on raise as 2000-01 and 2001-02 years

Table-1: Status of Primary Education in Vizianagaram District during 1996-1997 to 2005-2006

Year	*School Age Population (in lakhs)*	*Index*	*No. of Schools*	*Index*	*No. of Children Enrolled (in lakhs)*	*Index*	*Rate of Enrolment*	*No. of Children Per School*
1996-97	303227	100.00	2124	100.00	260888	100.00	86.04	123
1997-98	308026	101.58	2219	104.47	270832	103.81	87.93	122
1998-99	312900	103.19	2409	113.42	277944	106.54	88.83	115
1999-00	317852	104.82	2386	112.34	245258	94.00	77.16	103
2000-01	247483	81.62	2364	111.30	236346	90.60	95.50	100
2001-02	224749	74.12	2344	110.36	218763	83.85	97.34	93
2002-03	226136	74.58	2395	112.76	201593	77.27	89.15	84
2003-04	216620	71.44	2452	115.44	182242	69.85	84.13	74
2004-05	206593	68.13	2379	112.01	168216	64.48	81.42	71
2005-06	197039	64.98	2379	112.01	164808	63.17	83.64	69

Source: Commissioner and Director of School Education, Hyderabad & District Educational Officer, Vizianagaram.

witnessed 97.50 and 97.34 per cent respectively. After 2001-02 it has been on decline for the 3 consecutive years as 89.15, 84.13 and 81.42 per cent and then with a little growth in the year 2005-06 it stood at 83.64. But the analysis shows that the district still has a backlog of about 18 per cent in the universalisation of primary education. A peculiar trend has been occurring in the number of students per school. It has been fluctuating during the total period of study as the number of enrolled children, school age population and number of schools either decreasing or increasing due to various social, political and economic factors.

Status of Upper Primary Education

The Indian Constitution guarantees free and compulsory education to the children till they attain 14 years. It means that the enrolment should be universal up to upper-primary stage. In order to find out the achievement of the targets in the compulsory elementary stage that is up to upper primary stage, the enrolment figures and the number of schools established in the district during the period 1996-97 to 2005-06 are provided in Table-2.

From the table, it can be seen that there are only 170 upper primary schools in 1996-97 and the number has substantially increased to 497 by 2005-06. There was 26 per cent increase in the number of schools during 1996 - 2000 and 168 per cent growth is recorded during the period 2001-2006. On the whole, the growth of schools recorded an increase of 192 per cent during 1996-97 to 2005-06. The enrolment of students in the upper primary schools has recorded a slower growth when compared with the number of schools during 1996-2000. The year 2000-01 to 2001-02 can be treated as 'great year of achievement' as it recorded high growth from 48.31 to 78.08. In 2005-06 the growth rate of enrolment in upper primary schools increased with a steady speed and stood at 96.83.

It can be seen from the table that the total number of students enrolled in upper primary schools were 43,308 in 1996-97 and the number has slightly increased and decreased upto 2001-02 and there after the number has been on steady increase and recorded 68,747 in 2005-06.

Table-2: Status of Upper Primary Education in Vizianagaram District during 1996-1997 to 2005-2006

Year	*School Age Population*	*Index Schools*	*No. of*	*Index*	*No. of*	*Index*	*Rate of Enrolment*	*No. of Children Per School*
1996-97	115350	100.00	170	100.00	43308	100.00	37.54	255
1997-98	117176	101.58	173	101.76	43992	101.55	37.54	254
1998-99	119029	103.19	201	118.24	59773	138.02	50.22	242
1999-00	120909	104.82	219	128.82	58432	134.92	48.33	267
2000-01	115192	99.86	214	125.88	55650	128.50	48.31	260
2001-02	112684	97.69	389	228.82	59516	137.42	78.08	153
2002-03	113726	98.59	421	247.65	66115	152.66	77.69	157
2003-04	101274	87.80	442	260.00	67636	156.17	82.40	189
2004-05	96010	83.23	462	271.76	68850	158.98	86.21	149
2005-06	91021	78.91	497	292.35	68747	158.74	96.83	138

Source: Commissioner and Director of School Education, Hyderabad & District Educational Officer, Vizianagaram.

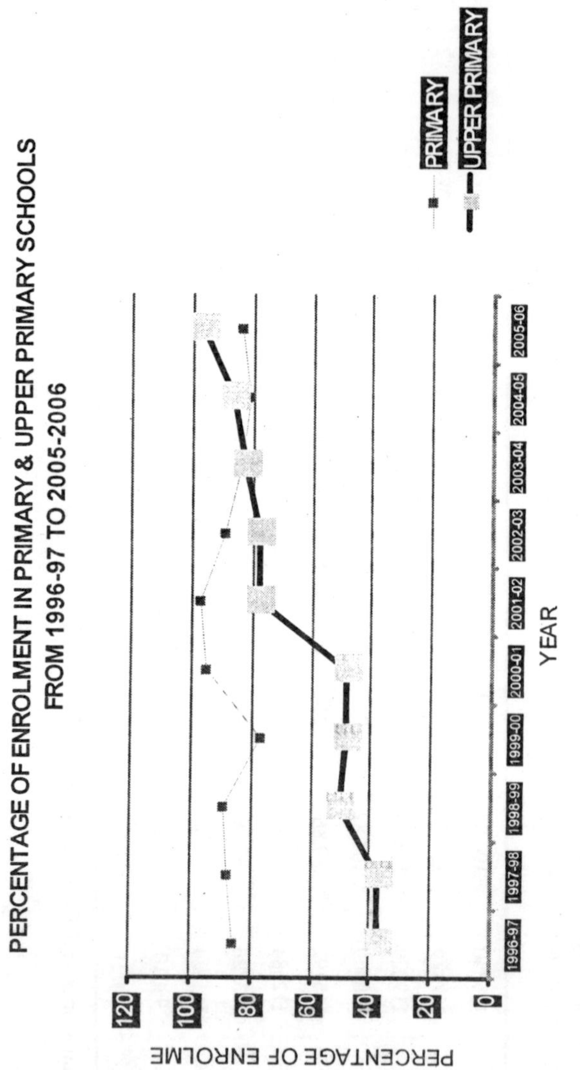
PERCENTAGE OF ENROLMENT IN PRIMARY & UPPER PRIMARY SCHOOLS
FROM 1996-97 TO 2005-2006
PERCENTAGE OF ENROLME
0
20
40
60
80
100
120
1996-97
1997-98
1998-99
1999-00
2000-01
2001-02
2002-03
2003-04
2004-05
2005-06
YEAR
PRIMARY
UPPER PRIMARY

FIGURE (A)

The rate of enrolment in upper primary schools to the corresponding age group has shown a dismal picture with 37.54 per cent for two years - 1996-97 and 1997-98 as there was no increase for these two years. However contrary to these two years 1998-99 witnessed growth recording 50.22 per cent enrolment to the corresponding age group. Again there was a little decrease during 1999-2000 to 2000-01 when compared to 1998-99 registering enrolment rates 48.33 and 48.31 respectively. There was a great increase in the year 2000-01 to 2001-02 as the rate of enrolment to the corresponding age group jumped from 48.31 to 78.08 and since 2001-02 the rate of enrolment has been on increase and stood at 96.83 per cent in 2005-06. This is a positive sign towards the achievement of universalisation of elementary education. A more or less similar picture emerged from number of children per school during the period of the study. A welcoming feature of the study is, despite the fact that number of children enrolled in schools is on the decline and a more or less stagnation in the number of schools, the number of children per school has been on the decline. This calls for an examination of the student-teacher ratio. Percentage of enrolment in Primary and Upper Primary schools was shown in Figure (A).

Pupil-Teacher Ratio in Primary Schools

So far, we have examined the size and growth of primary education in Vizianagaram district during the period 1996-97 to 2005-06. But, they do not really signify the quality of education. Hence an attempt has been made to verify the student-teacher ratio, which generally signifies the quality of education. It is also aimed to examine the number of teachers employed in primary schools in the district and the growth rate of teachers during the period of study. The data are presented in Table-3.

The number of teachers was found to be fluctuating during the period. It is observed that there were 4,922 teachers employed in primary schools in 1996-97 of which 3,560 were men and 1,362 women who constitute 72.33 and 27.67 per cent respectively to the total number of teachers. The total number has increased to 6,125 in 1998-99. Later for the following two consecutive years 1999-2000 and 2000-01 the total number has decreased to 5,875 and 5,714 respectively. There was a high rise in the total number of teachers in 2001-02 which has gone to 6,451 which is the highest number in the period of study. Though the total number is high in 2001-02 of the whole study period, lowest 'pupil-teacher ratio' is not recorded in this year since it was only 33.91 and the lowest 'pupil-teacher ratio' of the study period is 16.49 which is recorded in 2002-03. Again the total number of teachers decreased to 5,934 in 2003-04. With a modest increase, it was 5,940 in 2004-05; the number has decreased to 5,826 in 2005-06, the last year of study period. The growth of women teachers during the entire period is found to be high.

Women teachers recorded highest during the study period in 2001-02 with 2,678 numbers who constituted 41.51 per cent of the total number of teachers. This was a welcoming feature of Government of Andhra Pradesh in recruiting teachers. The policy of more women teachers in primary education may improve quality, as they are generally more sincere and hard working.

Table -3: Number of Teachers Appointed in Primary Schools of Vizianagaram District during 1996-1997 to 2005-2006

Year	*Men*	*Index*	*Women*	*Index*	*Total*	*Index*	*Pupil-Teacher Ratio (No of students per teacher)*
1996-97	3560	100	1362	100	4922	100	53.00
1997-98	3765	106	1165	86	4930	100	54.94
1998-99	4568	128	1557	114	6125	124	45.38
1999-00	4349	122	1526	112	5875	119	41.75
2000-01	4202	118	1512	111	5714	116	41.36
2001-02	3773	106	2678	197	6451	131	33.91
2002-03	4209	118	1914	141	6123	124	16.49
2003-04	4090	115	1844	135	5934	121	30.71
2004-05	4052	114	1888	139	5940	121	28.32
2005-06	3949	111	1877	138	5826	118	28.29

Source: Commissioner and Director of School Education, Hyderabad & District Educational Officer, Vizianagaram.

But, a more interesting picture emerges when the rate of growth of teachers is examined. It is reported that the index of growth of men and women teachers does not indicate any trend. The index of growth of men teachers has increased to 128 in 1998-99 which is the highest in the study period and then after it started decreasing for the next three consecutive years viz 1999-2000, 2000-01 and 2001-02 with 122, 118 and 106 respectively. However, it increased to 118 in 2002-03 and decreased for the following three consecutive years viz 2003-04, 2004-05 and 2005-06 with 115, 114 and 111 respectively. But, there is some positive change 'in the case of women teachers.

The positive change for women teachers started from 1998-99. The index has first decreased to 86 in 1997-98 and in 1998-99 the index increased to 114 and almost stagnant for the next two consecutive years with 112 and 111. But in 2001-02 the index for women teachers has gone to 197 which is an all time record of the study period. The index of women teachers is high rather than the men teachers, because of implementation of a policy of the government of Andhra Pradesh of 33.3 per cent reservation for women. During the period i.e., from 1996-97 to 2005-06 the increment in number of teachers has been encouraging but the enrolment in primary schools showed a declining trend except for 2 or 3 intervals over a period of time. This resulted in a change in the pupil-teacher ratio.

It is found that the pupil-teacher ratio was 53.00 and 54.94 in 1996-97 and 1997-98 respectively. Then after pupil-teacher ratio has been declining continuously till 2002-03 and finally the year witnessed all time low with 16.49 students per teacher, which is a good sign. Later, it has finally stood at 28.29 students per teacher in 2005-06 with 28.29 'pupil-teacher ratio', Vizianagaram district realised the ideal ratio as government has been insisting on pupil-teacher ratio of 40 for aided schools.

Education of Scheduled Caste (SC) and Scheduled Tribe (ST) Children

In all developing countries, education of the disadvantaged is the main concern. India too is concerned about the education of these disadvantaged children. So many sections of educationally backward population have been identified. But it may be pertinent to mention here that scheduled castes and scheduled tribes are the most deprived sections of the society in India. As such, they have been provided statutory safeguards under the Constitution of India there by making it obligatory on the part of the State to take special measures for their educational interest and upliftment.

We have analysed the enrolment data related to Scheduled Castes, Scheduled Tribes and others in Vizianagaram district to learn about the state of these deprived sections. Enrolment pattern of Scheduled Castes, Scheduled Tribes and others (including backward classes) at primary level is examined using the data relating to 2002-03 to 2005-2006. Children on rolls during this period are classified on the basis of schools run by management. Caste-wise enrolment and management-wise details are provided in Tables - 4, 5, 6 and 7.

In 2002-03, Scheduled Castes and Scheduled Tribes children in State government schools constitute 91.65 per cent of the total enrolment. Observing this high rate of enrolment one may assume that school going Scheduled Castes and Scheduled Tribes children are more when compared to others in all schools. But this is not true. This high rate of enrolment is due to the high number of exclusive schools for Tribes of all schools run by the State government. It is proved when we observe that Scheduled Tribes children enrolment is 85.63 per cent of 91.65.

Backward Classes and others constitute 8.35 per cent. A similar pattern could be observed in respect of the other periods of study viz., 2003-04 through 2005-2006. It is gratifying to note that the percentage of Scheduled Castes and Scheduled Tribes children on rolls in Municipal and Mandal Praja Parishad schools is near stagnant, while their enrolment in Private-Aided schools is on decline and in Private-Unaided schools is slightly increasing. This clearly shows that SC and ST children are enrolled in private schools mostly in urban areas, though the data available with us do not provide a break-up of rural-urban private schools.

Table-4: Percentage of SCs and STs in Total Enrolment During 2002-03 at Primary Level (6-11 Years) in Vizianagaram District

Management	*Percentage of SCs and STs*	*Percentage of others*	*Total percentage*
Central Government	40.52	59.48	100
State Government	91.65* (85.63)	8.35	100
Mandal Prajaparishad	23.84	76.16	100
Municipal	25.82	74.18	100
Private - Aided	41.90	58.10	100
Private - Un-Aided	8.55	91.45	100
Total	27.59	72.41	100

* Percentage of ST Enrolment.

Source: District Educational Officer, Vizianagaram.

Table-5: Percentage of SCs and STs in Total Enrolment during 2003-04 at Primary Level (6-11 Years) in Vizianagaram District

Management	*Percentage of SCs and STs*	*Percentage of others*	*Total percentage*
Central Government	36	64	100
State Government	92.24* (86.88)	7.76	100
Mandal Prajaparishad	22.14	77.86	100
Municipal	26.17	73.83	100
Private - Aided	38.71	61.29	100
Private - Un-Aided	9.06	90.94	100
Total	28.58	71.42	100

*Percentage of ST Enrolment.

Source: District Educational Officer, Vizianagaram.

Table-6: Percentage of SCs and STs in Total Enrolment During 2004-05 at Primary Level (6-11 Years) in Vizianagaram District

Management	*Percentage of SCs and STs*	*Percentage of others*	*Total percentage*
Central Government	47	53	100
State Government	93.90*(89.42)	6.10	100
Mandal Prajaparishad	23.42	76.58	100
Municipal	25.95	74.05	100
Private - Aided	38.70	61.30	100
Private - Un-Aided	9.40	90.60	100
Total	28.45	71.55	100

* Percentage of ST Enrolment.

Source: District Educational Officer, Vizianagaram.

Table-7: Percentage of SCs and STs in Total Enrolment during 2005-06 AT Primary Level (6-11 Years) in Vizianagaram District

Management	*Percentage of SCs and STs*	*Percentage of others*	*Total percentage*
Central Government	43.69	56.31	100
State Government	93.34*(88.36)	6.66	100
Mandal Prajaparishad	23.30	76.70	100
Municipal	26.79	73.21	100
Private - Aided	37.45	62.55	100
Private - Un-Aided	9.58	90.42	100
Total	27.97	72.03	100

*Percentage of ST Enrolment.

Source: District Educational Officer, Vizianagaram.

Mandal-wise Trends of Enrolment at Primary Level

Further, the analysis was carried out to examine the growth of enrolment of children in V class for the period 2001-02 to 2005-2006 mandal-wise in the district for both boys and girls. Any increase in absolute terms of children in V class for 2005-06 over 2001-02 is taken as growth in enrolment in V class. All the 34 mandals are considered for the analysis. Out of 34 mandals, only 4 mandals have registered a positive growth for boys and 3 mandals for girls. In other words, there is decline in enrolment in as many as 30 mandals for boys, 31 mandals for girls. Tables - 8 and 9 present the situation.

As could be seen from Table -8, there are 9 mandals namely Komarada, Jiyyammavalasa, Makkuva, Seethanagaram, Bobbili, Gajapatinagaram, Bondapalli, Bhogapuram and Vizianagaram have registered a decline below 10 per cent of enrolment of boys during 2001-02 and 2005-06 and as much as 13 mandals viz., Kurupam, Garugubilli, Balajipeta, Pachipenta, Therlam, Cheepurupalli, Pusapatirega, Denkada, Gantyada, Srungavarapu Kota (S Kota), Vepada, Lakkavarapukota and Kothavalasa have registered a decline between 10 to 20 per cent which is an alarming situation. Further, 5 mandals viz., Parvathipuram, Dathirajeru, Garividi, Nellimarla and Jami have registered a decline between 20 to 30 per cent and 3 mandals viz., Badangi, Merakamudidam and Gurla have registered a decline between 30 to 40 per cent vis-à-vis same is the case with the girls.

Girls have registered a decline 0-10 per cent in 10 mandals namely Komarada, Garugubilli, Makkuva, Ramabhadrapuram, Mentada, Gajapathinagaram, Bondapalli, Srungavarapu Kota, Vepada and Kothavalasa, whereas boys have registered a decline in 9 mandals one mandals in this range. In the range of 10-20 per cent girls have registered a decline in 8 mandals namely Parvathipuram, Balajipeta, Bobbili, Cheepurupalli, Bhogapuram, Denkada, Vizianagaram and Gantyada, whereas boys have registered a decline in 13 mandals in this range which is deplorable situation for boys and better situation for girls. In the range of 20-30 per cent girls have registered a decline in 10 mandals namely Jiyyammavalasa, Seethanagaram, Badangi, Therlam, Gurla,

Table-8: Negative Growth of V Class Enrolment of Boys and Girls during 2001-02 to 2005-2006

Range of Enrolment	No. of Mandals	Boys Name of the Mandal	No. of Mandals	Girls Name of the Mandal
0-10	9	Komarada, Jiyyammavalasa, Makkuva, Seethanagaram, Bobbili, Gajapati Nagaram, Bondapalli, Bhogapuram & Vizianagaram	10	Komarada, Garugubilli, Makkuva, Ramabhadrapuram, Mentada, Gajapatinagaram, Bondapalli, SrungavarapuKota, Vepada & Kothavalasa
10-20	13	Kurupam, Garugubilli, Balajipeta, Pachpenta, Therlam, Cheepurupalli, Pusapatirega, Denkada, Gantyada, Srungavarapu Kota, Vepada, Lakkavarapukota & Kothavalasa	8	Parvathipuram, Balajipeta, Bobbili, Cheepurupalli, Bhogapuram, Denkada, Vizianagaram & Gantyada
20-30	5	Parvathipuram, Dathirajeru, Garividi, Nellimarla & Jami	10	Jiyyammavalasa, Seethanagaram, Badangi, Therlam, Gurla, Garividi, Nellimarla, Pusapatirega, Lakkavarapukota & Jami
30-40	3	Badangi, Merakamudidam & Gurla	2	Merakamudidam & Dhatirajeru
40-50	–	-----	--	-----
50-60	–	-----	--	-----
60-70	–	-----	1	Pachipenta
Total	30		31	

Table-9: Oisutuve Growth of V Class Enrolment of Boys and Girls during 2001-02 to 2005-06

Range of Enrolment	*Boys*		*Girls*	
	No. of Mandals	*Name of the Mandal*	*No. of Mandals*	*Name of the Mandal*
0-10	2(5.88%)	Ramabhadrapuram & Mentada	2(5.88%)	Kurupam & Saluru
10-20	2(5.88%)	Gummalakshmi Puram & Saluru	--	-----
20-30	–	---	1(2.94%)	Gummalakshmi Puram
Total	4(11.76%)		3(8.82%)	

Note: Figures in brackets indicate percentages.

Garividi, Nellimarla, Pusapatirega, Lakkavarapukota and Jami, whereas boys have registered a decline only in 5 mandals which is good case for boys and alarming situation for girls. Further in the range of 30- 40 per cent girls have registered a decline in 2 mandals namely Merakamudidam and Dattirajeru, and boys have registered a decline in 3 mandals which is almost the same situation for both the sexes. The most alarming situation for girls is found in Pachipenta mandal where girls have registered a decline of 64.22 per cent. A study of the geographical nature and topography of these mandals reveals that some are tribal areas viz.,Gummalaxmipuram, Kurupam, Pachipenta, Jiyyammavalasa and Makkuva. In spite of the best efforts of the government it is distressing to note a declining trend in enrolment of boys in V class even in Vizianagaram, which is the district head quarter.

Positive enrolment growth for both boys and girls in V standard can be seen from Table -9. Here, it has been observed that out of 34 mandals in Vizianagaram district only 3 mandals are recorded with positive growth of girls' enrolment and 4 mandals are recorded with positive growth of boys' enrolment. Highest enrolment growth for boys is recorded in two mandals i.e., Gummalakshmi Puram and Saluru, and lowest is recorded in two mandals viz., Ramabhadrapuram and Mentada. In the case of girls highest enrolment growth is recorded in Gummalakshmi Puram and the lowest is recorded in Kurupam and Saluru.

Conclusion

This paper analyses the status of primary and upper primary levels of education for the period 1996-97 to 2005-06. The rate of enrolment to the corresponding age group of 6-11 years has almost been stable except in few cases over the period. Number of children per school showed a declining trend at primary level because of increasing number of schools due to various programmes initiated by the government and decrease in enrolment. However, this is not a welcome sign.

The average rate of enrolment at the upper primary level

to the corresponding age group 11-13 years during the study period is at 53 per cent. Here the ratio of the children per school is high. The pupil-teacher ratio has declined from 53.00 in 1996-97 to 28.29 in 2005-06, which is a welcome sign. However, the universalisation of elementary education is yet to be realised. Enrolment ratio varies for different categories in various management schools. The ratio is highest for scheduled castes and scheduled tribes in government schools and the lowest in private schools due to their poor economic status. Both positive and negative trends in the growth of enrolment have been observed in the district during the study period. This resulted in poor quality of education. Thus, the universalisation of elementary education in Vizianagaram District is, yet, a distant dream.

REFERENCES

1. George Psacharopoulous (1987): *Economics of Education Research and Studies*, Pergamon Press, Oxford.
2. Gopinathan Nair, P.R. (1981): *Primary education, population growth and socio-economic change*, Allied Publishers, New Delhi.
3. Govinda, R. (2002): "India education report: A profile of basic education", NIEPA, Oxford, New Delhi.
4. Govinda, R. and Varghese (1992): "Quality of primary education: an empirical study", *Journal of Educational Planning and Administration*, Vol.6, No.1, January, New Delhi.
5. Naik, J.P. (1975), *Elementary Education in India – A promise to keep*, Allied Publishers, Bombay.
6. Pulla Rao, D. (2008): "Development of the Primary and Upper primary Education in India", *Orient Journal of Law and Social Sciences*, Secunderabad, August, Vol. II, Issue-9. Pp: 79-91.
7. Pulla Rao, D. (2007): "Strategies for the Development of Education among Scheduled Tribes: An Assessment", *Indian Journal of Training and Development*, New Delhi, July-September, Vol. 37, No. 3, pp: 31-38.
8. Pulla Rao, D. (2005): "Development of Primary Education during Post-Independent India", *Human Endeavour*, Bhimavaram, April-September, Vol. 1, No. 2, pp: 21-28.

7

DEVELOPMENT OF THE PRIMARY AND UPPER PRIMARY EDUCATION IN INDIA

P. Jayanand Kumar & A. Vamsi Krushna***

Introduction

India is the largest democratic country in the world. Geographically, the country is vast spread over 329 million hectares of land and is supporting 1045 million people (2002 estimate), about 1.25 times the total population of Europe. During the last five decades, our number has tripled. With the birth of 48,000 children per day, 18 million are added every year to our population. This addition is more than the total population of Australia. With only 2.4 per cent of the total global land and 2 per cent of the total world's income, we bear the burden of 16.7 per cent of the total population of the World. We are essentially the land of youth and children as about 50 per cent of Indians are below the age of 20 years. Population explosion is one of the most serious problems facing our nation, which tends to nullify our progress on several socio-economic fronts. Even after 50 years of sustained efforts to develop and expand education, about 35 per cent of the people are illiterate. The corresponding figure for women is 46 per cent. According to NSSO Report

* Lecturer, Govt. Junior College, Chagallu, West Godavari District, A.P.

** Research Scholar, Department of Economics, Andhra University, Visakhapatnam, A.P.

(1999-2000), 26 per cent of our people live under the poverty line.

One of the important characteristic features of democracy is that it presupposes an educated and enlightened society. Democracy, both as a form of the government and as a way of life, cannot function when the society is uneducated and ignorant. Education and modernization are the two wheels of the same cart. Both, when combined together, lead to a rapid socio-economic development of a nation.

Economists have been arguing with sufficient empirical evidence that education contributes positively to development. A number of studies have been undertaken by researchers to establish the relationship between literacy and socio-economic development. It is, however, necessary to remember that primary education is pivotal for achieving literacy. Primary education constitutes a very important part of the entire structure of education. It is at this stage, the child starts going to a formal institution and formal education starts. Primary education in India has been under the control of a number of agencies. It is still under the management of number of private agencies, though, the State is increasingly taking the responsibility of providing free and compulsory elementary education to all. Article 45 of the Constitution provides for free and compulsory education for all children in the age-group 6-14 years, up to a minimum level. The whole idea has been woven into the concept of Universalization of Elementary Education (UEE). The level of compulsory education as envisaged in this Article corresponds to the elementary education of eight year's duration from class I to class VIII for the children aged 6-14 years. The universalization of Elementary Education has been recognized as a constitutional obligation in India by the year 1960 but the target has not been achieved even after 44 years of the target year. Now the government's target is, that all children should complete five years of primary schooling by 2007, and eight years of elementary schooling by 2010.

Present Structure of School Education in India

India, being a union of states, has accepted a uniform structure of school and college education popularly known as 10+2+3 pattern of school and college education. This pattern visualized 10 years of general education including 8 years of elementary followed by 2 years of secondary education; 2 years of senior secondary followed by 3 years of college education leading to the award of the first degree. Until recently there existed several different patterns such as 8+3+3, 10+1+3, or 10+2+2. But, in pursuance of the recommendations of the Education Commission (1964-66) and the proposals of the National Policy on Education, 1968, most of the States have adopted 10+2+3 pattern. The National Policy on Education (NPE)-1986 also reiterated the need for adopting a common pattern, namely, the 10+2+3 in the whole country. The NPE-1986 also proposed adopt of a common structure of elementary education consisting of 8 years of schooling – 5 years of primary and 3 years of upper primary education. Therefore, the present structure of school education can be represented as {(5+3)+2+2}. A child admitted to class I, normally, at the age of 6 years and is supposed to complete primary education up to Class V at the age of 11 years, and elementary education up to Class VIII, at the age of 14 years. Up to this stage the state is constitutionally obliged to provide for free and compulsory education to all children under Article 45 of the Constitution of India. Elementary education is followed by 2 years of secondary education popularly known as 'High School'.

Objectives

1. To examine the growth of enrollment of students in primary & upper primary schools by sex and the corresponding growth in the number of schools
2. To estimate the trends in the student-teacher ratio in both primary and upper primary education

The Data

The secondary data relating to the number of recognized schools, enrollment by sex and number of teachers appointed by sex in both primary and upper primary schools for selected years of five decades period from 1950-1951 to 2004-05 are obtained from annual reports for various years, Ministry of

Human Resource Development, Government of India and from Selected Educational Statistics for various years, Ministry of Human Resource Development, Government of India. In as much as the terminal year of our study is 2004-05, it cannot adequately reflect upon the phenomenal changes that have taken place in the primary educational set up in the more recent past. This is a limitation of the study.

The progress of UEE in India may be analysed in terms of three identifiable periods in history after independence.

1. Before Education Commission (1966)
2. Between Education Commission and the National Policy on Education - 1986, and
3. After National Policy on Education - 1986.

On the basis of the above identifiable periods, our study period (1950-51 to 2004-05) has been divided into 3 phases for estimation of annual compound growth rate of schools, enrollment and teachers by sex. The phases are

Phase-I 1950-1951 to 1965-1966.

Phase-II 1970-1971 to 1985-1986.

Phase-III 1990-1991 to 2004-05.

Development of Primary Education

In Table-1, the growth of the number of primary schools and the enrollment into primary education (schools), and the number of children per school for selected years during the period of our study is provided. The First Five Year Plan (1951-1956) began on 1st April, 1951. At the beginning of the First Plan in 1950-51, there were 2, 09,671 primary schools in the country. By 1965-1966, when the education commission submitted its report, the number of primary schools had increased to 3, 91,064. When the progress was reviewed in 1985-1986, it was found that the number of primary schools had increased to 5, 28,872. The period from 1986 onwards has been the period of implementation of the NPE-1986. Therefore, it is expected that elementary education might have developed considerably, both

Table -1: Enrollment and Number of Recognized Primary Schools in India: 1950-1951 to 2004-05

Year	Primary Schools	Index	% growth rate over previous period	No. of boys enrolled (6-11 years) (in millions)	Index	% growth rate over previous period	No. of girls enrolled (6-11 years) (in millions)	Index	% growth rate over previous period period	Total enrollment (in millions)	Index	% growth rate over previous	No. of children per school
1950-51	209671	100	–	13.8	100		5.4	100		19.2	100		91
1955-56	278135	133	32.65	17.1	124	23.91	7.5	139	38.89	24.6	128	28.12	88
1960-61	330399	157	18.79	23.6	171	38.01	11.4	211	52.00	35.0	182	42.28	106
1965-66	391064	186	18.36	32.2	233	36.44	18.3	339	60.53	50.5	263	44.28	129
1970-71	408378	195	4.43	35.7	259	10.87	21.3	394	16.39	57.0	297	12.87	139
1975-76	454270	217	11.24	40.6	294	13.72	25.0	463	17.37	65.6	342	15.09	144
1980-81	494305	236	8.81	45.3	328	11.58	28.5	528	14.00	73.8	384	12.50	149
1985-86	528872	252	6.99	52.2	378	15.23	35.2	652	23.51	87.4	455	18.43	165
1990-91	560935	267	6.06	57.0	413	9.19	40.4	748	14.77	97.4	507	11.44	174
1995-96	590421	281	5.26	62.4	452	9.47	47.4	878	17.33	109.8	572	12.73	186
1999-2000	641695	306	8.68	64.1	464	2.72	49.5	917	4.43	113.6	592	3.46	177
2004-05	767520	366	19.61	69.7	505	8.74	61.1	1131	23.43	130.8	681	15.14	170

Annual Compound Growth Rate				
1st phase	4.24	5.81	8.48	6.66
2nd phase	1.74	2.56	3.40	2.89
3rd phase	2.11	1.35	2.80	1.98
Total period	2.39′	2.99	4.50	3.55

Sources: 1. Annual reports of Ministry of Human Resource Development, Government of India.

2. Selected Educational Statistics, Ministry of Human Resource Development, Government of India.

5. Increase in number of students per teacher in primary schools

qualitatively and quantitatively. The total number of primary schools stood at 7, 6 7,520 in 2004-05. It is better not to over emphasise changes in growth rates over different phases because for reasons of arithmetical property, when one starts with a low base (as in 1951) the period immediately succeeding 1951 will have high rate and the subsequent periods lower rates. But comparison between the growth rates of boys and girls in any one phase assumes importance. In the analysis below, the differences in the growth rates of boys and girls receive greater attention compared to differences between periods. The index of growth of schools taking 1950-1951 as the base shows that the increase is not substantial as compared to the enrollment of children in primary schools. The annual compound growth rate of primary schools over a period of our study recorded 2.39 per cent. But the annual compound growth rate of primary schools in first phase is recorded 4.24 per cent; it is much higher than that of second phase (1.74%) and in third phase (2.11%). The total enrollment in primary schools in the year 1950-1951 was 19.2 million children of which 13.8 million were boys and 5.4 million were girls. It constitutes 28.12 per cent of the enrollment of girls to the total enrollment. The enrollment had increased to 50.5 million children in 1965-1966. The enrollment of girls was 18.3 million, which constituted 36.24 per cent of the total enrollment. The total enrollment in primary schools had increased to 87.4 million children in 1985-1986 of which 52.2 million boys and 35.2 million girls. The girls enrolled constituted 40.27 per cent to the total enrollment. Ultimately in 2004-05 the total enrollments of children stood at 130.8 million of which 69.7 million were boys and 61.1 million were girls. Here the girls enrolled constituted 46.71 per cent to the total enrollment. An interesting trend which can easily be observed is that enrollment of girls has grown at a higher rate than that of boys during the entire period of study. The annual compound growth rate of enrollment of total students was 6.66 per cent in first phase. This rate is much higher than that of the second and the third phases. The growth rate of enrollment in the case of girls is much higher than in the case of boys over the period of our study, in all the phases. The enrollment of students has increased at a higher rate than the number of schools and teachers.

So far, we have examined the size and growth of primary education in the country during the period of five and a half decades. But, they do not really indicate the quality of education. One indicator of the quality is the student-teacher ratio. So we, as a first step examine the number of teachers employed in the primary schools in the country and the rate of growth of the teachers by sex during the period of the study.

Table-2 shows that there were 5, 38,000 teachers employed in primary schools in 1950-1951 of which 15.24 per cent were women. By 2004-05, the total number of teachers posted in primary schools increased to 21, 61,000 of which 38.96 per cent were female. It is interesting that the index of female teachers increased at higher rate than that of male teachers through out the period under study.

The annual compound growth rate of total teachers in the first phase recorded 3.82 per cent, then the growth rate decreased gradually in second and third phases. The growth rate of female teachers was 5.38 per cent in the first phase against the growth rate of 3.50 per cent for male teachers. The growth rate of female teachers was much higher than that of male teachers in all the phases as well as for the total study period.

Note, however, that the number of teachers has not increased in the country in consonance with the increase in the number of students enrolled. This has resulted in an increase in student-teacher ratio over time except in 1955-1956, 1975-1976 and 1999-2000. It shows that the ratio was 36:1 in 1950-1951 and the ratio was constant in 1955-1956. Later it increased to 54:1 in 1970-1971 then the ratio continuously increased to 60:1 in 1990-1991. Later it was constant in 1995-1996 and it reached to 60:1 in 2004-05. Though the government has been insisting on a student-teacher ratio of 40 students per teacher for aided schools, it has never been possible for the government to achieve this objective. The data presented in Table-2 indicates only the country's average, but in most of the schools, the student teacher ratio is observed to be more than 100:1. This adversely affects the quality of education at primary level, because the school teacher does not find any motive to teach such a huge number, let alone paying

Table -2: Number of Teachers Employed by Sex in Primary Schools in India: 1950-1951 to 2004-05

(in 000s)

Year	*Male*	*Index*	*% growth rate over previous period*	*Female*	*Index*	*% growth rate over previous period*	*Total*	*Index*	*% growth rate over previous period*	*Student-Teacher Ratio*
1950-51	456	100		82	100		538	100		36
1955-56	574	126	25.88	117	143	42.68	691	128	28.25	36
1960-61	615	135	7.14	127	155	8.55	742	138	7.38	47
1965-66	764	167	24.23	180	219	41.73	944	175	27.22	53
1970-71	835	183	9.29	225	274	25.00	1060	197	12.29	54
1975-76	965	212	15.57	283	345	25.78	1248	232	17.73	53
1980-81	1021	224	5.80	342	417	20.85	1363	253	9.21	54
1985-86	1094	240	7.15	402	490	17.54	1496	278	9.76	58
1990-91	1143	251	4.48	473	577	17.66	1616	300	8.02	60
1995-96	1187	260	3.85	553	674	16.91	1740	323	7.67	60
1999-2000	1232	270	3.80	687	838	24.23	1919	357	10.29	59
2004-05	1319	289	7.06	842	1027	22.55	2161	402	12.61	60

Annual Compound Growth Rate			
1st phase	3.50	5.38	3.82
2nd phase	1.82	3.94	2.32
3rd phase	0.96	3.92	1.96
Total period	1.95	4.32	2.56

Sources: 1. Annual reports of Ministry of Human Resource Development, Government of India

2. Selected Educational Statistics, Ministry of Human Resource Development, Government of India.

the much needed individual attention at the stage of primary education.

Development of Upper Primary (Middle) Education

From Table-3 it may be observed that there were only 13,596 upper primary schools in the country in 1950-1951 and this number continuously increased to 2, 74,731 in 2004-05. The index of upper primary schools recorded a much higher increase than that of index of primary schools.

The annual compound growth rate of upper primary schools was 5.62 per cent for the entire period of study. The rate is much higher in phase one (12.14%) than in phase two (2.68%) and in phase three (4.05%).

There were 3.1 million children enrolled in upper primary schools in 1950-1951, of which 0.5 million were girls. They constituted only 16.13 per cent of total enrollment. Later the total enrollment raised to 10.5 million in 1965-1966. The enroliment of girls was 2.8 million, or 26.67 per cent of the total enrollment. The total enrollment in these schools had increased to 27.3 million in 1985-1986 in which they were 17.7 million boys and 9.6 million girls. The enrollment in upper primary schools ultimately reached to 51.2 million in 2004-05, of which 22.7 million were girls or 44.33 per cent of the total enrollment. An interesting trend which can easily be observed is that enrollment of girls has grown at a higher rate than boys during the period of study in upper primary education. It is emphasized that the index of girls' enrollment in upper primary education is much higher than that of index of girls' enrollment in primary education. It is a positive sign and shows the improvement of upper primary education in the country during the study period.

The annual compound growth rate of enrollment of total children in phase one was 8.47 per cent and it is much higher than that of the growth rate in phase two (4.91%) and phase three (2.77%). It is interesting that the growth rate of enrollment in the case of girls is more than that of boys over the period.

Student-Teacher Ratio in Upper Primary Schools

As noted earlier, the student-teacher ratio shows the quality of education. Here, we examine the growth in the number of teachers employed in the upper primary schools in the country during the period under study. The data are presented in Table-4. It is observed that there were 86,000 teachers employed in upper primary schools in 1950-1951, of which 13,000 were women, or 15.12 per cent of the total. By 2004-05 the total number of teachers in upper primary schools increased to 15, 89, 000.

The number of women teachers reached on all time high in 2004-05 (5, 97,000) and they constituted 37.57 per cent of the total teachers, indicating that women teaching community has been on the increase all through. One should consider this to be a healthy sign for the reasons (1) that it contributes to gender equality and (2) that women teachers exhibit care and patience, their general traits, in teaching children. The number of both in male and female teachers in upper primary schools shows an increasing trend over the period of our study. The index of female teachers recorded a much higher increase than that of the male teaches. This may be due to implementation of reservation policies in some states in the country in favour of women.

The annual compound growth rate of total teachers was 12.86 per cent in first phase. It is higher than the growth rate of second phase (2.82%) and third phase (2.65%). It is interesting that the recorded growth rate of female teachers at 17.11 per cent was higher than that of the male teachers at 11.80 per cent in phase one. The growth rates gradually decreased in phase two and phase three among both male and female teachers, but the growth rates of female teachers have been higher than that of male teachers in all the phases.

During the period under study, the increase in the number of teachers was 15, 03,000 (15, 89,000 - 86,000). As the enrollment in upper primary schools showed an increasing trend, it resulted in a favourable change in student-teacher ratio. It is observed that the ratio was 36:1 in 1950-1951 and it decreased to 19:1 in 1960-1961. Later the ratio gradually increased to 35:1 in 1995-

Table – 3: Enrollment and Number of Recognized Upper Primary Schools in India: 1950-51 to 2004-05

Year	Primary Schools	Index	% growth rate over previous period	No. of boys enrolled (6-11 years) (in millions)	Index	% growth rate over previous period	No. of girls enrolled (6-11 years) (in millions)	Index	% growth rate over previous period period	Total enrollment (in millions)	Index	% growth rate over previous	No. of children per school
1950-51	13596	100		2.6	100		0.5	100		3.1	100		228
1955-56	21730	160	59.83	3.8	146	46.15	1	200	100.00	4.8	155	54.84	221
1960-61	49663	365	128.54	5.1	196	34.21	1.6	320	60.00	6.7	216	39.58	135
1965-66	75798	557	52.62	7.7	296	50.98	2.8	560	75.00	10.5	339	56.72	138
1970-71	90621	666	19.55	9.4	361	22.08	3.9	780	39.28	13.3	429	26.67	147
1975-76	106571	784	17.60	11	423	17.02	5	1000	28.20	16	516	20.30	150
1980-81	118571	872	11.26	13.9	535	26.36	6.8	1360	36.00	20.7	668	29.37	174
1985-86	134846	992	13.72	17.7	681	27.34	9.6	1920	41.18	27.3	881	31.88	202
1990-91	151456	1114	12.32	21.5	827	21.47	12.5	2500	30.21	34	1097	24.54	224
1995-96	171216	1259	13.05	25	961	16.28	16	3200	28.00	41	1322	20.59	239
1999-2000	198004	1456	15.64	25.1	965	0.40	17	3400	6.25	42.1	1358	2.68	212
2004-05	274731	2021	38.75	28.5	1096	13.54	22.7	4540	33.53	51.2	1652	21.61	186

		Annual Compound Growth Rate		
1st phase	12.14	7.51	12.17	8.47
2nd phase	2.68	4.31	6.19	4.91
3rd phase	4.05	1.90	4.06	2.77
Total period	5.62	4.45	7.18	5.23

Sources: 1. Annual reports of Ministry of Human Resource Development, Government of India

2. Selected Educational Statistics, Ministry of Human Resource Development, Government of India.

1996. By 2004-05 the ratio decreased and stood at 32:1. Anyhow this figure is less than the student-teacher ratio of 40 recommended by the government for aided schools.

Conclusion

It is a common knowledge that India achieved freedom from the British imperialism on 15th August, 1947. Many decades have elapsed since. Yet in matters of education in general and primary education in particular the country is enviably placed. Economic backwardness of the country may have to do with mass illiteracy and ignorance of the people. But economic backwardness alone cannot explain educational backwardness. Kerala, though not particularly a rich state in the country, has achieved the objective of universalisation of primary education. The population explosion in the country could not have been unrelated to the illiteracy of its people.

We have examined here the effect of the initiatives of the government in the field of primary education. More specifically, we examined the trends in primary education in particular since 1950-1951. The focus is on (1) enrollment of children by sex (2) size of the teaching staff by sex, and (3) student-teacher ratio at the primary and upper primary stages.

Our data on the trends in the enrollment of children at the primary level showed that it was not commensurate with the growth of population in the relevant age group, notwithstanding the fact that universalization of primary education has been the avowed objective of the government. The quantitative growth of enrollment has been faster in the case of girls than in the case of boys throughout the period of five decades in both primary and upper primary education. Besides, the enrollment of students has increased at a higher rate than the number of schools and teachers.

To reflect upon the quality of education we arrived at student-teacher ratios. Let it be told that the significance of women teachers has been increasing over time and this should contribute positively to the growth and development of children. The student-teacher ratio at the primary level as it stood in 2004-05 was 60:1

and this compares highly unfavourably with the accepted norm of 40:1 ratio. What is more, in some schools the student-teacher ratio is in excess of 100:1The outcome of such ratio would be that the quality of education suffers.

As regards upper primary education the situation has been relatively better as compared to primary education. Even the student-teacher ratio on an average for the latest year of the survey is 32:1. This no doubt augurs well for upper primary education. There is, however a further need to effect improvements in upper primary education. As the child goes into the upper primary set up from primary set up there will be greater demands on the quality of teachers, of school buildings, of other infrastructure including toilets. These need to be strengthened. Mere increase in the number of teachers does not satisfy the demands of the pupils. This aspect has to be borne in mind if we want to ensure that the upper primary set up expands fast.

The expansion of both primary and upper primary education had been the highest during the 1st phase than 2nd and 3rd phases in enrollment, teachers and schools. One important reason of the downfall in the quality and standard of school education during the recent decades may be the uneven growth of enrollment, number of teachers and number of schools, the enrollment growing faster than the other two.

As a conservative estimate, the population of children in the age group 6-14 years, at present, may be about 200 million of which about 160 million (2001-2002 estimate) might be attending elementary schools. This leads to the conclusion that about 40 million children are still out of school, which constitute about 20 per cent of the relevant age group. It is reported that 22 per cent of the total out of school children of the world are in India.

According to our study, we have not been able to achieve the goal of the UEE as guaranteed in article 45 of our constitution. Though, there has been a massive expansion of schooling facilities during the last 55 years, the goal has moved farther with the number of out of schools children increasing. Moreover, there are glaring disparities in what has been achieved, which are

Table – 4: Number of Teachers Employed by Sex in Upper Primary Schools in India: 1950-51 to 2004-05

(in 000s)

Year	Male	Index	% growth rate over previous period	Female	Index	% growth rate over previous period	Total	Index	% growth rate over previous period	Student-Teacher Ratio
1950-51	73	100		13	100		86	100		36
1955-56	132	181	80.82	19	146	46.15	151	175	75.58	32
1960-61	262	359	98.48	83	638	336.84	345	401	128.48	19
1965-66	389	533	48.47	139	1069	67.47	528	614	53.04	20
1970-71	463	634	19.02	175	1346	25.90	638	742	20.83	21
1975-76	554	759	19.65	224	1723	28.00	778	905	21.94	21
1980-81	598	819	7.94	253	1946	12.95	851	989	9.38	24
1985-86	663	908	10.87	305	2346	20.55	968	1125	13.75	28
1990-91	717	982	8.14	356	2738	16.72	1073	1248	10.85	32
1995-96	756	1036	5.44	409	3146	14.89	1165	1355	8.57	35
1999-2000	829	1136	9.66	469	3608	14.67	1298	1509	11.42	32
2004-05	992	1359	19.66	597	4592	27.29	1589	1848	22.42	32

		Annual Compound Growth Rate	
1st phase	11.80	17.11	12.86
2nd phase	2.42	3.77	2.82
3rd phase	2.19	3.51	2.65
Total period	4.86	7.20	5.44

Sources: 1. Annual reports of Ministry of Human Resource Development, Government of India

2. Selected Educational Statistics, Ministry of Human Resource Development, Government of India.

based on caste, sex, religion, and rural-urban areas. There are good reasons to believe that India will not be able to achieve this goal of UEE even by 2030 unless some effective and efficient alternative strategies are planned and implemented.

REFERENCES

1. Anand, C.L. (1983), "The Constitution of India in the Teacher and Education in Emerging Indian Society", NCERT, New Delhi.
2. Gadgil, V.R. and Dandekar, V.M. (1955): *Report of Two Investigators: Primary Education in Satara District,* Gokhale Institute of Politics and Economics, Poona.
3. George Psacharopoulous (1987): *Economics of Education Research and Studies,* Pergamon Press, Oxford.
4. Gopalan, K (1996): "Education for all – new initiatives", *University News,* AIU, Jan 1, New Delhi.
5. Gopinathan Nair, P.R. (1981): *Primary Education, Population Growth and Socio-economic Change,* Allied Publishers, New Delhi.
6. Government of India (1969): *Education and National Development,* NCERT, New Delhi.
7. Government of India (1994): *Development of Education in India (1993-94),* MHRD, New Delhi.
8. Govinda, R. (2002): *India education report: A profile of basic education,* NIEPA, Oxford, New Delhi.
9. Govinda, R. and Varghese (1992): "Quality of primary education: an empirical study", *Journal of Educational Planning and Administration,* Vol.6, No.1, January, New Delhi.
10. Govinda, R. and Varghese, N.V. (1993): "Quality of primary schooling in India: A case study of Madhya Pradesh", International Institute for Educational Planning, Paris and National Institute of Educational Planning and Administration, New Delhi.
11. Naik, J.P. (1975), "Elementary Education in India – A promise to keep", Allied Publishers, Bombay.NIEPA (1990): "Development of Education in India 1988-1990", MHRD, Government of India, New Delhi.
12. NIEPA (1990): *Education for All by 2000 A.D.,* New Delhi.
13. Pulla Rao, D. (1998): *Economics of Primary Education,* Rawat Publications, Jaipur.

14. Rajput, J.S. (1994): "Elementary Education - Alternative Strategies", *The Hindustan Times*, June 10, New Delhi.

15. Saini, S.K. (1980): "Development of Education in India", Cosmo Publications, New Delhi.

16. Saiyadain, K.G. et al. (1966), *Compulsory Education in India*, Universal Book House, New Delhi.

8

TRENDS IN THE GROWTH OF SECONDARY EDUCATION IN INDIA

P.S.K. Sudheer, Y. Ravini** & D. Pulla Rao****

Introduction

One of the important characteristic features of democracy is that it presupposes an educated and enlightened society. Democracy, both as a form of the government and as a way of life, cannot function when the society is uneducated and ignorant. Education and modernization are the two wheels of the same cart. Both, when combined together, lead to a rapid socio-economic development of a nation. Economists have been arguing with sufficient empirical evidence that education contributes positively to development. A number of studies have been undertaken by researchers to establish the relationship between education and socio-economic development.

India is a vast country covering about 329 million hectares of land and providing shelter for a population of over 1,000 million. Since the total population of the world is a little more than 6,000 million, India has to support about 16 per cent of the world's population on only 2.4 per cent of land and 2 per cent of the world's total income. As far as population is concerned, we are the largest democracy of the world. During the last 50 years our population has tripled. With the birth of 48,000 children

*Research Scholar, Dept. of Economics, Andhra University, Visakhapatnam.

, * Dept. of Economics, Andhra University, Visakhapatnam.

per day, 18 million are added every year to our teeming millions. This annual addition is more than the total population of Australia. It is reported that by 2001 census our population has risen to about 1,027 million. Thus, the welfare of the people of India is the welfare of over one-sixth of mankind. The majority of this large population - about 73 per cent, live in 5,79,000 rural habitations, meaning thereby that we are predominantly a rural society. According to the 2001 census about 65 per cent of the people were literate. If the population aged 7 years and above is concerned, the level of illiteracy was 35 per cent. It was 46 per cent for women.

The Structure of School Education in India

India, being a union of states, has accepted a uniform structure of education popularly known as 10+2+3 pattern of school and college education. This pattern visualizes 10 years of general education including 8 years of elementary followed by 2 years of secondary education, 2 years of senior secondary followed by 3 years of College Education leading to the award of first degree. A child is admitted to Class I, normally, at the age of 6 years and is supposed to complete primary education up to Class V at the age of 11 years, and elementary education up to class VIII, at the age of 14 years up to this stage the state is constitutionally obliged to provide for free and compulsory education to all children under Article 45. Elementary education is followed by two years of secondary education popularly known as 'High School'. At this stage also there is no diversification of courses and there is common curriculum for all children. The main purpose of this stage is to build a strong foundation in the fundamental principles of all basic subjects. At the end of this stage, that is, after 10 years of general education, the first public examination is held. This stage is followed by two years of senior secondary education. The senior secondary or +2 stage consists of two streams, academic and vocational.

Curriculum Framework for School Education

The present structure of school education in India is largely based on the National Curriculum for Primary and secondary

Education. A framework brought out by the NCERT in 1985 and another similar document published in 1988.

Curriculum for Secondary Stage

The curriculum of secondary stage consists of (1) three languages (2) mathematics (3) science, (4) social sciences, (5) contemporary India (6) work experience, (7) art education (8) health and physical education. The objectives of curriculum at secondary stage are two-fold. One is to prepare the students to join the higher (senior) secondary stage followed by college, and the other is to prepare them for the world of work. This stage is expected to be terminal for a large number of students who want to join the world of work.

Curriculum for Senior Secondary Stage

At this stage, diversified courses are introduced for preparing the students either to enter the university education for the first degree or to enter into job market after undergoing the vocational training. The senior secondary or +2 stage consists of two streams, one is academic and the second one is vocational.

The academic streams, which includes the study of elective courses chosen for in-depth study, consists of (1) science (2) mathematics (3) commerce (4) social sciences (5) humanities. The vocational stream, which is designed to prepare students for careers in agriculture, industry, or government services as well as for self-employment, consists of (1) one or two languages (2) general foundation courses (3) elective subjects related to specific vocations, and is designed to provide intensive training. The first public examination is held after ten years of schooling at the end of class X. Another public examination is held at the end of Senior Secondary Stage (Class XII). The examinations, which are held at the end of the secondary and senior secondary school stages, are conducted by the School Education Boards, established for this purpose.

Objectives

1. to examine the growth in the enrollment of students by sex and the corresponding increase in the number of schools

2. to examine the trends in number of teachers by sex employed in secondary schools and to estimate the student-teacher ratio.

Methodology and Data Sources

The quinquennial data relating to the number of recognized schools (for classes IX to XII), enrollment by sex and number of teacher employed by sex in secondary schools from 1950-1951 to 1999-2000 are obtained from annual reports of Ministry of Human Resource Development, Government of India and also from Selected Educational Statistics for various years, Ministry of Human Resource Development, Government of India.

We have estimated index numbers and percentage growth rates over previous periods for number of schools, enrollment and teachers by sex. Later we have estimated annual compound growth rates of schools, enrollment and also teachers for our study period.

Progress of Secondary Education

In Table-1, the growth of the number of secondary schools and the enrollment into secondary education, and the number of students per school for selected years during the period of our study is provided. The First Five Year Plan (1951-1956) began on 1st April, 1951. At the beginning of the First Plan in 1950-1951, there were 7,416 secondary schools in the country. This figure increased to 1, 16,820 in 1999-2000. These figures include high schools, higher secondary schools, intermediate colleges, Junior colleges, community colleges and PUC sections wherever they exist. The index of growth taking 1950-1951 as the base shows that the increase is not substantial as compared to the enrollment of students in secondary schools. As per the percentage growth rate over previous period in the case of secondary schools, the growth of the schools in the period 1951-1961 is the highest record i.e., 133.67. The table shows that the growth rate of schools for the period from 1950-1951 to 1970-1971 are much higher than that of the remaining period of our study. The annual compound growth rate of schools is recorded 5.67 per cent.

Table-1: Number of Recognized Schools and Enrollment by Sex in Secondary Schools in India, 1950-1951 to 1999-2000

Year	*Secondary Schools (units)*	*Index*	*% growth rate over previous period*	*No. of boys enrolled (lakhs)*	*Index*	*% growth rate over previous*	*No. of girls enrolled (lakhs)*	*Index*	*% growth rate over previous period*	*Total enroll-ment (lakhs)*	*Index*	*% growth rate over Previous period*	*No. of children per school*
1950-51	7416	100		13	100		2	100		15	100		202
1960-61	17329	234	133.67	27	208	107.69	7	350	250.00	34	227	126.67	196
1970-71	37051	500	113.81	49	377	81.48	17	850	142.86	66	440	94.12	178
1980-81	51624	696	39.33	76	585	55.10	32	1600	88.23	108	720	63.64	209
1990-91	78619	1060	52.29	140	1077	84.21	69	3450	115.62	209	1393	93.52	266
1992-93	84086	1134	6.95	150	1154	7.14	77	3850	11.59	227	1513	8.61	270
1995-96	98134	1323	16.71	161	1238	7.33	88	4400	14.28	249	1660	9.69	254
1999-00	116820	1575	19.04	172	1323	6.83	110	5500	25.00	282	1880	13.25	241

% growth rate in 1999-00 over 1950-51	1475.24	1223.08	5400.00	1780.00
Annual compound growth rate	5.67	5.30	8.34	6.04

Sources: 1.Annual reports of Ministry of Human Resource Development, Government of India.
2.Selected Educational Statistics, Ministry of Human Resource Development, Government of India.

Table-2: Number of Teachers Employed by Sex in Secondary Schools in India: 1950-51 to 1999-2000

Year	*Male (000s)*	*Index*	*% growth rate over previous period*	*Female (000s*	*Index*	*% growth rate over previous period*	*Total(000s)*	*Index*	*% growth rate over previous period*	*Student-Teacher Ratio*
1950-51	107	100		20	100		127	100		12
1960-61	234	219	118.69	62	310	210.00	296	233	133.07	11
1970-71	474	443	102.56	155	775	150.00	629	495	112.50	10
1980-81	658	615	38.82	254	1270	63.87	912	718	44.99	12
1990-91	857	801	30.24	416	2080	63.78	1273	1002	39.58	16
1992-93	908	848	5.95	445	2225	6.97	1353	1065	6.28	17
1995-96	982	918	8.15	511	2555	14.83	1493	1175	10.35	17
1999-00	1142	1067	16.29	578	2890	13.11	1720	1354	15.20	16
% growth rate in 1999-00 over 1950-51	967.29			2790.00			1254.33			
Annual compound growth rate	4.85			6.96			5.35			

Sources: 1. Annual reports of Ministry of Human Resource Development, Government of India Selected Educational Statistics, Ministry of Human Resource Development, Government of India.

The total enrollment in secondary stage in the year 1950-1951 was 15 lakhs students of which 13 lakhs were boys and only 2 lakhs were girls. Girls constituted only 13 per cent to the total enrollment. The total enrollment had increased gradually and reached to 282.00 lakhs in 1999-2000. The enrollment of girls was 110.00 lakhs which constituted 39 per cent of the total enrollment.

An interesting trend which can be observed is that enrollment of girls has grown at a higher rate than that of boys during the entire period of our study. The annual compound growth rate of total enrollment at secondary stage was 6.04 per cent. The growth rate was 8.34 per cent for girls and 5.30 per cent for boys during the study period. The enrollment of girls has increased at a faster rate than that of boys throughout.

Student-teacher Ratio in Secondary Schools

So far, we have examined the size and growth of secondary education in the country during the period of five decades. But, they do not really indicate the quality of education. One indicator of the quality is the student-teacher ratio. So we, as a first step we examine the number of teachers employed in the secondary schools in the country and the rate of growth of the teachers by sex during the period of the study.

Table-2 shows that there were 1, 27,000 teachers in secondary schools in 1950-1951 of which only 20,000 were women, and they constituted only 16 per cent to total. The total teachers increased gradually over a period of time and reached to 17, 20,000 in 1999-2000 of which 5, 78,000 were women and they constituted 34 per cent to total teachers. The index of female teachers increased at higher rate than male teachers through out the period under study. The annual compound growth rate of total teachers between 1950-51 and 1999-00 was 5.35 per cent. The growth rate was 6.96 per cent for female teachers and 4.85 per cent in the case of male teachers. Reservation policies in some states in the country must have favoured women to form increasing part of the total teachers.

The number of teachers has not been increasing in the country in consonance with the increase in the number of students enrolled. This has resulted in the increase in the student-teacher ratio over time except in 1960-1961, 1970-1971 and 1999-2000. The ratio was 12:1 in 1950-1951, 11:1 in 1960-1961 and 10:1 in 1970-1971. Later it increased gradually and reached 17:1 in 1995-1996. It is stood at 16:1 in 1999-2000. This figure is less than the student-teacher ratio recommended by the government. One should consider this to be a healthy sign.

Conclusion

We examined the effect of the initiatives of the government in the field of secondary education. More specifically, we examined the trends in the growth of secondary education since 1950-1951. The focus is on (1) enrollment of students by sex (2) size of the teaching staff by sex, and (3) student-teacher ratio at the secondary stage.

Our data on the trends in the enrollment shows that enrollment in the case of girls is progressing faster than in the case of boys throughout the period of five decades. The enrollment of students has increased at higher rate than the number of schools and teachers. To reflect upon the quality of education we arrived at student-teacher ratios. Let it be told that the significance of women teachers has been increasing over time and this should contribute positively to the growth and development of students. The student-teacher ratio at the secondary level as it stood in 1999-2000 was 16:1 and it is highly favourable situation compared to the accepted norm of the government. This no doubt augurs well for secondary education. There are however certain needs that the secondary educational set up has to fulfill. As the student goes into the secondary setup from elementary setup there will be greater demands on the quality of teachers, of school buildings, of other infrastructure including toilets. These need to be strengthened. Mere increase in the number of teachers does not satisfy the demands of the students. One important reason of the downfall in the quality and standard of school education during the recent decades may be the uneven growth of enrollment, number of teachers and number of schools, the enrollment growing faster than the other two.

REFERENCES

1. Chalam, K.S. (1993): *Educational Policy for Human Resources Development*, Rawat Publishers, Jaipur.
2. Government of India (1952-53): *Report of the Secondary Education Commission*, Ministry of Education, New Delhi.
3. Government of India (1968): *National Policy on Education*, 1968, Ministry of Education and Culture, New Delhi.
4. Government of India (1986 & 1992): *National Policy on Education (NPE)*, 1986 and its revised version - 1992, MHRD, New Delhi.
5. Government of India (1994): *Development of Education in India (1993-94)*, MHRD, New Delhi.
6. NCERT (1985), *National Curriculum for Primary and Secondary Education: A framework*, December, New Delhi.
7. NCERT (2000): *National Curriculum Framework for School Education*, New Delhi.
8. NIEPA (1990): *Development of Education in India 1988-90*, MHRD, Government of India, New Delhi.
9. Saini, S.K. (1980): *Development of Education in India*, Cosmo Publishers, New Delhi.
10. Singhal, R.P. (1992): "Implementation of Ten plus Two: the Indian experience of School Education", *Journal of Educational Planning and Administration*, Vol.VI, No.3, pp.251-265.

9

CHILD LABOUR: PERILS AND PREVENTIVE STRATEGIES

*G. Venkata Ramana**

Child Labour: A Pervasive Problem

Child labour is one of the oldest professions of the world and has remained as the most neglected phenomenon for the last few centuries. It has moved from a matter of regional and national concern to one of the international debates and possible global persuasion and policy interventions. Child labour is a harsh reality, fostered by socio-economic and historical compulsions. It is a pervasive problem throughout the world, more so in developing countries like India.

The use of child labour, in one of its most exploitative forms during the early years of the industrial revolution. The extent of mobilization and development of this form of labour in the society moves between two extremes from the environment and physically hazardous industrial activities to seasonal labour on family forms and the more common household chores.

Child Labour: Concept and Meaning

Child labour is a global phenomenon and it has been there since olden days. There is no universally accepted definition of

* Associate Professor and Head, Department of Sociology, Dy. Director, Centre for Distance Education, Sri Krishnadevaraya University, Anantapur, Andhra Pradesh.

the concept 'Child Labour'. Varying definitions of the term are used by International Organizations, Government and Non-Government Organizations, Trade Unions and other interested groups. According to Indian Constitution (as described in Child Labour Prohibition and Regulation Act, 1986) Child Labour can be defined as that segment of the child population, which participates in work either paid or unpaid. A comprehensive definition on child labour is given by the International Labour Organisation (ILO). According to it, "Child labour includes children prematurely adult lives, working long hours for low wages, under conditions damaging to their health and to their physical and mental development, some times separated from their families, presently deprived of meaningful education and training opportunities that would open for their better future.

Child Labour: Global Scenario

Globally, out of estimation, 211 million children between the ages 5-14 who are engaged in some form of economic activity, 186 million children fall with in the accepted ILO definition of child labour. An often 50 million children are child labourers in the age group of 15-17. the Asian Pacific region harbors the largest number of child workers in 5-14 age group 123 million, constituting 19 per cent of the total population of children (ILO, 2002). An estimated 171 million children between the ages 5-17 work in hazardous conditions.

Overall, more than 2/3 of the child labourers are still in hazardous activities. In addition, it is estimated that about 8.4 million children are engaged in forms of child labour like trafficking (1.2 million), forced and bonded labours (5.7 million) and illicit activities (0.6 million) (ILO,2002).

ILO counted the number of working children below the age of 10 and 14 moreover, the increase of 177 million comes from six developing countries. Of which, India and Pakistan are a part of 250 million, about 120 million are working full time, while 130 million work part-time. The report, child labour - targeting the intolerable says that Asia accounts for 153 million working children, Africa about 80 million and Latin America about 17.5 million. 61 per cent in Asia, 32 per cent in Africa, and 7 per cent in Latin America, 1 per cent in US, Canada, Europe and Other wealthy nations. In Asia, 22 per cent of the work force is children. In Latin America, 17 per cent of the work force is children. The proportion of the child labourers varies a lot among countries and even regions inside those countries.

Child Labour: Indian Perspective

The child labour has been in practice in Indian society since time immemorial. Children help their parents in the household chores and also in family occupations. On the basis of historical experiences, the problem of child labour lies in the process of industrial revolution. According to National Commission on Labour, "the employment of children is nonexistent in organized industries. It presents in varying degrees in unorganized industries. Ironically India's child labour laws prohibit children being engaged in factories where wages are high, but not in cottage industries, restaurants in households and agricultural sector where wages are low. In fact, the agricultural sector stands out as the biggest single source of the child labour in India (Koteswara Rao, 2003).

India has the largest number of child labourers in the world and greater incidence of child labour than any of the countries. As a matter of fact, Pakistan and Bangladesh account for the highest percentage of child labourers in the world. Nearly twenty five per cent of the working children of the world are the Indians. Child labour contributes significantly to the Indian economy. It contributes twenty per cent of GNP and eight per cent of work force. Most of our export oriented industries like carpets, brassware, diamond, glass, match and fire works etc., are banking upon child labour (Rajeshwari Panigrahi & Kamalun Nabi, 1999).

Magnitude of Child Labour

The nature and magnitude of child labour in India is complex and gigantic. Millions of children are working in a large number of different industries and occupations all over the country. Child labour in India is a mass phenomenon occupying an important place in the economy in terms of national wealth and growth. So it is more difficult to give exact estimate of overall magnitude of the problem. However, an attempt has been made by various agencies to estimate the extent of child labour.

The magnitude of child labours in India indicates that some fluctuating trends during three decades between 1971 and 2001. The total number of child labour has been of a substantial magnitude.

Table 1: Child Labour in India

Census	*Child labour engaged in different sectors*
1971	1,07,53,985
1981	1,36,40,874
1991	1,12,85,349
2001	1,26,66,377

Source: Census of India 1971, 1981, 1991 and 2001.

It is clear from Table 1 that the 1971 census recorded the number of child labour as 10.75 millions, but for 1981 the number rose to 13.64 millions. Over the decade there has been a substantial increase in the number of child labour both in absolute numbers as well as in terms of percentage.

The magnitude of child workers has registered a steep decline from 11.28 millions in 1991 to 13.64 million in the previous decade. However, there has been further increase to 12.66 million as per the census of 2001. It is significant to note that the census of 1981 recorded the highest number of child workers during the period of three decades between 1971 and 2001.

State-wise Distribution

Child labourers are found working almost everywhere starting from the Himalayas in North and ending at the Kanyakumari in the south. In reality, the children have become indispensable in almost every kind of industry. In India working children are engaged in different organized and unorganized sectors i.e. rural and urban. In rural sector they are engaged in fields, plantations, domestic jobs, fishing forestry, brick fields, leather tanning and cottage industry. In urban sector they are employed at houses, shops, tea stalls, hotels, restaurants, canteens, railway platforms, bus terminuses, small and large industries like carpet weaving, glass manufacturing, sports goods industry, mines, slate, lock manufacturing units, fire works, and matches, diamond and gem stone cutting and polishing units etc. They also work as hawkers, milk boys, vegetable vendors, shoe shine boys, rap pickers, porters, rickshaw pullers etc.. In India the highest concentration of child labour is however, still in agricultural sector which provides livelihood to about seventy per cent of the India's population.

Table 2: Details of States with more than one million Child Workers

State	*1971*	*1981*	*1991*	*2001*
Andhra Pradesh	1627492	1951312	1661940	1363339
Bihar	105739	1101964	-	1117500
Karnataka	-	1131530	-	-
Madhya Pradesh	1112319	1698597	1353563	106259
Uttar Pradesh	1326726	1434675	1410086	1927997

Source: Ministry of Labour, GoI, 2003.

It is seen from the table 2 that there are six states with more than one million child workers

Table 3: Details of State with 5 Lakhs to 10 Lakhs Child labour

State	*1971*	*1981*	*1991*	*2001*
Gujarath	518061	616913	523585	485530
Karnataka	808719	1131530	976247	822615
Maharastra	988357	1557756	1068427	764075
Rajasthan	587389	819605	734199	1262570
Tamil Nadu	713305	975055	578889	418801
West Bengal	511443	605263	711691	857087

Source: Ministry of Labour, Government of India, 2003.

Causes of Child Labour

There are a number of causes behind the wide spread prevalence of child labour in India. Child labour is a symptom of the underlying problem of the wide spread poverty and inequality in society. It is also a cause of poverty. Children who join the workforce at an early stage do so without any formal education or skills that will help them to be upwardly mobile. In most cases, they are involved in monotonous and laborious tasks. They grow up as illiterates devoid of any skills for further development. Consequently they get into low paid unskilled work when they become adults. As adults, when they marry and have children, they are already in a poor economic condition and are forced to send their children for work. Therefore the cycle of child labour-poverty-illiteracy - child labour (Sekhar, 1993).

According to Anandharaja Kumar (1999) children are sent to work due to sheer necessity in the family. Wherever literacy levels are low, the size of the family is large and a family is compelled to send their children to work. Poverty forces the parents to send their children to seek employment because of augmentation of their income is essential for the survival of the families. However, the burgeoning population growth, increasing rural migration, family disintegration, in a devote measures of social security, lack of avenues for education, social choices, social policies and shortcomings in institutional arrangements and ineffective law enforcement machinery are some of the contributory factors for the increase of child workers in India.

More specifically the following are the important causes:

1. *Growth of Population:* It is one of the main causes of child labour in India. India possesses about 2.3 per cent of total global land with which she has to support about 16 per cent of the world population. India with 935.8 million people is still the second populous country after China. The present birth and death rates of population of India are 2.75 per cent and 0.9 per cent per annum respectively. This implies that currently while about 88

lakh people die in a year, abut 268 lakh children are born during the same period. The difference of about 180 lakh persons constitutes the additional number of children which is being added to our teeming population. According to the United Nation's Population found that (UNFPA) India alone accounts for a fifth of the population has been growing; India will be the world's most populous country by 2050 i.e. after.

2. *Poverty:* Poverty is a major factor which has given rise to the problem of child labour. On an average 30 per cent of Indian population live below poverty live. The situation is far more worse in the states of Orissa and Bihar where roughly half of the population live below the poverty line followed by Uttar Pradesh, Maharastra and Andhra Pradesh. It is a matter of great shock that even after 61 year's attainment of independence, we have not yet been able to eliminate poverty from India. Large number of families suffering from the malady of poverty are forced to involve their children as labourers out of desperation and in order to supplement the family income.

3. *Illiteracy:* It is another reason behind the prevalence of child labour. It is really a matter of great shame that we have not yet been able to make primary education compulsory. India is ranked the lowest in the world as far as literacy is concerned. As a result of it and also because of massive poverty the children generally get the chance of making themselves available for employment at so early age.

4. *Wage Structure:* Children's work for less remuneration than adult labourers.

5. *Lack of Unions:* The working children are usually not associated with any trade union or federations. As such, they have no voice and strength to fight for their dues, rights and privileges.

6. *Inequitable Distribution of Land Assets:* In India, nearly 10 per cent of the privileged class holds 90 per cent of the agricultural land. The rest of the farmers are actually from labourers who work for wages. In spite of forty - five years of enforcement of tenancy laws, there has been practically no reform at this brought. The poor families on account of their low earnings compel their children to take up jobs in order to supplement their meager family income.

Above all, ineffective enforcement machinery, increase of rural migration, lack of political commitment and willingness to implement the child labour laws are the some of the burning issues adding to the child labour.

Consequences of Child Labour

A tender age has many adverse consequences especially for children. Children employed in carpet weaving, glass and bangles, match and fire work, slate or pencils, diamond cutting and polishing, bathos, slaughter Houses, lock making etc., are continuously exposed to various hazard, including at times, physical, social, sexual and psychological abuse. Children can be seen working underground, under water, dangerous heights or in confirmed spaces, handling dangerous machines, equipment, tools and some times, heavy loads. There is continuous exposure to hazardous substances or extreme temperature or noise levels. They also work for long hours or during the night. Through child labour, the child's potentials are put improper use for the employer's benefits (Singh and Sekhar, 2003).

Health Effects: According to Bimal (2000), many of the associated diseases can be attributed to extreme poverty situations, chronic semi-starvation and healthy environments do contribute to ill health in all children whether working or otherwise. The adverse conservancies of children working in hazardous occupations are many. Firstly it poses a challenge to the safety of the workers. Secondly health hazards have more long term implications in terms of making the person invalid for any work at an early age. Various studies have shown that the impact of the hazardous work begins to show in it severe from only after 2-3 years in terms of morbidity, fever, cold, cough, dysentery, body ache and weakness, TB and other respiratory problems.

The ILO report of the Director General in its 68th session of the International Labour Conference 1983 observed that the vulnerability of working children to health hazards is increased by the high incidence of malnutrition and under non-nourishment in contrast to their increased requirement for energy utilization to perform heavy work activities. The incidence of communicable disease is always higher among these children. Children come into close contact in work situations with infective cases of Tuberculosis and other similar diseases. Before malnutrition anemia, hard labour, fatigue and in a deviate sleep make other more susceptible to infections diseases.

Psychological Effects: According to Koteswara Rao M (2003), leisure, play and recreation are absolutely essential for healthy psychological growth of children. Those children who have restricted social interaction, long hours of daily work extending to 12 - 15 hours a day without any holidays, suffer from the inevitable crippling effects on their emotional development. In general, it is detrimental to their education, training, development towards maturity and integration in the society.

Many psychologists believe that childhood is the critical period for late development of personality and the exploitative situations of child labour exert strong influence on the child's self-concept and self-esteem. Child growing up in such a negative atmosphere feels incompetent, rejected and un-wanted. It leads to deficits in there physical, mental, social and emotional development.

Child labour degenerates socio-economic structure, affects the social infrastructure, causes health hazards and vitiates the ecology of civil welfare. The huge number of child labourers have adversely affected the quality of Indian labour force and narrowed down the scope of adult employment is responsible for the increase of child labour. Child labour also effects the migration of labour to a certain extent. In rural areas, the participation of children in the household and economic activates allows the elder member to migrate to other places in search of seasonal or permanent employment. Besides, the prevalence of child labour leads to formation of delivering gangs, anti-social elements and finally ends up with human resource under development.

Preventive Measures

Number of child labour study groups and committees i.e. Harbans Singh Committee, Gurupadaswami Committee, Sanad Mehta Committee, Singh Committee etc. have given them valuable suggestions. Casteism, poverty, income, family size and levels of education are some of the major factors that have intensified the problem of child labour in India. Gurupadaswarmi committee has revealed in its report that the child labour problem is a result of poverty and elimination of poverty in itself a great problem.

Various organizations including NGOs have joined the campaign to stop the exploitation of child workers and protect the child rights. As the magnitude of the child labour is more scary in India, it cannot be solved, by legislations alone. In fact, India alone constitutes 25 per cent of worlds working children. Hence, it calls for multi dimensional approach to overcome the problem of child labour. Child labour problem is an intense socio-economic problem in India that requires a long term multi-pronged strategy to be carried out on a continuous basis.

The following are the important remedial strategies to prevent and eradicate child labour:

1. Implementation of poverty eradication programmes
2. Compulsory schooling for children in non-hazardous jobs.
3. Withdraw / stopping all subsidies to industries employing children.
4. Continuous monitoring of the enforcement of law.
5. Offering up of free vocational and industrial training institutes for poor children after the completion compulsory primary education.

Legal Initiatives as Strategies to Prevent Child Labour

The history of child labour legislation in India has traversed a long path with the recognition of the child labour issue as a serious concern in the late nineteenth century. In India, too many laws like pledging the children Act.1957, Employment of children Act 1938, and later child labour (Prohibition and Regulation) Act 1986. Laws like Factories Act 1948, Mines Act 1952 and Plantation Labour Act 1957, The Merchant Shipping Act 1958, The Motor Transport Workers Act 1961, The Beedi and Cigar Workers (Conditions and Employment) Act 1966, Employment of Children (Amendment) for 1978, The Child Labour (Prohibition and Regulation) Act 1986 are the important initiatives and efforts taken up by the Government for the case of child labour.

Despite the fact that these Acts facilities to regulate and prevent the child labour none of them stresses upon the strategies to eliminate child labour.

Conclusion

The future of the nation depends on the present day children. So efforts are to be made to provide the children a pleasant, present and a bright future. Despite legislative measures, government efforts and sizeable NGO interventions, the problem of child labour continues. Child labour in India has been a fact and harsh reality in the socio-economic fabric of the nation. This problem needs adoption of suitable measures in the socio-economic structure of the society supplemented by legal measures.

Child labour is one of the social problems especially in developing countries like India. Poverty, illiteracy, alarming population, socio-economic disparities are some of the perennial causes for the growth of population. The concrete efforts in the form of legislations, Acts, stringent actions have been initiated and implemented at national and international level. Despite of all the efforts and measures, it appears that all these have regulated and to some extent monitored but could not completely eliminated. Besides, the growing urbanization, industrial development, growing private establishment the problem is likely to be increased. Therefore, it is high and right time to identify the ground causes for child labour, review the magnitude of the problem and suggest the suitable strategies to eliminate the child labour. In this regards, it is the moral responsibility of the policy makers, politicians, administrators, Government and NGO, philanthropists, sociologists, academicians including researchers to strive for, plan out and formulate suitable policy - measures to eliminate child labour.

REFERENCES

1. Sekhar, H. R., "Girl Child labour in the match industry of Sivakasi: No light in their lives", Child Labour Cell, V. V. Giri National Labour Institute, Noida, 1993.
2. Rajeshwari Panigrahi and Kamalun Nabi Md., "Child labour: the Harsh Reality", *Southern Economist*, Bangalore, June 1, 1999, pp 11-12.
3. Anandharaja Kumar. P., "Child Labour issues and Solutions" - *Kurukshetra*, Delhi, July, 1999.
4. Bimal. K. *Problems of Working Children*, APH Publishing Co. New Delhi, 2000.
5. Daman Ahuja, Community Action against child exploitation, *Social Welfare*, Delhi, July 2000, pp 29-32.
6. Koteswara Rao M, "Consequences of Child labour: A Study", *Southern Economist*, Bangalore, August 15, 2003, pp 5-7.
7. Census of India, 1971, 1981, 1991, 2001, Registrar General of India, New Delhi.

10

DISPARITIES OF FEMALES IN LITERACY RATES AND EDUCATION IN INDIA

S. Ramesh Babu, Y. Venkata Naidu** & K. Ravi Kumar****

Introduction

Gender discrimination or inequality from womb to tomb is a well-known fact in the traditional cultures of the developing countries. In India too, discrimination on the basis of sex often starts at the earliest stages of life. The Vedic era, however, was the golden era as far as equality of status and freedom women are concerned. In this era woman was considered as equal partner and enjoyed equal status and prestige in the society. The couple was called 'Dampati' which means that the husband and wife are the joint owners of the household. The position of the girl child seems to have deteriorated after the first millennia, especially in the north Indian states, due to a change in political equations. Early marriage, low status in marriage due to widespread polygamy and practice of seclusion among upper class women became rampant. Access to education was also limited. The reforms of the nineteenth century, however, advocated a ban on early marriage of girls, supported widow remarriage and opened

* Professor, ** Research Scholar, Dept. of Economics, Andhra University, Visakhapatnam, Andhra Pradesh.

*** Centre for Women Studies, Andhra University, Visakhapatnam, Andhra Pradesh.

schools for girls. This effort was continued more vigorously in the twentieth century with the support from the Indian National Congress, which led the struggle for independence. Though the constitution and a vast body of legislation have promoted gender equality, the status of the girl child continues to be low.

Education is the process that liberates mind. It is liberation from all forms of darkness and ignorance. Women's literacy is essential for economic viability and independence. Acquisition of knowledge is one of the prerequisites for human development. Today all development agencies agree on the importance of educating women in order to promote and maintain family education, health, nutrition and general well being. The aim of education should be to train women in such a way that they apply their acquired knowledge to the pursuits of daily life and fit them for the position they have to fill. Education for women should always be directed towards their holistic development. Education enhances a woman's sense of her own health needs and perspectives, and her power to take any health and family planning decisions. This, in turn, helps reduce child and maternal mortality and morbidity rates. Increased women education leads to greater empowerment of women, to a postponement of the age of marriage and to a reduction in the size of the families etc.

Historical Perspectives on Women Education in India

In ancient India women enjoyed a high status in the society. They were provided educational opportunities comparable to men. The social evils like purdah, sati, enforced widowhood and child-marriage crept into the society much later and resulted in the degradation of their status. There were no institutions for education of girls during Muslim period, but girls did receive religious education in the recitation of the Quran in their homes.

Under the British rule, the East India Company was reluctant to take up the responsibility of girl's education for a long time, due to the doctrine of religious neutrality, which was adopted by the Government so as not to offend the natives even on social customs that had nothing to do with religion. The Indian Education Commission (1882) took a serious note of the status and education of women and rated it to be extremely backward, and recommended measures for improvement. But, because of certain socio-political reasons, no noticeable progress could be made. After Independence, the University Education Commission (1948-49), set up by the government of India, laid special emphasis on the education of women.

During the post-Independence period, the main strategy adopted to achieve equalization of educational opportunities has been to make school accessible to every child. It was thought that expansion of educational facilities, as a part of providing universal elementary education for all would make education available to the weaker sections of the society including women.

Gender inequality has become one of the major areas of concern for educationists and policy makers in the developing countries in the 21st century. Gender inequality in India stems from two important sources of differences between men and women i.e. (1) earning capacity that make women utterly dependent upon men and (2) cultural taboos and traditions that greatly restrict the autonomy of women. Biological differentiation has perpetuated a structure, which has deprived women of normalcy of life chances as available to men.

As long as Indian society remains male dominated, the constitutional provisions for legal equality of women with men matters very little. Perhaps, in no area are the laws so openly and widely violated as in the case of women, whether it is a question of education, health, and securing employment or equal wages for equal work. The prevailing mindset of the people of the society is primarily responsible for the gender inequalities, which force women to be submissive.

Women are discriminated against notwithstanding the important role in several aspects of human life and materially contribute significantly for the development of the family, society and the country. Women account for a large percentage of unpaid work, both at home and outside. They actively participate themselves in work on the family farms and in household enterprises. Where they do participate in paid work, their earnings are low employment, irregular and insecure, support services inadequate, opportunities for improvement and growth few and collective organization weak.

It is a well-known fact that women play a very important role in agriculture, as it is largely a household enter-prise. They are engaged in agriculture both as main workers and as marginal workers also. Women perform a variety of tasks in agriculture transplantations, such as fertilizer application, weeding harvesting. Their role in the allied activities like management of dairy, poultry, sheep breeding etc is also well known. Indian women are major producers of food in terms of value, volume and hours of work.

Women, of late, have been increasingly involving themselves in work outside agriculture - in the secondary and tertiary sectors. Increasing levels of educational attainments have facilitated such involvement. To carry forward this trend, it is necessary that education of females should continue to be accorded greater and greater priority. Fortunately, the changing norms in the society are now enabling more and more women to actively seek education. Now they can be found in large numbers in the fields of Information Technology, science and space research and in other such fields that demand high level of skills.

As per the National Policy on Education (NPE) - 1986, the government of India launched several programmes. One such programme was the Mahila Samakhya. Its main emphasis was on the empowerment of women. The programme endeavours to create a learning environment where women can collectively affirm their potential, gain the strength to demand information and knowledge and move forward to change and take charge of their lives. Following the implementation of programmes specially directed at improving the educational status of women it is possible that women may be fast catching up with men in respect of educational attainments and may also be gaining access to employment in ever increasing numbers. We propose to examine whether this has really been happening. In other words, we propose to examine whether the policies of the government of Andhra Pradesh and of India have contributed to progressive trends - in the sense that they have aided the disadvantaged females more than their counterpart males.

Objectives

1. To arrive at the index of disparity between males and females in the literacy rate in India using inter-temporal data between 1901-2001.
2. To estimate the growth of educational institutions (from primary to higher education level) in India between 1950-51 and 2001-2002.
3. To analyze the growth of enrollment of females vis-à-vis males in primary, upper primary, secondary and higher education in India between 1950-51 and 1999-2000.
4. To analyze the faculty-wise enrollment of females in higher education during the year 2001-02.

The Data

The secondary data relating to the literacy rates of male and female, number of educational institutions from primary to higher levels and enrollment of students by sex in primary, upper primary, secondary and higher education level in India are obtained from the Census reports, Selected Educational Statistics, Ministry of HRD, Government of India and Annual reports, Ministry of HRD, Government of India.

Gender-wise Disparities in Literacy Rates in India

The most important characteristic of population is literacy, which is a pre - requisite for the overall development of the country both socially and economically. Female literacy is considered to be a more sensitive index of social development compared to overall literacy rates. Female literacy is negatively related with fertility rates, population growth rates, infant and child mortality rates, and shows a positive association with female age at marriage, life expectancy and participation in modern sectors of the economy. In spite of all the special constitutional provisions and governmental efforts, in the field of education, the disparities between male and female are still large. The gap between the literacy rates of males and females has been presenting since 1901 when the female literacy rate was only 0.60 per cent as against 9.83 per cent among males. The disparity index (ratio of male literacy rate to female literacy rate) in 1901 was 16.38. On the eve of the initiation of planned economic development in 1951 the literacy rate of women was 7.93 per cent. And women education received a phenomenal jerk from 1961. One can notice a double-digit growth rate in that year and it continued to grow at an increasing rate thereafter and even surpassed the cutoff level of 50:50 by the year 2001 (Table - 1).

Table-1: Sex Differences in Literacy Rates in India (1901 to 2001)

Year	*Male literacy rate*	*Female literacy rate*	*Disparity index*
1901	9.83	0.60	16.4
1911	10.56	1.05	10.1
1921	12.21	1.81	7.6
1931	15.59	2.93	5.3
1941	24.90	7.30	3.4
1951	24.95	7.93	3.1
1961	34.44	12.95	2.6
1971	39.45	18.69	2.1
1981	56.50	29.85	1.9
1991	64.13	39.29	1.6
2001	75.85	54.16	1.4

Source: Census Report, 2001.

Inter-State Disparities in Literacy Rates in India

Now an attempt is made to analyze the inter-state disparities

Table 2: Literacy Rate in States by Sex: 1991-2001

Sl. No.	*State*	*Females*			*Males*			*Persons*		
		2001	*1991*	*Variation*	*2001*	*1991*	*Variation*	*2001*	*1991*	*Variation*
1.	Andhra Pradesh	51.2	32.7	18.5	70.9	55.1	15.7	61.1	44.1	17.0
2.	Arunachal Pradesh	44.2	29.7	14.6	64.1	51.5	12.6	54.7	41.6	13.2
3.	Assam	56.0	43.0	13.0	71.9	61.9	10.1	64.3	52.9	11.4
4.	Bihar	33.6	22.0	11.6	60.3	51.4	9.0	47.5	37.5	10.0
5	Goa	75.5	67.1	8.4	88.9	83.6	5.2	82.3	75.5	6.8
6.	Gujarat	58.6	48.9	9.7	80.5	73.4	7.1	70.0	61.6	8.4
7.	Haryana	56.3	40.5	15.8	79.3	69.1	10.2	68.6	55.9	12.7
8.	Himachal Pradesh	68.1	52.3	15.8	86.0	75.4	10.6	77.1	63.9	13.2
9.	Karnataka	57.5	44.3	13.1	76.3	67.3	9.0	67.0	56.0	11.0
10.	Kerala	87.9	86.2	1.7	94.2	93.6	0.0	90.9	89.8	1.1
11.	Madhya Pradesh	50.3	29.4	20.9	76.8	58.5	18.3	64.1	44.7	19.4
12.	Maharashtra	67.5	52.3	15.2	86.3	76.6	9.7	77.3	64.9	12.4
13.	Manipur	59.7	47.6	12.1	77.9	71.6	6.2	68.9	59.9	9.0
14.	Meghalaya	60.4	44.9	15.6	66.1	53.1	13.0	63.3	49.1	14.2
15.	Mizoram	86.1	78.6	7.5	90.7	85.6	5.1	88.5	82.3	6.2
16.	Nagaland	61.6	54.8	6.9	71.8	67.6	4.1	67.1	61.7	5.5

17. Orissa	51.0	34.7	16.3	76.0	63.1	12.9	63.6	49.1	14.5
18. Punjab	63.6	50.4	13.1	75.6	65.7	10.0	70.0	58.5	11.5
19. Rajasthan	44.3	20.4	23.9	76.5	55.0	21.5	61.0	38.6	22.4
20. Sikkim	61.5	46.8	14.7	76.7	65.7	11.0	69.7	56.0	12.8
21. Tamil Nadu	64.6	51.3	13.2	82.3	73.8	8.6	73.5	62.7	10.8
22. Tripura	65.4	49.7	15.8	81.5	70.6	10.9	73.7	60.4	13.3
23 Uttar Pradesh	43.0	24.4	18.6	70.2	54.8	15.4	57.4	40.7	16.7
24. West Bengal	60.2	46.6	13.7	77.6	67.8	9.8	69.2	57.7	11.5
25. Chattisgarh	52.4	27.5	24.9	77.9	58.1	19.8	65.2	42.9	22.3
26. Uttaranchal	60.3	41.6	18.6	84.0	72.8	11.2	72.3	57.8	34.5
27. Jharkhand	39.4	25.5	13.9	67.9	55.8	12.2	54.1	41.4	12.7
28. Jammu & Kashmir	41.8	NA	-	65.8	NA	-	54.5	NA	-

Source: Compiled from Population of India 2001. Census Results and Methodology by Ashish Bose.

in the literacy rates for females, males and total persons at census of India, 1991 and 2001. The state-wise information on literacy rates for females, males and persons is presented in Table - 2.

As can be seen from the table, Kerala retained its position by being on top with a 90.9 per cent literacy rate in the county. The rate among males was 94.2 per cent and among females it was 87.9 per cent. Bihar stood at the bottom with a literacy rate of 47.5 per cent (60.3 per cent for males and 33.6 per cent for females). Among the three new states Uttranchal has the highest literacy rate of 72 per cent for the total population, male literacy rate of 84 per cent and female literacy rate of 60 per cent. Chattisgarh has an overall literacy rate of 65 per cent (males 78 per cent and females 52 per cent); Jharkhand has an overall literacy rate of 54 per cent (68 per cent males and 39 per cent females). Six out of the 28 states in India have a female literacy rate of less than 50 per cent. These states are Rajasthan (44 per cent), Jammu & Kashmir (42 per cent), Jharkhand (39 per cent) and Bihar (34 per cent). The female literacy rate in Madhya Pradesh is 50 per cent.

The gap between male and female literacy rate is the highest in Rajasthan (32 per cent), followed by Uttar Pradesh (27 per cent), Madhya Pradesh (27 per cent), Jharkhand (27 per cent), Chattisgarh (26 per cent) and Bihar (26 per cent). It is distressing to note that the male - female literacy gap is high in Gujarat (22 per cent). Maharashtra and West Bengal (18 per cent each) including social backwardness.

In terms of progress on the female literacy front during the last decade, Chattisgarh has the best record (the increase in the literacy percentage by 25 points between 1991-2001, followed by Rajasthan (24 per cent), Madhya Pradesh (21 per cent). In the case of males, Rajasthan has the best record (increase of 21.5 points) followed by Chattisgarh (20 points) and Madhya Pradesh (18 points). There is no doubt that special programmes launched by the Government and NGOs in Rajasthan and Madhya Pradesh have succeeded in stepping up literacy rates mostly among males.

Special Schemes and Programmes for Promoting Education of Females

Several strategies were adopted to promote education of girls in independent India. Theoretically, all formal and non-formal education and training programmes are open to women also along with their male counterparts. However, separate provisions are made for opening of separate institutions or separate wings for women / girls exclusively. Education is free for girls up to the higher secondary stage and several states have made education free for girls' right up to the university level as well. Besides, there are other incentives like free noon meals, free books, free uniforms, scholarships for good attendance, bicycles, etc.

In the first three Five Year Plans, girls' education was covered under special component plans with additional allocations. In the Eighth Five Year Plan, a central scheme was introduced to provide funds to the state governments to hire a woman teacher for all single teacher primary schools and also towards cash awards and prizes for villages, blocks and districts with good performance in female education / literacy. Girls belonging to scheduled castes and scheduled tribes received additional benefits for showing better school attendance. In some states girls/women receive a little high amount of scholarship particularly at the post matric and technical educational level as a special incentive for promotion of women education. As a result of the protective discrimination policies under constitutional provisions, the enrollment of the SC and ST girl children has considerably improved.

Committees and Commissions on Women Education after Independence

After Independence, the government of India appointed various committees and commissions to promote the cause of women's education. They are:

1. University Education Commission (1948-49)
2. Secondary Education Commission (1952-53)

3. National Committee on Women Education (1958-59)
4. Committee on differentiation of curricula for boys and girls (1961)
5. Committee to look into causes for lack of public supports for girl's education and enlist public cooperation (1963).
6. Education Commission (1964-66)
7. Committee on status of women (1971-74)
8. National Policy on Education (1986) and Programme of Action (1992)
9. National Perspective Plan for Women's Education (1988-2000 AD)

The above committees and commissions though, differ in their focus, all of them agree on the basic issues like (a) improvement of girl's enrollment in schools, (b) female literacy rate and (c) women empowerment through education.

Despite the near universal and far-reaching benefits through female education, female literacy rates are still low and the school dropout rates are high. There are gender differentials in education at all levels and so are the resulting differentials in employment.

Growth of Educational Institutions

After independence, the government took serious steps to establish a large number of primary, upper primary, higher secondary, colleges for general education, colleges for professional education and universities in the country. Table – 3 provides data on the number of recognized educational institutions in the country between 1950-51 to 2001-02.

During the last five decades the establishment of educational institutions increased in primary, upper primary, higher /high secondary, colleges for general education, colleges for professional education and universities/deemed universities from 209671 to 664041, from 13596 to 219626, from 7416 to 133492, from 370 to 8737, from 208 to 2409 and from 27 to 272 respectively. The growth rates are calculated for the periods 1950-51 to 2001-02. The rates are 316.7 for primary, 1615.4 for upper primary, 1800.1

for high / high secondary, 2361.4 for colleges for general education, 1158.2 for colleges for professional education and 1007 for universities / deemed universities.

Table-3: Growth of Recognized Educational Institutions from 1950-51 to 2001-02

Year	*Primary*	*Upper Primary*	*High/Hr. Sec/Intr Pre.Jr. Colleges*	*Colleges for General Education*	*Colleges for Professional Education (Engg., Tech., Arch., Medical & Education Colleges)*	*Universities Deemed Univ./Instt. of National Importance*
1	2	3	4	5	6	7
1950-51	209671	13596	7416	370	208	27
2001-02	664041	219626	133492	8737	2409	272
Growth	316.7	1615.4	1800.1	2361.4	1158.2	1007.0

Source: (www.education.nic.in)

Percentage Share of Female Enrollment to Total

Let us now examine the progress of girls' enrollment in primary, upper primary, secondary / higher secondary and higher education stages. As shown in Table-4 in 1950-51, the enrollment of girls was 28.1 per cent at primary school stage, 16.1 per cent at the upper primary stage, 13.3 per cent at secondary/ higher secondary level and 10.0 per cent in higher education level compared with the corresponding percentage of 71.9, 83.9, 86.7 and 90.0 per cent among boys. By 1999-2000, the situation has considerably improved at all levels, in favour of females to 43.6 per cent at primary level, 40.4 per cent at upper primary level, 38.9 per cent at secondary / higher secondary level and 39.9 per cent in higher education as against 56.4 per cent in primary stage, 59.6 per cent in upper primary stage, 61.1 per cent in secondary / higher secondary level and 60.1 per cent in higher education stage among boys.

Table - 4: Percentage of Girls Enrollment to Total Enrollment by Stages 1950- 51 to 1999-2000

Year	*Primary Stage (I-V)*	*Upper Primary Stage (VI-VIII)*	*Secondary / Higher Secondary (IX-XII)*	*Higher education*
1950-51	28.1	16.1	13.3	10.0
1960-61	32.6	23.9	20.5	20.4
1970-71	37.4	29.3	25.0	20.0
1980-81	38.6	32.9	29.6	26.7
1990-91	41.5	36.7	32.9	32.3
1999-2000	43.6	40.4	38.9	39.9

Sources: 1. Selected Educational Statistics, Ministry of HRD, Govt. of India
2. Ministry of HRD, Govt. of India, Annual Report, 2000.

Table-5: Annual Compound Growth Rate of Enrollment by Stages 1950-2000

Stage	*Annual compound growth rate during 1950-51 to 1999-2000*	
	Boys (%)	*Girls (%)*
Primary	3.12	4.53
Upper Primary	4.31	7.31
Secondary / higher secondary	5.30	8.34
Higher education	6.87	10.66

Note: Computed on the basis of enrollment of boys and girls in different stages.

It is evident from the growth rates shown in Table–5, the enrollment of girls has increased at a faster rate than that of boys at primary, upper primary, secondary / higher secondary and higher education level. During our study period (1950-51 to 1999-2000) the Annual Compound Growth Rate of enrollment of girls was 4.53 per cent as against 3.12 per cent of boys in primary stage. The corresponding figures were 7.31 and 4.31 in upper primary stage, 8.34 and 5.30 in secondary / higher secondary stage and 10.66 and 6.87 in higher education respectively. The foregoing analysis shows that during the whole period of 50 years after implementation of our constitution, the growth rate of enrollment of girls has been higher than that of boys.

Enrollment of Females in Higher, Professional and Technical Education

By 1999-2000 there are 7494 colleges for general education, 540 engineering colleges, 755 medical colleges, 818 Colleges of Teacher Training, and 308 universities including institutions of national importance and research institutions serving more than six million students and scholars in India. There are 1066 Polytechnics, TTIs 4171 and 1319 Teacher Training Schools in 1999-2000.

Though, the share of girls in various faculties has increased very substantially during the last four decades, they continued to be way behind in Arts with 44.7 per cent, Science with 35.6 per cent, Commerce with 31.6 per cent, Education with 47.0 per cent, Engineering and Technology with 19.5 per cent, and Medicine with 38.0 per cent to reach the ideal 50:50 ratio (Please see Table-6).

Table - 6: Enrollment of Females as Percentage to Total Enrollment in Higher Education by Faculty

Year	*Arts*	*Science*	*Commerce*	*Education*	*Engg. / Tech.*	*Medicine*
1960-61	18.6	0.0	1.1	32.5	0.8	20.4
1970-71	33.5	18.8	2.8	37.3	1.0	21.3
1980-81	37.5	27.9	15.2	46.7	4.6	23.8
1990-91	39.8	36.8	24.0	44.4	10.9	34.3
1999-2000	44.7	35.6	31.6	47.0	19.5	38.0

Source: Dept. of Education, Human Resource Development Govt. of India.

Conclusion and Suggestions

The position of the girl child has deteriorated after the first millennia; consequently, access to education was also limited. The most important characteristic of population is literacy, which is prerequisite for the overall development of the country both socially and economically. As per 2001 census, women constitute about 54.16 per cent of the total population in India. In the field of education the disparities between males and females are still larger.

The literacy rate among females has increased at a faster rate than among males. This is evident from the successively decreasing trend of disparity index from 16.4 in 1901 to 1.4 in 2001 in the country. In literacy rate Kerala retained its supremacy position by being on top with a 90.9 per cent literacy rate in 2001 in the country. The rate among males was 94.2 per cent and among females it was 87.9 per cent. Bihar stood at the bottom with a literacy rate of 47.5 per cent (60.3 per cent for males and 33.6 per cent for females).

Several strategies were adopted to promote education of girls in independent India. The Government of India has been appointing various committees and commissions to promote the female education as and when required. Separate provisions are being made for opening of separate institutions or separate wings of women/girls exclusively. The Government of India had established a large number of educational institutions in the country by 2002.

The enrollment of girls in primary education increased from 28.1 per cent in 1950-51 to 43.6 per cent in 1999-2000; in upper primary education it was increased from 16.1 per cent in 1950-51 to 40.4 per cent in 1999-2000; in secondary education it was increased from 13.3 per cent in 1950-51 to 38.9 per cent in 1999-2000; and in higher education it was increased from 10.0 per cent in 1950-51 to 39.9 per cent in 1999-2000. The enrollment of females has considerably improved at all levels of education in favour of females during the period of our study.

Career counseling is being actively promoted to ensure that the skills acquired by girls are appropriately utilized. These positive initiatives have helped in improving the participation of girls/women at all levels of education especially in higher education since the post-independent period. It is evident that the enrollment of girls/ women has increased at a faster rate than that of boys/men at primary, upper primary, secondary/ higher secondary and higher education stage.

The foregoing analysis suggests that during the whole period of five decades after implementation of our constitution, the growth rate of enrollment of girls/women in all stages of education has been higher than that of boys / men. The share of girls/ women enrollment in various faculties has also increased very substantially during the last four decades. Yet, their share in the educational facilities is less than 50 per cent in the total.

In the above context there is a need for rethinking about the higher education for women. There is a general agreement that the enrollment of women to higher education must be raised at least to cover their share in the total population, which is around 50 per cent. Efforts must be directed to retain the girls in primary and secondary educational levels and enable them to pursue higher studies. And again, in the field of higher education, enrollment into technical, medicine, veterinary sciences and law should be increased through special measures in favour of women.

REFERENCES

1. Chalam, K.S. (1988): *Education and Weaker Sections,* Inter-India Publications, New Delhi.
2. Chalam, K.S. (1993): *Educational Policy for Human Resources Development,* Rawat Publications, Jaipur.
3. Chauhan, C.P.S. (2000): 'Contemporary Issues In Higher Education', *University News,* AIU, New Delhi, December 2004.
4. Chauhan, C.P.S., (1990) *Higher Education In India: Achievements, Failures and Strategies,* Ashish Publishing House, New Delhi.
5. Government of India. *National Policy on Education (NPE), 1986* and its revised version 1992, MHRD, New Delhi, 1986 And 1992.
6. Mira Seth (2001): *Women and Development – The Indian experience,* Sage publications, New Delhi.
7. Nurullah, S and Naik, J.P. (1943): *History of Education in India during the British period,* Macmillan & Co. Ltd., Bombay.
8. Power, K.B. (2000): 'Higher Education in the Twenty-First century', *University News,* AIU, New Delhi, December 4.

9. Sakuntala Narasimhan (1999): *Empowering Women – An alternative strategy from rural India,* Sage publications, New Delhi.

10. Sangeetha Purushothaman (1998): *The Empowerment of Women in India – grassroots women's networks and the state,* Sage publications, New Delhi.

11. University Grants Commission. *Annual Reports,* 1959-60, 1993-94, 1995-96, 1998-99 and 2001-02, UGC, New Delhi.

11

DROPOUTS IN PRIMARY EDUCATION IN VIZIANAGARAM DISTRICT OF ANDHRA PRADESH – MANDAL LEVEL ANALYSIS

D. Francis, S.M. Khasim** & D. Pulla Rao****

Introduction

Economists have been arguing with sufficient empirical evidence that education contributes positively to development. A number of studies were undertaken by researchers to establish the relationship between literacy and socio-economic development. It is, however, necessary to remember that primary education is pivotal for achieving total literacy. Primary education constitutes a very important part of the entire structure of education. It is at this stage, the child starts going to a formal institution and formal education starts. Primary education in India has been under the control of a number of agencies. It is still under the private management by and large, though, the State is increasingly taking the responsibility of providing free and compulsory elementary education to all. Article 45 of the Constitution provides for free and compulsory education for all children in the age-group 6-14 years, up to a minimum level. The whole idea has

* Teaching Associate, Department of Economics, Dr. B.R. Ambedkar University, Etcherla, Srikakulam, Andhra Pradesh.

** Research Scholar & *** Professor, Department of Economics, Andhra University, Visakhapatnam, Andhra Pradesh.

been woven into the concept of Universalization of Elementary Education (UEE). The level of compulsory education as envisaged corresponds to the elementary education of eight year's duration from class I to class VIII for the children aged 6-14 years. The universalization of Elementary Education has been recognized as a constitutional obligation in India by the year 1960 but the target has not been achieved even after 48 years of the target year.

The Problem of Dropouts

Efforts are being made, but we have not yet fulfilled our National development goal of UEE so far. Although, the policy intentions were articulated well, there was no comprehensive operational plan. Though efforts are being made to improve the status of primary education in India in reality, the child in the classroom is not focused fully. Unless the child is focused as the centre of classroom activity, dropouts and stagnation will continue to exist. An analysis of data on primary education reveals that there is failure both on enrollment and dropout fronts. The educational policies could neither ensure a cent per cent enrollment nor prevent the incidence of dropouts. Among the failures in the achievement of compulsory primary education the two dominant factors appear to be (i) dropouts, and (ii) repeaters. Some pupils leave the system at different points without completing primary stage and it is designated as dropouts or push outs while some pupils repeat the same grade and it is called stagnation or repeaters, while the concept of stagnation is simple and straight forward, the dropout phenomenon creates certain conceptual problems.

The National Policy on Education (NPE), 1986 and the Programme of Action, 1992 reiterate the commitment or retaining the children in schools up to at least class VIII. The question of dropouts may represent the insufficiency of the Educational System and this leads to the wastage of the scarce resources in a developing country like India. We consider enrollment as the indicator for various levels or stages as well as various classes. The target is still to enroll all children of 6 years in class 1 and ensure their continuance till they get through class V. Then only the dreams of universalisation of Elementary/Primary Education be realised. In this paper, the dropout rates are discussed at primary level in Vizianagaram District for the period 2001-2002 to 2005-2006.

Objectives

(i). To examine the dropout situation at the mandal level in the district.

(ii). To elicit the causes of the dropout of the children before completing their primary education in the district.

Methodology and Sources of Data

The data for this study were collected from both primary and secondary sources. Primary data were collected for studying causes for dropouts. The secondary data consist of enrolment of students in each mandal have been collected from the records of the District Educational Officer, Vizianagaram and from Commissioner and Director of School Education, Hyderabad. Causes for dropouts have been hypothesized by direct interview method with coverage of 180 households of dropouts in three mandals of Vizianagaram District. The three mandals have been selected on the basis of socio-economic and geographical conditions, these are: (1) Vizianagaram - Urban area (2) Bobbili-Semi-urban area, and (3) Kurupam - Tribal area. The survey was conducted in 2008 with reference to the period from 2001-2002 to 2005-2006.

In this paper, the dropout rates are calculated for all the 34 mandals in Vizianagaram District. Dropout rates are taken as 100 minus the ratio of enrolment in Class V in the year 't' to the enrolment in Class I in the base year i.e., (t-4) for primary level in calculating the dropout rate mandal wise the standard formula has been used, i.e.. Dropout rate for Class I to (1+n) in the year t to (t+n)

$$\text{Dropout rate} = 100 - \frac{\text{Enrolment in class } (1 + n) \text{ in the year } (t+n)}{\text{Enrollment in class 1 to year t}}$$

The Study Area of Vizianagaram District

Vizianagaram district is one of the North-Eastern Coastal districts of Andhra Pradesh. The population of the district is about 22.49 lakhs as per 2001 census and this constitutes 2.95 per cent of total population of the State. There are about 9.97 lakh literates forming 44.33 per cent of total population of the district. Among literates, male literates constitute 60.68 per cent while female literates form 39.32 per cent as per 2001 census. There are 2,364 primary schools with 2.36 lakhs children on rolls and 214 upper primary schools with an enrolment of 55, 650 lakhs in 2001. The focus of the study is on the dropout rates of primary education in Vizianagaram District, which is one of the most backward districts of the Coastal Andhra Pradesh. Vizianagaram District was divided into 34 Revenue mandals.

Results of the Analysis

The analysis has been carried out for primary classes i.e. I to V during the period 2001-02 to 2005-06. Mandal wise dropout rates for boys and girls are shown separately in Table-1.

It is found that the dropout rate for boys and girls put together for primary education in the district is 14.92 per cent. For boys it is 14.35 per cent and for girls it is 15.51 per cent in the district. Further it is found that there are about 17 mandals whose dropout rates are found to be above the district average. For boys there are about 17 mandals, which are found to be above the district average and for girls 18 mandals are found to be above the district average. Firstly, regarding dropout rates among mandals, the highest dropout rate is recorded in Kurupam mandal with 40.04 per cent followed by Pusapatirega with 36.83 per cent and the lowest is recorded in Bobbili with 3.56 per cent and Nellimarla with 4.53 per cent. There are 3 mandals where no drop outs are recorded. They are Gumma Lakshmi Puram, Garugubilli and Rambhadrapuram.

The thinly populated and with large number of villages in Kurupam mandal recorded the highest dropout rates with 40.04 per cent and for girls with 43.60 per cent respectively. But contrary to the situation in Kurupam, Gumma Lakshmi Puram mandal in the district with the highest inhabited villages recorded nil dropouts. Garugubilli and Ramabhadrapuram followed Gummalakshmi Puram in recording nil dropouts. This is due to geographic characteristics, economic status and literacy levels of the particular population. For example, literacy rate in Garugubilli in 2001 is 53.73 per cent and in the case of males it is 68.1 per cent.

Secondly, dropout rates among girls are the highest in Kurupam mandal with 43.60 per cent. Second, third and fourth positions in highest dropouts are occupied by Pusapatirega, Dathirajeru and Saluru with 43.36 per cent, 25.13 per cent and 23.54 per cent respectively. If we observe the lowest dropouts among girls, Nellimarla with 2.47 per cent occupies first position. Vizianagarm with 4.87 per cent, Gummalakshmi Puram with 4.93 per cent and Balajipeta with 5.33 per cent occupy second, third and fourth places respectively. Nil dropouts are found in Garugubilli, Ramabhadrapuram and Kothavalasa mandals in Vizianagaram district during the period 2001-02 to 2005-06.

Thirdly, if we observe dropout rates among boys, Kurupam occupies the first position with the highest dropout rate 36.64 per cent. Srungavarapu Kota with 32.85 per cent, Vepada with 32.23 per cent and Pusapatirega with 30.16 per cent occupy second, third and fourth positions respectively in the district. If we observe the lowest dropout rates among boys, Mentada with 2.12% occupies the first position, Garugubilli with 3.03 per cent, Jiyyammavalasa with 4.94 per cent and Nellimarla with 6.64 per cent occupy second, third and fourth positions in recording lowest dropouts in the district during the study period 2001-2002 to 2005-2006. It is noteworthy that there are three mandals which have not recorded any dropouts namely; Bobbili, Ramabhadrapuram and Gummalakshmi Puram.

From the above analysis it can be easily identified that the highest dropout rate is commonly recorded in Kurupam and Pusapatirega mandals for both boys and girls in the district. In the case of Srungavarapu Kota mandal which recorded third highest dropout rate in the district for the period 2001-02 to 2005-06 are 32.85 per cent (boys) 22.53 per cent (girls), and the average of the boys and girls comes to about 27.83 per cent. In the same way the lowest dropouts are recorded in Bobbili mandal with 3.56 per cent; nil dropouts among boys and 7.90 per cent dropouts among girls.

Table -1
Mandal-wise Dropout Rates at Primary Level in Vizianagaram District from 2001-02 to 2005-06

Sl.No	Name of the Mandal	Boys	Girls	Total
1	KOMARADA	21.00	21.86	21.43
2	G.L.PURAM	0.00	4.93	0.00
3	KURAPAM	36.64	43.60	40.04
4	JIYYAMMAVALASA	4.94	12.69	8.81
5	GARUGUBILLI	3.03	0.00	0.00
6	PARVATHIPURAM	15.79	17.85	16.82
7	MAKKUVA	13.28	22.77	18.12
8	SEETHANAGARAM	21.39	19.43	20.44
9	BALIJIPETA	12.06	5.33	8.74
10	BOBBILI	0.00	7.90	3.56
11	SALURU	19.72	23.54	21.61
12	PACHIPENTA	13.19	7.07	10.24
13	RAMABHADRAPURAM	0.00	0.00	0.00
14.	Badagni	9.66	19.27	19.46
15	THERLAM	10.56	17.79	14.29
16	MERAKAMUDIDAM	15.65	15.07	15.36
17	DATHIRAJERU	23.22	25.13	24.15
18	MENTADA	2.12	9.26	5.75
19	GAJAPATHINAGARAM	8.24	11.56	9.92
20	BONDAPALLI	18.82	22.37	20.63
21	GURLA	15.53	17.66	16.61
22	GARIVIDI	20.74	22.77	21.75
23	CHEEPURUPALLI	17.20	21.27	19.26
24	NELLIMARLA	6.64	2.47	4.53
25	PUSAPATIREGA	30.16	43.36	36.83
26	BHOGAPURAM	10.65	19.44	14.87
27	DENKADA	22.17	23.51	22.84

28	VIZIANAGARAM	6.71	4.87	5.82
29	GANTYADA	7.97	12.25	10.05
30	SRUNGAVARAPUKOTA	32.85	22.53	27.83
31	VEPADA	32.23	8.61	20.81
32	LAKAVARAPUKOTA	9.64	13.41	11.54
33	JAMI	13.04	8.79	11.03
34	KOTHAVALASA	20.38	0.00	10.36
	Total	14.34	15.51	14.92

Source: District Educational Officer, Vizianagaram District.

There are only 2 (5.88 %) mandals with dropout range of 30 to 40 per cent and 9 (26.47 %) mandals which are in the range of 20 to 30 per cent dropout rate. As many as 13 mandals are there with dropout range of 10 to 20 per cent in the district during the period 2001-2002 to 2005-06. Details of range-wise dropout rates for all pupils (both boys and Girls) of mandals are presented in Tables-2.

Table -2: Range-wise Distribution of Dropout Rate for All Pupils

Range of Dropout Rate	*Number of Mandals*	*Name of the Mandals*
0-10	10	Gummalakshmi Puram, Garugubilli, Ramabhadrapuram(nil), Bobbili, Nellimarla, Mentada, Vizianagaram, Balajipeta, Jiyyammavalasa, Gajapathinagaram
10-20	13	Gantyada, Pachipenta, Kothavalasa, Jami, Lakkvarapukota, Therlam, Bhogapuram, Merakamudidam, Gurla, Parvathipuram, Makkuva, Cheepurupalli, Badangi
20-30	9	Seethanagaram, Bondapalli, Vepada, Komarada, Saluru, Garividi, Denkada, Dathirajeru, Srungavarapu Kota
30-40	2	Pusapatirega, Kurapam
Total :	34	

It is found from Table-3 that there are only 2 (5.88%) mandals whose dropouts for girls are in the range of 30 to 40 per cent. And the remaining 32 (94.12%) mandals are in the range of 0-30 per cent. This clearly shows that, there is less dropout rate in the district.

Table -3: Range-wise Distribution of Dropout Rate for Girls

Range of Dropout Rate	*Number of Mandals*	*Name of the Mandals*
0-10	12	Garugubilli, Ramabhadrapuram, Kothavalasa (nil),Nellimarla, Vizianagaram, Gummalakshmi Puram, Balajipeta, Pachipenta, Bobbili, Vepada, Jami, Mentada
10-20	11	Gajapathinagaram, Gantyda, Jiyyammavalasa, Lakkavarapukota, Merakamudidam, Gurla, Therlam, Parvathipuram, Badangi, Seethanagaram, Bhogapuram
20-30	9	Cheepurupalli, Komarada, Bondapalli, Srungavarapu Kota, Makkuva, Garividi, Denkada, Saluru, Dathirajeru
30-40	2	Pusapatirega, Kurapam
Total :	34	

Range-wise distributions of dropout rate for boys of mandals are presented in Table - 4. There are about 10 mandals (29.41%) which are in the dropout range of 20 to 40 per cent and the remaining 24 mandals (70.59%) are below 20 per cent drop out range.

From the above analysis it can be concluded that out of 100 children who took admission in class I in the year 2001-02, as high as 40 Pupils in Kurupam mandal, 37 pupils in Pusapatirega and 28 pupils in Srungavarapu Kota mandal dropped out of school without reaching class V by 2005-06. It is evident from above data that dropouts are at medium level in the district. However, it can not be neglected in view of reaching the goal of Universalisation of Primary Education.

Table - 4: Range-wise Distribution of Dropout Rate for Boys

Range of Dropout Rate	Number of Mandals	Name of the Mandals
0-10	11	Gummalakshmi Puram, Ramabhadrapuram, Bobbili(nil), Mentada, Garugubilli, Jiyyammavalasa, Nellimarla, Vizianagaram, Gantyada, Gajapathinagaram, Lakkavarapukota
10-20	13	Therlam, Bhogapuram, Balajipeta, Jami, Pachipenta, Makkuva, Gurla, Merakamudidam, Parvathipuram, Cheepurupalli, Bondapalli, Badangi, Saluru
20-30	6	Kothavalsa, Garividi, Komarada, Seethanagaram, Denkada, Dathirajeru
30-40	4	Pusapatirega, Vepada, Srungavarapu Kota, Kurapam
Total :	34	

It is observed from the study that only 60 per cent of the enrolled children completed primary education in Kurupam, and 63 per cent in Pusapatirega and 72 per cent in Srungavarapu Kota mandals. It means that for Universalisation of elementary education the coverage has been about two third in 2005-06 of the target set for the year 2010 as per the Sarva Siksha Abhiyan. It is clear that, despite a high coverage of enrolment in class I the target of achieving Universalisation of primary education does not seem to be possible in the near future in the wake of medium dropout rates as seen in Vizianagaram district.

Reasons for Dropouts

The preceding analysis shows a medium dropout rate at primary level. In order to understand the reasons for dropout and non-enrolment and also identify the socio-economic barriers at the primary stage itself a sample survey of 180 households of dropouts in three mandals selected purposively viz., Vizianagaram, Bobbili and Kurupam has been conducted. These three mandals represent urban, semi-urban and tribal situations in the district. In Bobbili the dropout rates have been less and in the Kurupam the dropout rates have been quite high, and Vizianagaram is a model situation. All the details are presented in Table -5.

(a) Literacy Level of the Head of the Family

Literacy level of the parents of the child is the most influencing factors of dropout rate. It is possible to hypothesize that higher the literacy level of the head of the family, the lower is the chance of the child dropping out of the school. Our data clearly show that, out of 60 households in each mandal, the heads of 12 children, 21 children and 38 children are illiterate in Vizianagaram, Bobbili and Kurupam mandals respectively. They constitute 20, 35 and 63 per cent of illiterates respectively. It indicates how illiteracy contributes to dropouts. It can clearly be understood, if we compare this with the Table -1, we can easily come to the conclusion that illiteracy of the head of the family is the primary reason for higher dropout rate.

Table 5: Reasons for Dropouts in Vizianagaram District

Reasons for Dropouts	*Vizianagaram (Urban)*	*Bobbili*	*Kurupam*
I. Literacy level of the head of the family			
a) Literates	48(80.00)	39(65.00)	22(36.67)
b) Illiterates	12(20.00)	21(35.00)	38(63.33)
II. Occupation of Parents			
a) Agriculture	15(25.00)	27(45.00)	44(73.33)
b) Industry	18(30.00)	12(20.00)	4(6.67)
c) Others	27(45.00)	21(35.00)	12(20.00)
III Caste Factor			
a) SC/ST	18(30.00)	22(36.67)	42(70.00)
b) BC	25(41.67)	29(48.33)	11(18.33)
c) OC	17(28.33)	9(15.00)	7(11.67)

IV	Economic Status of Parents			
	a) Below Rs.12000	12(20.00)	21(35.00)	37(61.67)
	b) Above Rs.12000	48(80.00)	39(65.00)	23(38.33)
V	Negligence of Girls Education	9(15.00)	20(33.33)	28(46.67)

Note: Figure in parentheses indicate percentages

(b) Poor Economic Conditions of the Family

As per the study 70 per cent of people in Kurupam belong to the low income group. They are small farmers and daily wage labourers. Due to poor economic conditions, parents, instead of sending their children to school, seek assistance from their children at home and on the agricultural farm in Kurupam. But the case is different for Bobbili and Vizianagaram where the family conditions are better and dropouts are less. Hence it can be concluded that poverty is the most significant and determining factor for dropouts.

(c) Involvement of Children in Domestic Work

Teachers opine that most of the dropouts are due to the activities assigned to the children like watching the cattle, assisting their parents at farms and looking after the younger brothers or sisters at home. This reason has been significant in Kurupam mandal. As such it can be concluded that excessive involvement of children in domestic work and chores is the most dominating factor influencing the dropout rates in Vizianagaram district.

(d) Negligence of Parents

Even today, most of parents do not show interest in educating their children, especially in rural areas like Kurupam mandal and more so in the case of girls. Most of the parents in this mandal, due to lack of education, awareness and for some beliefs and customs, neglected their children's education, particularly girls, whereas the situation is different for Vizianagaram and Bobbili. Highest dropout rate for girls in the district is recorded in Kurupam mandal.

(e) Caste Factor and Dropout Rates

Some communities like Scheduled Castes and Scheduled Tribes face social discrimination which may vary in intensity, place to place and caste to caste. In Kurupam mandal about 85 per cent of the population is Scheduled Tribes and other disadvantaged communities. This clearly reflected in high drop out rate of 40 per cent in this mandal which is highest in the district (Table-1). According to local teachers most of the drop outs belong to ST, SC and BCs. This is mostly due to both economic and social reasons.

Conclusion

Universalisation of primary education means enrolment of 100 per cent children of 6 years age in class I and ensuring their continuance till they complete their primary education i.e. class V. In this paper, we calculated dropout rates for all the mandals in Vizianagaram district and have examined how distant the target is. It is found from the analysis that the highest dropout rate is recorded in Kurupam mandal for both boys and girls with 36.64 per cent and 43.60 per cent respectively. This shows that girl's dropout rate is relatively higher than that of boys because of many reasons like customs and traditions etc.

The lowest dropout rates are recorded in Bobbili mandal for both boys and girls. There is no dropout rate recorded for boys and girls recorded 7.90 per cent during the period of study. In addition to lowest dropouts in Bobbili, three mandals, Gummalakshmi Puram, Garugubilli and Ramabhadrapuram recorded no drop outs. It can be easily understood that dropout rate is influenced by urbanisation and it leads to decrease in dropout rates.

As a whole, the highest dropout rate is recorded in Kurupam mandal (40.04%) and the lowest is recorded in Bobbili mandal (3.56%). The results show that tribal mandals are not ready to realize the target of Universalisation of primary education except Gummalakshmi Puram which is a highly tribal populated mandal without any dropouts. It is observed that the local authorities also failed to fulfill the target. Except few urban mandals, the coverage of the concept of universalisation of primary education is about only one third of the set target.

The study shows that dropout rate is the highest for backward mandals and the lowest for urban mandals in general. In our sample survey, some of the reasons for dropout rate has been examined that literacy level of the head of the family is one of the predominant factors. It is higher for Bobbili mandal when compared to the other two mandals i.e., Vizianagaram and Kurupam. Occupation, economic status of parents, negligence of girl child education and social and religious barriers are also causes for higher dropout rates. For reaching the goal of universalisation of elementary education (UEE) all the above said causes should be overcome.

REFERENCES

1. Brimer, M.A. and Pauli, C. (1971): "Wastage in education – a world problem", UNESCO.
2. Chalam, K.S. (1988): *Education and Weaker Sections,* Inter India Publications, New Delhi.
3. Chauhan, C.P.S. (2004): *Modern Indian Education, Policies, Progress and Problems.* Kanishka Publishers, New Delhi.
4. Chickermane, D.V. (1962): "A study of wastage in primary education", *Education and Psychology Review,* Vol.II, January.
5. Pulla Rao, D. (1998): *Economics of primary education,* Rawat Publications, Jaipur.
6. Rajaiah, B. (1987): *Economics of Education,* Mittal Publications, New Delhi.
7. Rajput, J.S. (1993): "A problem of dropouts", *The Hindustan Times,* New Delhi, July 10.
8. Sharma, R.C. and C.L. Sapra (1969): *Wastage and stagnation in primary and middle schools in India,* NCERT, New Delhi.
9. Pulla Rao, D. (2008): "Educational Dropout of Children at Primary Stage in East Godavari District of Andhra Pradesh", in Rasure K.A (Ed.) *Economics of Education, Health and Human Resource Development, (Vol. I),* Abhijeet Publications, Delhi, pp. 165-177.
10. Pulla Rao, D. (2005): "Dropouts in Primary Education in East Godavari District of Andhra Pradesh – Mandal level Analysis", 23rd Annual Conference of Andhra Pradesh Economic Association, February, pp. 358-367.
11. Pulla Rao, D. (2008): "Development of the Primary and Upper primary Education in India", *Orient Journal of Law and Social Sciences,* Secunderabad, August, Vol. II, Issue-9. pp: 79-91.

12

LITERACY IN INDIA: SOME OBSERVATIONS

R.V.L.N. Ratnakara Rao & V. Krishna Murthy***

Introduction

According to UNESCO, "40-60 percent of the literacy rate is necessary for the development of a country. For rapid development it requires 60 and above percent". In the census a person is defined as literate if he or she can read and write with understanding in any language. In the Census 1991, the literacy percentage was calculated for the first time based on the total population including children below seven years.

Literacy Rate

1. The literacy rate was very low, 18.33% in 1951 and through successive planning and programmes, the literacy rate could achieve 64.84 % by 2001 Census. Yet, about 35% o India's population is illiterate and there is variation in literacy rate.

2. The literacy rate in 2001 census was 65.44% and among the states, Kerala had the highest literacy rate of 90.86% and Mizoram holds the second position with literacy of 88.80%, Bihar had the lowest literacy of 47.0%, Rajasthan

* Dept. of Physical Education, Andhra University.

** Professor, Dept. of Education, Andhra University, Visakhapatnam.

** Retd. Professor, Department of Education, Andhra University, Visakhapatnam, Andhra Pradesh.

has improved its literacy rate significantly to 60.41% but its female literacy is abysmally low at 43.85%.

3. Himachal Pradesh (77.1%), Maharashtra (76.8%), Tripura (73.6%), Tamilnadu (73.5%), Manipur (70.53%), Gujarat (70.0%), Sikkim (68.81%), Haryana (68.6%), Karnataka (67.0%), Nagaland (66.59%), Assam (64.3%) have literacy rates slightly above the average for India.
4. On the other hand Madhya Pradesh (63.74%), Meghalaya (63.3%), Orissa (63.08%), Andhra Pradesh (61.1%), Uttar Pradesh (57.4%), Arunachal Pradesh (54.7%) had literacy rate of less than the average for India.
5. All the Union Territories except Dadar Nagar Haveli (60.0%) had literacy rates higher than the average for India.
6. the literacy percentage varied from a minimum of 25.1% per rural females (Bihar) to a maximum of 97.55% for Urban males (Mizoram).

Women Literacy

At the time of independence, 14% of the population in India was literate, but now the Literacy rate has increased to 65.38% with 75.96% for males and 54.28% for females as per 2001 Census Report. The 2001 Census shows that the sex ratio for India is 933 which is the lowest in the world.

The rate of literacy among women has gone up from 39.29% in 1991 to 54.16% in 2001.

1) In fact the increase in female literacy by 14.87% out paced that of male literacy (11.72%).
2) The male -female literacy gap has reduced from 24.84% in 1991 to 21.7% in 2001. Still the rate of literacy among males 175.85% is higher than females (54.16%) and hence much remains to be done to improve the female literacy and narrow the male-female gap in literacy rate.
3) At least 60 million girls lack access to primary education in India. According to a recent National Sample Survey

Organization(NSSO) Report, the literacy rate in India during 2004-05 was just 64%, with Kerala having 83% of its rural population and 85% of its urban residence as literates.

4) In India as a whole the gender gap in literacy has been decreasing.

Development of Primary Education in India (1950-51 to 2004-05):

Based on the information available in Annual Reports for various years and other selected educational statistics: Ministry of Human Resource Development, Govt. of India, the following can be said about the development of Primary and Upper Primary Education.

1. The annual compound growth rates indicates a gap between the increase in Primary Schools (2.39) and increase in the total number of children (3.55) enrolled during the period; It indicates the need for establishing more primary schools taking additionally the annual compound growth rates by 1.20. so that it is sufficient to meet the annual compound growth rate in the total number of children.
2. The annual compound growth rate of female teachers was recorded at 4.32 %, which was much higher than the rate of (1.95) during the period.
3. The teacher - student ratio at the primary level in 2004-05 stand at 1:60, which is highly un-favourable with the accepted norm of 1:40 ratio. Further, under the pretext of rationalization of teacher - student ratio, some of the state government have closed down even such primary schools with favourable teacher-student ratio of 1:40.

Ranking in Primary Education:

Based on different aspects like school accessibility, creation of facilities, teacher recruitment, announcement of results etc., the status of different states were declared for primary and upper primary school levels. For the year 2007-08, the declared levels were as follows:

First Rank	Second Rank	Third Rank	Fourth Rank
Karnataka	Puducherry(Pondicherry)		Tamil Nadu
Andhra Pradesh			

For the year 2006-07, Andhra Pradesh was in the Sixth Rank

PROGRAMMES

A) Sarva Siksha Abhiyan (SSA)

SSA is a Government of India's flagship programme for achievement of Universalisation of Elementary Education (UEE) in a time bound as mandated by 86th amendment to the constitution of India making free and compulsory education to the children of 6-14 years age group a fundamental right.

SSA is being implemented in partnership with state governments to cover the entire country and address the needs of 192 million children in 1.1 million habitations. The objectives of SSA are the following:

a) To bring all children in School, Education Guarantee centre, alternate school, Back-to-School camp by 2003. b) All children complete 5 years of primary schooling by 2007. c) All children complete 8 years of elementary schooling by 2010. d) Focus of elementary education of satisfactory quality emphasis on education for life. e) Bridge all gender and social category gaps at primary stage by 2007 and f) Universal retention by 2010.

B) Mid Day Meal Scheme (MDMS)

MDMS involves provision of lunch free of cost to school children on all working days. Key objectives of the programme are:

a) protecting children from class room hunger. b) Increasing school enrollment and attendance. c) Improved socialization among children belonging to all castes. d) Addressing mal-nutrition and e) Social empowerment through provision of employment to women.

The scheme has a long history especially in Tamil Nadu and Gujarat, and has been expanded to all parts of India after a land mark direction by the Supreme court of India on November 28, 2001. So far, 17 crore children are covered under the Mid-Day Meal Scheme which is the largest school lunch programme in the World. Allocation for this programme has been enhanced from Rs. 3010 crore to Rs. 4813 crore.

Conclusion

Elementary education in India, as J.P. Naik says "is a promise to keep", so that India achieves its position in the developing world, which is already ahead of others in computer education etc.

SECTION - B: HIGHER EDUCATION

13

ROLE OF HIGHER EDUCATION IN RURAL AREAS OF INDIA

I. Narendra Kumar, C.P. Kasaiah** & A. Siva Sankar****

Higher education refers to education in post-higher secondary institutions, colleges and universities. It is called higher because it constitutes the top most stage of formal education and it is concerned with processes in more advanced phases of human learning. The age of entrants is 18 years and therefore they are mentally matured and capable of performing the task at the abstract level. They can analyze synthesize and evaluate the concepts, facts, ideas of all kinds. Their creativity is at peak level. The growth of the Indian higher education system is a result of the nation policy adopted immediately after independence to promote education amongst the masses. The National Policy in Education visualizes education to be:

- A process of empowerment, which is to be promoted through the development of knowledge, skills and values (Education for development),

* Academic Consultant, Dept. of Econometrics, S.V. University, Tirupati, Andhra Pradesh.

** Professor of Econometrics, Dept. of Econometrics, S.V. University, Tirupati, Andhra Pradesh.

*** Academic Consultant, Dept. of Econometrics, S.V. University, Tirupati, Andhra Pradesh.

- An instrument of social change that provides means for upward economic and social mobility through enhancement of qualification. (Education for equality), and
- The Indian Higher Education scenario provision of access and promotion of equity are important considerations. It has become necessary to balance these against the demand for quality. Admittedly in the whole process, quality suffers.[1]

Higher education occupies an important position in shaping the way in which future generations learn to cope with the complexities of sustainable development. It prepares the future decision-makers of society for their entry into the labour market and it actively contributes to the society. It is important to note that the system of higher education has to play a crucial role in the development of economy and society. It has to play a significant part in the making of productive people as well as strong nation. Hammadi viewed the kind of higher education will play a vital role in determining the shape of social, economic, political and industrial development of the country in the years ahead. Thus, the colleges and universities are key players in the development of science and technology. Because the world economy is changing fast as knowledge society, technology is driving much of this process, with information technology, biotechnology and other innovations leading to remarkable changes in the way we live and work.[2] As knowledge becomes more important, so does higher education. Countries need to education more of their young people to a higher standard. In this context former prime minister Jawaharlal Nehru says if all is well with the universities all would be well with the be nation. Because the higher education: (1) teach that life has a meaning, (2) awaken the connate ability to love the life of soul by developing wisdom, (3) acquaint with social philosophy, (4) train for democracy and (5) acquaint the cultural heritage. In India there has been a considerable demand for higher education since Independence. Democratization of education system boosted the growth of higher education in India. It has been accelerating rapidly over the past 150 years since the inception of Calcutta, Bombay and Madras Universities in 1857. There has been significant quantitative expansion in terms of institutions, enrollment and teachers.

Higher Education is of paramount importance for economic and social development. Institutions of higher education have the main responsibility of equipping individual with advanced knowledge and skills required for positions of responsibility in Government, business and professions. Science and technology which was essentially a tool for economic development in the industrial economy has emerged as a major force and exerts an all pervasive influence in every sphere of human life. Possession of relevant knowledge, creation on new knowledge and capacity for its application has become the determinants in the strength of a nation. Consequently, education has come to the centre stage and is today the most important agent for change and development. The dominance of education and the emergence of the concept of human resource development are most significant developments of this century. The new role that education might play, the new gates it might open, and the unknown world it might bring to light, are in the womb of the future. We need the highest of education for a few to master existing knowledge, as well creating new knowledge, and basic education for all at the society to be able to absorb and apply knowledge to social, political and economic development. Added to the general trend of the last century, certain policy changes of our government in early 1990s brought new compulsion to keep our education system rejuvenated according to timely needs. Our India has, with whatever reservation there may be accepted liberalization and globalization of our economy. It means that we open our market to the world and we gain access to the world market, employment opportunities have transcended the state boundaries as well as national boundaries and therefore we have to improve our competitiveness, which in concrete terms mean excelling in productivity and quality. In this context, education faces three challenges universalization, equity and ability to be the frontiers of knowledge. Higher education has a decisive and dominant role to play in keeping our competitiveness high in every sphere of activity.[3]

As mentioned earlier, in the 1940 and 1950 very few students and graduates from rural areas characterized education in India. Today, however there has been a dramatic shift from class to mass, with students of higher education drawn from rural areas. As there is awareness about compulsory and free education, more and more children complete their primary and secondary education. Many of them wish to attain a degree. Rural areas in India started to cope up the growing demand of youth by opening new colleges at their doorstep. However, this kind of rapid expansion has caused negatively towards the quality of higher education in rural areas. Because, most of these higher educational institutions have not so far prepared to face the challenges of changed structure of world economy. It is important to note that we are living in a period where market forces determine the fate of the country. We are moving from manufacturing centered to knowledge-centered society. Information technology revolution made easy access to the information of the world round the clock. Those who have skills to use it have access to extraordinarily valuable resources. Therefore to participate in the knowledge economy, requires a new set of human skills. People should have higher qualifications and intellectual capacity. But the education system of rural areas in India is to be equipped and fully prepared to face the new realities. Unless youth develops expertise, they fall behind and may be marginalized and isolated. Therefore colleges in rural areas need to restructure their academic forces in tune with the winds of change. Otherwise the products (students) they produce may become rotten in job market. Now the higher education is facing the so many problems in rural India. The problems are: the quality of teachers/teaching, weak primary education system, medium of instruction and problem faced by the students, and specially all the colleges in the rural areas lack of basic infrastructure; most of the colleges established in rural areas belong to arts faculty; staff scarcity, lack of job oriented courses are lacking case of rural colleges, lack of library facilities, uneducated parents, problems of language and lack of funds to maintain the colleges.

Now a society requires the following from higher education:

- To train a skilled, intelligent, creative and responsible workforce,
- To transmit, sustain and extend the arts and humanities, the scientific tradition, the historical record and other aspects of our living culture,
- To support a citizenry that participates responsibly in community affairs, including public governance and cares about out country and the world,
- To provide forum for integrating a multitude of people and synthesizing a wealth of ideologies, political and scientific problems, and
- To give individual access to life long learning in changing world.[4]

Urban Areas in Higher Education

It is disheartening to note that our higher educational system is urban oriented in the matters of location of facilities, allocation of finance and content of curriculum. University prepares the syllabus, frames examination and admission rules. Teachers in rural areas are rarely consulted. Policy framers hardly realize the difficulties faced by rural teachers students. Most of the contents of the syllabus highlight the urban values and culture. Since most of the job opportunities are available in urban areas, the company owners prefer the city students than the rural. Most of the students in rural areas never study the problems pertaining to villages.

The Impact of WTO and GATS

This is going to be one of the major problems that affect the higher education system in the near future. After opening up various sectors like banking, insurance and communication to multi national companies the Indian Government has decided to open up the education sector for them. Finally globalization and commercialization of education is becoming reality. From January 1, 2005, India is obliged under WTO to open up its higher education sector to foreign providers and to end public subsidies. No doubt international education definitely has advantage like-regularly updated curricula, more practicality, learner-centric and more importantly it develops marketable skills.

The GATS will stress on drastic cut in public expenditure on education. Accordingly, the Committee in its report recommended that "there should be a freeze on recruitment of staff in all the autonomous institutions at all levels. This shows that GATS does not have any interest in improving the quality of education. They are only interested in exploiting the lucrative market. It is sad to note that our college syllabus is not international in nature and not upgraded according to the need of the hour. Most of the higher educational institutions lack basic infra structures which can cope up modern changes. Our educational policies are decided by political affiliations of ruling party and not by academicians who have rural exposure. Before implementing the recommendations of GATS, they should think of improving the problems of higher educational institutions in rural areas. Otherwise days are not far when a foreign University may start modern and highly sophisticated colleges with all kinds of ultra infrastructural facilities, which are to be fit in national and international job market. Even though they start these kind colleges in urban areas, students may migrate to city centers in search of these colleges.

From the above problems of higher education in society and rural areas are very peculiar in nature. The government is trying to tackle the problems by providing the reservation, quotas etc., to the rural students in professional colleges as well as employment opportunities. But this is not sufficient. To achieve the main objectives of higher education are developments and equity, the level of the rural students will rise to that of the main stream students. It is absolutely necessary to bring in the equity and equality between rural and urban students. All academicians, politicians and policy makers will join hands and prepare a good national and implemented the same with grater spirit and speed.

Suggestions

The problems of higher education in rural areas are more. Efforts will be made to expand the quantity and quality of higher education in rural areas.

- Provide increasing number of students especially from disadvantaged background with specialized skills, because specialists are increasingly in demand in all sectors of the world economy.
- Provide new technology-based tools for gathering knowledge and it must become central elements of their education, and curricula should be designed so that students lean how to earn.
- The emphasis on English language and communication skills should be doubled.
- Improve educational infrastructure especially access to computer and internet and scientific laboratories and also traditional infrastructure such as libraries, classrooms at both primary and higher educational levels.
- The recruitment, retention, motivation and long term development of well trained faculty.
- Increasing access for economically and socially marginalized population including women.

REFERENCES

1. Muktha.S.Adi, "Higher Education-Problems in Rural Areas", *University News,* 2007
2. Hammadi Ali, "University Administration in Developing Countries", Indian Bibliographies Bureau, New Delhi, 1984.
3. Varsha Parikh and Dimple Saluja, "Higher Education -Society and State", *University News,* 2007.
4. *Ibid.*
5. Shaukath Aziz, "Higher Education in Rural India", *University News,* 2005.
6. "Higher Education in Developing Countries: Peril and Promise", *The World Bank,* 2000.
7. Peer Mohammed, *Higher Education and Employment,* Rawat Publications, Jaipur, 1994.

8. Krishana Raj P.M, "GATS and its Implications of Higher Education in India", www.evesindia.indiainfo.com

9. Sarma vijendar, "WTO, GATS and Future of Higher Education India", *People Democracy*, 2002.

10. Tiwari, Murali Dhum, *Education and E-governance*, Macmillan Ltd. New Delhi, 2001.

11. Kuladai Swamy.V.C, *Higher Education in India, Crisis in Management*, Viva Books Pvt.Ltd, Delhi, 2003.

14

NEED FOR REFORMS IN EXAMINATION SYSTEM

*Rakesh A. Joshi**

Since 1950-51, it is believed that the real motive force of economic development is people. Over the years, perspectives on development and its rationale and measures have changed. Today, development focuses on people and their well-being. Education plays a crucial role in socio-economic development of a country. Investment in education increases the quality of people.

Education is of great importance for the balanced development of an economy and shall definitely have its effectiveness. In a welfare state like India, the state has the responsibility of education. The government in India is planning the entire education structure and various state governments are shouldering the task of providing education. The government through its education policy decides the structure of different strata of education. Most economists would agree that it is the human resources of a country that ultimately determine the character and pace of its economic and social development. According to the late Professor Harbison of Princeton University, "*Human resources constitute the ultimate basis for wealth of nations. Human beings are the active agents who accumulate capital, exploit natural resources, build social economic and political organisations and carry forward*

* Reader, Department of Economics, Saurashtra University, Rajkot (Gujarat).

national development." The more the education, the more speedy the development. Education is a vision, not calculation. After almost five decades of rapidly expanding enrolments and crores of dollars of educational expenditure, the plight of the average citizen of Asia, Africa and Latin America seems little improved. Education imparts values, ideas, attitudes and aspirations which is in the nation's best development interests. We can divide the whole education process into primary education, secondary education and higher education. The schools are shouldering the responsibilities of primary and secondary education while the universities render their duties towards the higher education. In the developing countries like India, the number of students engaged in higher education is smaller than that of primary and secondary levels. Though there are various institutions in higher education, the university is considered as the most significant apex body.

Higher education deals with a comparatively smaller mass of students. Talented students qualified in higher secondary education seek admission in colleges and institutions of advanced studies. There are about 300 universities in our country. There are more than 9000 graduate as well as postgraduate colleges affiliated to the universities getting either grants in aid or controlled and managed by state governments. Some of the universities are residential and some are open universities, especially for those students, who cannot remain present daily. There are so many prestigious institutions (e.g. IIM, IIT) famous for their quality and standards and doing research work of a very high order. A good university is that, which has a high standard and which is constantly engaged in the search for truth and striving for making original contribution to the field of research.

The word 'University' was taken from the Latin word 'universitas', which means institution, a community or a corporation. In fact, a university is a community consisting of teachers, students and researchers aiming at acquisition of knowledge, where thirsty youth come and quench their thirst. According to the famous educationist Cardinal Newman, *"University is a place, where new knowledge is discovered and there is an interaction of mind with mind. It is a temple of learning, the light of the world and the mother institution of progressive generations."*

In the recent times, the system as a whole of higher education in India has grown a lot. The number of universities has increased manifold. Enrolment in universities has also increased over the years although still far below that in developed countries, and even less than the South Asian countries like Malaysia, Philippines, etc. But, the vast growth of higher education over the years has failed to check its deteriorating quality. Now, a university is considered as a factory providing degrees to the disgruntled masses. Nowadays, it is a general impression that a university is supposed to be an institution with the main function of holding examinations and conferring degrees. According to Professor Earnest Barker, *"A university is an organized degree giving institution helping in spread of knowledge."*

Main Problems of the Universities

In our country, universities suffer from many problems, chief among them are the following:

i) Financial problem of universities are increasing.

ii) Most of the students are aimless

iii) Every year there is a problem of admission for the students.

iv) Indiscipline of the students is rampant.

v) Libraries and laboratories are having inadequate budget.

vi) The low standard of education has become an unsolvable problem.

vii) Educational institutions have to face so many hurdles in their day-to-day administration.

viii) Political interference increased in academic matters, and

ix) The examination system is faulty.

In this paper, I have tried to throw some light on:

i) Necessity of examination reforms, and

ii) Some reforms to set it right.

Examination demands a challenge. After providing proper information and knowledge to the students, it is necessary to test their grasping power. If the student is not quite up to the mark, then he should not be upgraded to the next standard. The teachers have implemented various methods for the examination since ancient times, but there is no proper solution about an appropriate examination system. The system of examination in practice suffers from several defects and there is indiscipline of students due to this defective examination system. It is not the true test of a student's knowledge. Teachers, parents and students are so much absorbed with examination, that they do not find time to think of the cause of the obsession. Failure in examinations is ultimately passed on to a student who, it is said, is incapable of coping with the curriculum. He is compelled to resort to cramming and use unfair means in the examination. Today, copying has become a student's birthright. Teachers are threatened and even beaten sometimes. Change in the system is overdue. It should undergo radical changes. There is need to adopt a new approach to evaluation. The cost of examination is too much. Some thinkers opine that there is no need to change the examination system, but the examination itself must be abolished. Actually, examinations are necessary, but some changes in the system and the changes in the aptitudes of the students are essential.

Suggested Reforms for the Examination System

1) In every faculty of higher education, one paper of moral (ethics) education should be introduced, so that virtues like truth, honesty, co-operation, and morality may be imbibed in the young minds. That will be helpful in creating a clean atmosphere of examination.

2) Unit tests should be introduced, so that the understanding of the students can be tested often.

3) Question Banks in various subjects should be prepared. A good question bank increases the confidence of the students as well as being useful to the question paper setters.

4) Most of the universities hold subjective type examination.

In these examinations, there are only four or five descriptive - answer oriented questions. Therefore, many students prepare only few topics and they do not study other portions of the syllabus. To cover the whole syllabus, there should be objective tests, which can cover all portions of the syllabus.

5) Oral examinations (Viva-voce) are also essential. The student has responsibility to improve the third world society, which is full of harmful customs, rituals, social evils, etc. So, it is necessary for any graduate to offer good ideas and information to the common people. Hence, oral test is essential too. This will increase the elocution power of the students.

6) Examinations must be given in atmosphere of peace and discipline. Otherwise, weak students will get good marks by unfair practices.

7) Assessment or evaluation must be centralized with necessary safe arrangement and it should be fully consistent and impartial.

8) Examinations should be valid and testing the knowledge of the students should be authentic. Setting of question papers need to be correct and appropriate.

9) Evaluation is a continuous process. It needs preparation and maintenance of progress report of every individual student.

10) To save the cost of examinations, online exams on computer should be introduced. It will save money as well as the valuable time.

11) In Gujarat, a new experiment will be started from the year 2009. The students of 8, 9 and 10th standard will be permitted to appear in examinations with books. In this context, only hard working students can write their answers in proper manner.

Such types of reforms are necessary to improve examination system.

REFERENCES

1. Bhayati Jamnalal, *Problems of Education in Third World* Uppal Publishing House, New Delhi.
2. Brubacher J. S. *Modern Philosophy of Education*, McGraw Hill Book Company, New York, 1962.
3. Ministry of Education, "Post-war educational development in India", New Delhi.
4. K.A.Rasure (Ed.) *Economics of Education, Health and Human Resource Development*, Abhijeet Publications, Delhi, 2008.
5. Oza N. B, and Joshi K.M. (Ed.) *Higher Education – Issues and Options*, Mangaldeep Publications, Jaipur, 2001.
6. Todaro, M.P. *Economic Development in the Third World*, Longman Publishers Ltd., Singapore, 1986.

15

HIGHER EDUCATION AND PRIVATE SECTOR

*K.A. Rasure**

Indian education has always ranked among the best in the world. As India's growth story and the boom in offshore research, software and business process outsourcing show a rising trend over the next few years. Indian education is going to be under presure to delive a large talent pool that is required to fuel this growth and insure that India remains competitive. Indians are now, more than ever before, feeling the strong need for good higher education. There has been a boom in education, sector with numerous private initiatives. While quality needs to be ensured through this growth , the education sector shows clear signs of maturing and becoming more competitive and quality driven.

Genesis of Indian Education System

India's organised education system was created during the British rule beginning in the early 1900s. Designed to bring in more Indian's into the governance formulated by the British government over India, the education system was elitist and based on the use of English as the medium of instruction. The education network was also created to serve the needs of the large number of British families and their children who resided in India as part of the government and armed forces.

* Nrupatunga Arts, Commerce, Management and Science College, Sedam 585222, Gulbarga Dist., Karnataka.

India however has also had a rich history of traditional education and this tradition spans over five thousand years. The arts, culture, theatre, spirituality and literature have for long been part of our Education system—a unique way of schooling that entailed one-to-one transfer of knowledge and learning under the Gurukul system where the student lived with the teacher and learned all that he needed to become a master in his profession in unique 'guru-shishya' or 'teacher-student' relationship.

Indian education, however, restricted learning to women and female children. Education was for centuries male-dominated and even within this, there was selective imparting of education based on profession and social status. India therefore has a rich culture and history of strong education and transfer of knowledge through mentoring.

In post-Independence era new education methods were developed and the system of education made more equitable and democratic. Thanks to several decades of intense focus by successive governments, India's education system has created a rich and large pool of skilled and knowledgeable talent that India has been able to reap rich harvests during the growth and globalisation decades of the 1990s and 2000s.

Higher Education in India

Higher education in India has evolved in divergent and distinct streams with each stream monitored by an apex body, indirectly controlled by the Ministry of Human Resource Development. The universities are mostly funded by the state government. Howerver, there are 12 important universities called central universities, which are maintained by the union government and because of relatively large funding, they have an economic edge over the others. The engineering colleges and business schools in the country are monitored and accredited by AICTE while medical colleges are monitored and accredited by the MCI. The NCTE was constituted a few years ago to monitor, organise and accredit in the country, and this apex body has started making its presence felt. Apart from these, the country has some engineering, management and medical institutions which are directly funded by the union government.

As on 31.3.2005, there were 342 universities including 18 central universities, 211 state universities, 95 deemed universities and 5 institutions established under the state legislation and 13 institutes of national importance. There were 17,625 colleges, of which 5,386 have been recognised by the UGC under Section 2(f) and 12(B) of the UGC Act.

In 2004-05, an estimated 104.81 lakh students were enrolled in the institutions of higher education as against 99.54 lakh in the previous year and the faculty strength was 4.71 lakh as compared to 4.57 lakh in the previous year.

Degree Structure

There are three principal levels of qualifications within the higher education system in the country. These are:

1. Bachelor/undergraduate level
2. Masters'/post-graduate level
3. Doctoral/pre-doctoral level.

Diploma courses are also available at the undergraduate and post-graduate level. At the undergraduate level, the duration varies between one to three years, while postgraduate diplomas are normally awarded after one year's study. Bachelor's degree in arts, commerce and sciences comprises three years of education (after 12 years of school education). In some places there are honours and special courses available. These are not necessarily longer in duration but indicate greater depth of study. Bachelor's degree in professional field of study in agriculture, dentistry, engineering, pharmacy, technology and veterinary medicine generally take four years, while in architecture and medicine, it takes five and five-and-a-half years respectively. There are other bachelor degrees like in education, journalism and library, that can be taken as an integrated degree lasting five years or as a three-year second degree course.

Master's degree is normally of two-year duration. It could be coursework based without thesis or research alone. Admission to post-graduate programmes in engineering and technology is on the basis of Graduate Aptitude Test in engineering or combined medical test respectively.

A pre-doctorial programme—Master of Philosophy(M.Phil.) is taken after completion of the Master's degree. This can either be completely research based or include course work as well.

A doctorial programme—Ph.D is awarded two years after the M.Phil or three years after the Master's degree. Students are expected to write a substantial thesis based on original reaearch which generally takes longer.

Indian universities offer various courses in the following disciplines:

1. Engineering and technology
2. Computer sciences, information technology, biotechnology and bio-informatics
3. Medical, dental,nursing pharmacy and paramedical
4. Agriculture/veterinary sciences, dairy tehnology and fisheries
5. Arts and fine arts, humanities, social sciences, commerce, science and management
6. Hotel management and catering technology, travel and tourism
7. Fashion design and technology.

Government Funding to Higher Education

(Rs crore)

Year	*plan*	*Non-plan*
Ninth plan		
1997-98	352.10	545.00
1998-99	360.35	1,009.00
1999-2000	376.00	975.00
2000-01	435.00	1,000.00
2001-02	467.78	1,020.68
Tenth plan		
2002-03	559.76	1,100.00
2003-04	516.75	1,132.30
2004-05	719.75	1,182.85
2005-06	374.41	609.17

Main Players in the Higher Education System

University Grants Commission (UGC). The government established the University Grants Commission (UGC) by an Act of Parliament in 1956. It discharges the constitutional mandate of coordination, determination, and maintenance of standards of teaching, examination and research in the field of university and higher education. UGC serves as a vital link between the union and state governments and the institutions of higher learning. It monitors developments in the field of collegiate and university education; disburses grants to the universities and colleges; advises central and state governments on the measures necessary for the improvement of university education; and frames regulations, standards of instruction. The UGC is responsible for coordination, determination and maintenance of standards, release of grants, etc.

Professional Councils. Professional councils are responsible for recognition of courses, promotion of professional institutions and providing grants to undergraduate programmes and various awards. The statutory professional councils are:

1. All Indian Council for Technical Education (AICTE)
2. Distance Education Council (DEC)
3. Indian Council for Agriculture Research (ICAR)
4. Bar Council of India (BCI)
5. National Council for Teacher Education (NCTE)
6. Rehabilitation Council of India (RCI)
7. Medical Council of India (MCI)
8. Pharmacy Council of India (PCI)
9. Indian Nursing Council (INC)
10. Dentist Council of India (DCI)
11. Central Council of Homeopathy (CCH)
12. Central Council of Indian Medicine (CCIM)

Central Government

The central government is responsible for major policies relating to higher education in the country. It provides grants to the UGC and establishes central universities in the country. The central government is also responsible for declaration of educational institution as deemed to be university on the recommendation of the UGC.

Presently there are 16 central universities in the country. In pursuance of the Mizoram Accord another central university in the state of Mizoram is planned. There are 99 institutions which have been declared as deemed to be universities by the Government of India as per the UGC Act, 1956.

State Governments

State governments are responsible for establishment of state universities and colleges, and provide plan grants for their development and non-plan grants for their maintenance. The coordination and cooperation between the union and the states is brought about in the field of education through the Central Advisory Board of Education (CABE).

Special Constitutional Responsiblity of the Central Government

Education is on the 'Concurrent list' subject to Entry 66 in the Union list of the Constitution. This gives exclusive legislative power to the central government for co-ordination and determination of standards in institutions of higher education or research and scientific and technical institutions.

Funding to Higher Education in India

The UGC has no funds of its own. It receives both plan and non-plan grants from the central government to carry out the responsiblities assigned to it by law. It allocates and diburses full maintenance and development grants to all Central universities, colleges affiliated to Delhi and Banaras Hindu Universities and some of the institutions accorded the status of 'deemed to be universities'. State universities, colleges snd other institutions of higher education, receive support only from the plan grant for development schemes. Besides, it provides financial assistance to universities and colleges under various schemes/ programmes for promoting relevance, quality and excellence as also promoting the role of social change by the universities. The details of the grants provided by the government to UGC during the ninth plan and the tenth plan both under plan and non-plan are shown in the table.

Pitfalls of Indian Higher Education System

The abysmal situation of education in India is a direct result of low levels of investment and the consequent absence of choice and competition. Our talented politicians sell it as a socialist virtue in the name of equality, while sending their own kids to well-run schools and oversease universities.The laws they continue to back guarantee slow progress.

The situation is even more complex in higher education.When Stanford University looked at higher education in India it was told that it would have to follow UGC norms in both teachers salaries and fees and clearly not a formula for quality.

According to the University Grants Commission only two percent of Indian colleges have the potential for excellence. Clearly our education system is not delivering in terms of quality, quantity or value for money. Economics tells us such a situation cannot last entrepreneurs will rush in to fill all the gaps-in quantity, quality and price points unless they are blocked by legislations.

What are the major pitfalls? Amartya Sen has answered that the pitfalls of illiteracy include functional handicap, intellectual deprivation and social disadvantages when large groups are systematically negleted, like girls especially from economic and social underdog families the social penalties are gigantic. This is the real situation of Indian education system.

In this globalised world private sector plays an important role in all activities. Thus private sector in education both domestic and foreign will be able to cater to excess demand and with increased competition be forced to provide better quality at competitive prices. Regulation in line with corporate social responsibility can be designed for private providers to maximise returns. Proactively liberalising higher education and designing suitable policies to minimise adverse effects can go a long way in sustaining India's competitiveness in services.

16

ROLE OF OPEN UNIVERSITIES IN THE DEVELOPMENT OF HIGHER EDUCATION IN INDIA

P. Raj Kumar, N. Someswara Rao** &
P.S.K. Sudheer****

Introduction

After Independence, India has made tremendous progress in the field of education, though mostly quantitative in nature. Earlier, education was available only to the elite classes of the society, and a large majority of the poor and marginalized people remained illiterate. Political considerations have an important role in the expansion of higher education, especially at the state level. The state governments experienced tremendous pressure from the public to establish more and more colleges and universities. In a democratic society, even the strong governments find it very difficult to resist such pressures and are compelled to succumb. These considerations have led to fast expansion of higher education in our country, which in turn, has adverse impact upon its quality. Therefore, in order to ensure access and education of a reasonably good quality, we must think of some

* Research Scholar, Department of Economics, Andhra University, Visakhapatnam, A.P.

** Lecturer, SSSS Degree College, Chodavaram, Visakhapatnam, A.P.

*** Research Scholar, Department of Economics, Andhra University, Visakhapatnam, A.P.

alternative system capable of supplementing the role of conventional system, and distance education is one of such alternatives.

Limitations of the Formal System of Education

As a result of unplanned expansion and scarcity of funds, the quality of education imparted in the institutions of higher education gradually deteriorated. The frustrated lot of students resorted to aggressive behaviour. The lopsided and unbalanced expansion of education diverted the efforts and resources of the government towards general education at the cost of vocational training. This process produced an enormous number of unskilled and unemployable graduates with devalued degrees.

Although, the quantitative development of higher education, during the post-Independence period, has been apparently very impressive, yet, it is inadequate to meet the growing demand of the people for higher education. Now, unlike the pre-Independence period, the benefits of higher education are reaped by a sizeable number of youth even from underprivileged sections of the society. At present, we have one college for every 11,000 and one university for every 4.7 lakhs of persons in the relevant age group (18-23 years). Yet, in the real terms, only about 6-7 per cent of the eligible age group is getting the benefit of higher education. This is insignificant compared to the corresponding figures of over 50 per cent for the countries belonging to the Organisation of Economic Corporation and Development (OECD), and about 30 per cent in the other developed countries.

Now let us examine the historical evolution of non-conventional educational system in India. During the third five-year plan period (1960-65) the demand for higher education raised high so much that the conventional university systems and other institutions of higher education in the country were facing a lot of pressure on the available seats. In the words of the higher education commission.

"If the present rate of expansion (10 per cent every year) is assumed to continue for next 20 years, the total enrollment in higher education would be between 10 and 8 millions by 1985-

86. At this escalation of scale, the need for higher educational institutions will be rising more than twice".

But spurred by the egalitarian ideals of providing educational opportunities for the wide spectrum of the populace could not be covered - even to provide those who had potential to take up higher education studies. This was a challenge to the conventional educational systems of India. In fact the existing educational system had reached a point of saturation beyond which it could not be stretched without damaging both the system and the economy of the country.

This led the Planning Commission to take note of the widespread success of the correspondence courses launched by the University of Delhi and recommended the adoption of these courses at the university levels throughout the country so as to open the doors of higher studies for all those who opted for it. Such an encouragement in fact triggered the growth and expansion of correspondence courses in India. The U.G.C. has set out guidelines for opening correspondence courses in universities all over India and came forward to offer liberal financial assistance to universities willing to adopt the UGC guidelines for operating correspondence courses. After these developments, many universities started establishing institutes of correspondence courses and continuing education.

Open Learning: The Concept

Due to limitations of the formal system of education, policy makers attracted towards non-conventional modes of education providing for non-residential studies like correspondence courses. The Distance Education (DE) mode, in which it was not necessary to bring all the students together to listen to the face-to-face lectures delivered by the teachers, rather, students while remaining away from their teachers would learn according to their own time, was considered worthwhile. However, in Distance Education system, the provision of occasional meetings between the teachers and the students is made. These meetings are popularly known as Personal Contact Programmes (PCPs). The learners receive their study material through correspondence modes (postal services) and study at home or at their workplace. The efforts of the students are supplemented by assignments, which are checked and evaluated by experts in respective fields of knowledge. Conceptually, Distance Education is a part and parcel of open learning. In fact, Distance Education system is known by a variety of names in India, such as "External Appearance" (private appearance), "Correspondence Education" and "Distance Education".

Origin of Distance Education in India

The open learning system in India originated in the form of "private appearance" of the candidates in public examinations under which a candidate who could not study as a regular student was also allowed to appear in the examination after undertaking necessary study at home or at their workplace. This system was probably introduced to help the poor, the needy and the disadvantaged sections of the society, particularly Scheduled Castes, Scheduled Tribes and women. Later on, in order to overcome the deficiencies of the private appearance and improve the quality of education, some universities started correspondence courses to cater to the requirements of such students. The term Distance Education received a formal recognition in 1982 when the four-decade old International Council for Correspondence Education changed its name to the International Council for Distance Education.

V.C. Kulandaiswamy in his article, "Open University" in (ed.) *Higher Education Reform in India* by Suma Chatnis and Phillip G. Altbach has observed that Distance Education is neither a supplement nor mere alternative to the conventional system, but a marked phase in the evolution of mass education. Its advantage lies in the fact that in every situation, it is much easier to transport knowledge to the people than transport the people to the place of learning.

Some Definitions of Distance Education

According to Hilary Prraton "Distance Education means an education process in which a significant proportion of teaching is conducted by some one removed in space and/or time from the learner".

Michael Moore observed that, "Distance teaching may be defined as the family of instructional methods in which teaching behaviours are executed apart from learning behaviors, including those that in continuous situations would be performed in the learner's presence, so that communication between the teacher and the learner must be facilitated by print, electronic, mechanical or other devices".

Tony Doddes defines Distance Education as a set of techniques of teaching and learning or any channels of communication which applies to almost any set of educational goals, and which enable learning to take place where teachers and students are, for the most part, at a distance from each other in space or time.

Components of Distance Education

The old concept of correspondence education was exclusively associated with print material while the new concept of distance education includes supplementary material being used through non-print media such as radio, television, computer and satellites. These institutions may be called the dual mode institutions. At present, India has two types of distance education institutions. They are (1) Correspondence Course Institutions (CCIs), and (2) Open Universities.

Electronic media (or multimedia), self-instructional materials, two-way communication and students support services, which are four major components of distance education system, have immense significance for distance education.

This system of education can help in diffusion of education and equalization of educational opportunity. Millions of people all over the world are able to fulfill their academic aspirations and satisfy unfulfilled desires of knowledge through this system.

Establishment of Open Universities

The establishment of the first Open University in UK served as source of inspiration as well as model for other developed and developing countries of the world. The government of India also considered the matter seriously. The first state level Open University was established in Andhra Pradesh in 1982 and a second national Open University Indira Gandhi National Open University (IGNOU) in November, 1985 at Delhi. By the end of 1999, the 'system' in India consisted of 10 Open Universities exclusively devoted to Distance Education and about 62 Institutes/ Directorates of Distance Education attached to traditional universities. Among the 10 Universities, the Andhra Pradesh Open University (1982), Indira Gandhi National Open University (1985), Kota Open University (1987) and Yashwant Rao Chavan Maharashtra Open University (1989) have made genuine progress. Six state open universities in Bihar, Gujarat, Karnataka, Madhya Pradesh, West Bengal and Uttar Pradesh have been of recent origin. These Open Universities and Distance Education institutes provide traditional courses along with professional courses.

Growth of Enrollment in the Open Universities in India

The enrollments in open universities indicate that there has been a continuous increase in their share in the total enrollment in higher education. By the end of the year 2000, there were 10 open universities in India, which is the largest number in the world. The long-term plan is to have an Open University in each state. It is being proposed that the correspondence education institutions attached to the conventional universities should be upgraded to level of open learning institutions or some of them may be merged into the State open universities. The 8th Five-Year Plan (1992-97) had proposed that in view of the increasing demand for higher education, 50 per cent of the admission seekers should be encouraged to join the Distance Education (DE) mode.

These open universities have had a tremendous impact on Indian education in respect of access, quality and equity. All the open universities together are offering about 300 programmes and over 1900 courses of conventional and non-conventional type at different levels. Earlier it was believed that through distance education only education in social sciences and arts could be imparted, but now this belief is over, and the DE mode has proved equally effective in imparting education of science subjects including medicine, engineering and technology also. Also the quality of education imparted through DE mode is comparable to the one imparted through the conventional face-to-face mode. The student enrollment in these institutions has increased very fast. When Andhra Pradesh Open University started functioning in 1983, it enrolled about 6,200 students. In 1986-87, the Andhra Pradesh Open University (APOU) and IGNOU together enrolled about 17,000 students. By 1989-1990, the number of open universities had gone up to 4, with a total enrollment of 83,600 students. During the later part of 1990s the open learning system attracted a very large number of students. In a short period of just three years 1995-98, the annual enrollment of Open Universities in India increased from 2.01 lakhs to 3.50 lakhs, the corresponding cumulative figures being 5.72 lakhs and 10.5 lakhs. In 1999-2000, the annual enrollment of students in all the open universities taken together is a little more than 6.18 lakhs, and the cumulative figure of enrollment has approached 17.85 lakhs (Table-1).

Table -1: Enrollment in the Open Universities in India (1984-2000)

Year	*Enrollment in Open Universities*	*Share of OUs in Total Enrollment*	*Enrollment in DE Institutions*	*Share of DE in Total Enrollment (%)*
1983-84	6,231	0.19	2,01,000	6.08
1985-86	17,004	0.47	3,35,090	9.00
1987-88	50,569	1.25	4,02,720	9.40
1989-90	83,603	1.83	5,17,148	10.90
1991-92	1,16,417	2.20	6,64,572	12.60
1993-94	2,28,338	3.92	7,52,773	12.94
1995-96	5,72,000	8.90	-	-
1997-98	10,50,000	14.83	-	-
1999-2000	17,85,000	23.08	26,85,000	34.72

Sources:
1. Anand, S.P., 1979.
2. Venugopal, V and Manjulika, S., 1996.
3. UGC Reports, 1986-87, 1999-2000.

Administrative Network

These universities have established a large network of Regional Offices and Study Centers all over the country in order to ensure effective delivery of instructional material and increase efficiency of student support services. About 38,000 academic counsellors, drawn from the conventional institutions, provide tutorial services through Regional Offices and Study Centers. The open universities have employed their own staff also for carrying out academic, ministerial and administrative business. The development of study material and designing of delivery mechanism is the responsibility of the academic and technical staff respectively.

As a part of its mandate for training of distance education personnel, Staff Training and Research Institute in Distance Education (STRIDE) has been set up at the IGNOU headquarters at New Delhi. This institute organizes national and international seminars and workshops to achieve its objectives. A proper mechanism has been evolved to coordinate the activities of the institutions of distance education. A coordinating council, known as Distance Education Council (DEC) has also been constituted for development of correspondence programmes offered by the traditional universities and for taking policy decisions so as to avoid duplication of efforts and ensure exchange of ideas and resources. This council has created network of open universities for joint programme development, sharing of material and delivery of programmes / courses. For example, the APOU is using the "Food and Nutrition" course evolved by the IGNOU, while the Nalanda University (Bihar) has decided to use the "Public Accountancy" programme developed by Kota Open University (Rajasthan). In order to promote cooperation among the Open Universities of Asian countries, the Asian Association of Open Universities has been formed. It is expected that by exchanging course materials among the member countries of the Association, both time and money can be saved.

One essential feature of distance education system is that the teacher and the student are at a distance apart. There is hardly any possibility of face-to-face interaction between the two. Obviously, the communication between teacher and the taught is essential for learning to take place. This communication is made possible through media. Correspondence education system largely depended on the print media through which learning material was sent to the learners. The usual procedure of transportation of the material involved the mailing of the material in packets through postal services. But, these days, conditions have completely changed. The system is now well-organized having a large network of Study Centers and Regional Centers along with other components of Student Support Services. These are the three major components of the methodology of Distance Education.

Emerging Challenges

We have seen that development and expansion of Distance Education is a worldwide phenomenon, and its popularity is due to its openness, flexibility, productivity, wider access, multimedia teaching and wide range of course openings relevant to the social needs. Distance Education has not only ushered a forerunner in an era of globalization, but is emerging as an effective tool in providing wide access to higher education. Presently higher education is in a state of crisis. It is hampered by several problems—degradation in quality and standard of education, increase in number of educated unemployed, lack of resources, increasing cost, fast changing technology and so on. Some of these major problems, coupled with recent resource crunch, have contributed to the prevalent chaotic situation of higher education in the country. The twenty-first century, being primarily an information age, is further going to mount new challenges. To survive in such an information society the educational institutions must increase efficiency, improve quality, reduce cost and introduce need based and job-oriented courses. The institutes of higher education should brace up to meet the challenges of the emerging age.

The conventional system alone cannot solve these problems of higher education. To some extent distance and open learning systems can meet some of these challenges through better planning and effective implementation. Tremendous efforts are needed to rectify the situation.

Following are some of the major challenges facing the distance education in the new millennium:

a) Lack of Accessibility

The conventional education system has reached a saturation point. Moreover, our financial resources do not allow any further expansion of this system. Distance Education has reduced the pressure on the government to establish additional conventional universities. Further, our education system has hardly done anything for people living below poverty-line and people living in remote areas. The percentage share of education for Scheduled Castes and Scheduled Tribes is low as compared to the total, reflecting inequality. Many persons are highly motivated, academically talented, but are unable to go for higher education due mainly to social, economic and geographical constraints. The distance education is capable of taking in-service persons, dropouts, retired personnel, women, persons who are unable to join formal education. Thus, distance education has assumed immense significance due to its potential for increasing accessibility, for promoting equality of educational opportunities and taking education to the doorstep of neglected or poorly served segments of population who live in remote rural areas.

b) Deterioration in Quality

Increasing access and decrease in quality have been major issues confronting higher education in India. We have provided mass education at lower levels without adequate emphasis on quality. The quality of education at lower levels directly affects higher education. Because of lack of flexibility in conventional system, and other constraints arising from lack of financial resources, inadequate infrastructure, unplanned expansion, undue political interference and so on, it is not easy to overcome the problem of quality.

c) Lack of Relevance

Another challenge facing our education system is lack of relevance of our course material to the changing needs of the society. In the wake of globalization most of our course materials have become outdated. Distance Education provides an opportunity to diversify courses to make education relevant to the needs of learners and society. Because of the changing nature of jobs, which now require continuous renewal, and updating of knowledge and skills, we must enrich and update our courses continuously for persons engaged in different vocations/ professions. The emergence of political will to transform education and to make it more relevant to the needs of the individual and the community is of great importance.

d) Growing Unemployment

Another challenge facing the country is growing unemployment. Since independence, India has built the third largest tertiary educational system in the world and yet, a sizeable number of the educated are unemployed. Further, every year we are adding to the numbers of unemployed and under-employed graduates. Thus mounting number of graduate unemployed pose a serious drag on our developmental process. In 1992, the total number of applications in the live register of employment exchange was 36.8 million. The distance education mode can provide courses and programmes, which should be need-based, employment-oriented and should help in self-employment generation.

Career orientation to education, therefore, seems to be a top priority of the National Policy on Education, 1986, updated in 1992. In 1999-2000, IGNOU launched five such new programmes i.e. Master's in Tourism Management, Bachelor's degree in Education, Bachelor's degree in Information and Technology, Advanced Diploma in Information and Technology and Certificate in Participatory Programmed Planning.

Distance Education can be used as an effective tool of development of rural India. We can introduce general and specialized programmes as per their requirement and make available the educational facilities to rural people. By introducing courses like forest and wild life management, agro-services, floriculture, horticulture, dairy farming, dairy technology etc., according to the need of the region, employment opportunities can be generated. Vocational orientation of education may enable the youth to gain skills, techniques and knowledge in line with the technological developments to become more employable and find job or go in for self-employment.

e) Lack of Financial Resources

Another challenge facing our education system is severe financial crunch. Recently drastic cuts have been imposed on grants for institutions of higher learning. The relative priority given to higher education in allocation of resources in the Five Year Plans nose-dived from 25 per cent in the Fourth Five Year Plan to 7 per cent in the Eighth Five Year Plan. The Government has asked these institutions to raise their own resources and be self-supporting in the forthcoming years. Accommodating the growing population for higher studies has become a challenging task. To meet this challenge self-financing education seems to be flexible solution. Distance Education system can partially help in overcoming this crisis by starting self-financing courses like B.Ed., M.Ed., IT, etc.

f) Shift in Educational Delivery System

Another biggest challenge facing higher education is in the field of information and technology. The revolution in information technology with tremendous explosion of knowledge has led to a change in teaching-learning process. With new revolution in every kind of technology, particularly communication technology, it has been found necessary to train the students in a manner that would enable them to keep pace with modern global requirements. The revolution in information technology has widened the scope of distance education. By integrating media with course structure, distance education increases enormously the productivity in education. The Internet technology and the networks will be powerful tools for delivering educational services. The coming of satellites into the communication areas has almost revolutionized the education delivery system. Thus, value-oriented education will emerge.

Internet has significantly modified the concept of distance. The world has come closer with the advent of tele-communication media viz. computer conferencing, audio graphics, and video-conferencing are available to distance educators. Realizing the potential of internet-based education IGNOU began to offer internet-based courses like CIC, BCA, MCA, BIT, and ADIT in January 1999. Web courses are exciting and, if designed properly, can provide valuable and active learning experiences. The distance education institutes will have to accept the new and dynamic role of "knowledge generator" if they want to meet the challenges of globalization.

Conclusion

It is apparent from the above analysis that the distance education mode has become more popular all over the world in general and in India in particular. It is catering to a wide range of aspirants willing to upgrade their educational qualification for one region or the other. Distance education is considered an appropriate response to many challenges. This system in India has tremendous scope to meet the challenges by optimizing the inherent potentialities of the system. Distance education institutes should supplement the efforts of traditional universities in promoting excellent higher education, particularly accessing the students from the rural areas. The planners, policy-makers and decision-makers will have to be very clear about the role of distance education in higher education development. Distance educational methods also will be more extensively used by conventional systems as a supplement to enrich their own teaching learning practices. Since it is relatively cheaper, it has become highly popular. Above all, the distance education mode had greatly reduced the distance between learning process and the student beyond the national boarders.

It is no wonder that in future the role of regular institutions for general education will be reduced in great extent and the distance educational institutions have to fill the void.

REFERENCES

1. Ambika Sharanjit Kaur (1996): *Managing Distance Education*, Deep & Deep Publications, New Delhi.
2. Inayat Khan (1989): *Distance Teaching*, Amar Prakashan, New Delhi.

3. Khan, A.W. (2000): "Distance Education in the Twenty-First century", in Venugopal Reddy, V and Manjulika, S (Ed.), *World of Distance and Open Learning,* Viva Books Pvt. Ltd., New Delhi.

4. Ram Reddy, G. (1988): "Distance Education: What, Why and How"? In Koul B.N., Singh B and Ansari M.M., *Studies in Distance Education,* AIU and IGNOU, New Delhi.

5. Sahu, P.K. (1993): *Higher Education at a Distance,* Sanchar Publishing House, New Delhi.

6. Sharma, I.P. (1985): *Adult Education in India,* National Book Orgnaisation, Delhi.

7. Singh, R.P. (1987): *Non-formal Education: An Alternative Approach,* Sterling Publishers Private Limited, New Delhi.

8. Venugopal Reddy, V. and Manjulika, S. (1996): *Distance Education in India: a Model for Developing Countries,* Vikas Publishing House Pvt. Ltd., New Delhi.

17

ACADEMIC STAFF DEVELOPMENT IN HIGHER EDUCATION: ROLE OF UGC-ACADEMIC STAFF COLLEGES

*Sai Ramesh, Thota**

Introduction

The higher education system in India is often criticized that it lacks relevance and significance and has not been able to contribute sufficiently to the national development. The reasons for such an attitude could be many. Prominent among them are unplanned proliferation of Universities and Colleges, lack of infrastructural facilities, educated unemployment, growing social imbalances, erosion of values.

University/College teachers in India take their jobs without any knowledge of pedagogy, educational psychology etc. They learn the techniques of teaching either by trial and error method or by following the ideas set up by their teachers. Neither the University nor the College has evaluated the teacher seriously. As a result there has been a steady erosion of academic standards both in the teaching fraternity and in the student community.

The urgent need of the day is to transform the value system- the basic structure and process of the educational system- to make it flexible and dynamic to move in the ultimate direction of providing opportunities for life long learning to every individual.

* Ex-Librarian, UGC - Academic Staff College, Andhra University, Visakhapatnam, Andhra Pradesh.

This transformation will emphasize ethical values and human welfare. For this, the teacher's role is quite significant. The teacher has to contribute to scholarship and advancement of the frontiers of knowledge. He has to play an important role in the transformation of the education system through active participation in such programmes as restructuring of courses, faculty improvement etc. for imparting practical and relevant education. Along with, he should have a commitment to the society based on justice and should strive for the inculcation of the values and extension of knowledge and skills to the society as a whole. In other words, the teacher has to be a key factor in the transformation of value system. Colleges and Universities are national Institutions supported by the resources of the society. Therefore, the teachers in these Institutions have a moral responsibility of maintaining a high degree of respect in the minds of the public. Hence, there is always a need for In-service education for teachers for their academic development.

In-Service Education for Teachers - Aims, Objectives and Purpose

In-service education programme is undoubtedly a significant programme, aiming at the continuous development of teachers in the desired direction.

Objectives of In-service Education for Teachers

a) to provide incentive to the teachers to function more efficiently.

b) to help teachers to know their problems and to solve them by pooling their resources and wisdom.

c) to help teachers to employ more effective methods of teaching.

d) to help teacher to get acquainted with modern techniques in education.

e) to broaden the mental outlook of teachers.

f) to upgrade the teachers knowledge and understanding of the contents.

g) to increase the professional efficiency of the teacher.

h) to increase the knowledge of teacher educators continuously so that they may remain aware with the progress of education in India and abroad and with the new knowledge of their subject.

i) to motivate teacher educators to self study, independent thinking and creativity.

j) to help to initiate new techniques and to analyse the existing techniques in order to prepare good perspective teachers.

k) to promote teacher educators to leave the useless methods and to accept the new scientific techniques and ideas.

l) to develop positive attitudes in order to make him able to help in progress of the nation.

It is well understood from the recommendations of the Education Committees that training of teachers at higher level is inevitable to keep the teacher abreast with new knowledge in the subject concerned and to train him in the latest methodologies and techniques of teaching. The various experiments in the training of teachers in India prove that no uniformity has been maintained in the content, nature and method of training course among different Institutes and Universities. The NPE in its Programme of Action (1986) explained that "the present system does not accord teachers proper orientation in concept, technique and value system to fulfill their role and responsibilities.

It is therefore proposed:

(i) to organize specially designed orientation programmes in teaching methodologies, pedagogy, educational psychology, etc., for all new entrants at all levels.

(ii) to organize refresher courses for serving teachers to cover every teacher at least once in 5 years.

(iii) to organize orientation programmes by using the internal resources of Universities and bringing a number of Colleges together, and

(iv) to encourage teachers to participate in Seminars, Symposia, workshops etc.

In order to achieve the above, a scheme of setting up Academic Staff Colleges (ASCs) in suitable Universities in the country was initiated by the University Grants Commission (UGC).

New Designs of Human Resource Development

The NPE 1986 emphasized the need for continuing education in general and orientation as well as refresher courses in particular. It has been aptly observed that the life in the coming decades is likely to bring new tensions with opportunities. To enable the people to benefit in the new environment will require new designs of human resources development. The coming generation should have the elasticity to internationalize new ideas constantly and creatively. In the context of the unprecedented explosion of knowledge, higher education has to become dynamic as never before, constantly entering unchartered areas. Provision would be made for minimum facilities in the Colleges for up-gradation of course. A major effort would be directed towards the transformation of teaching methods, introduction of audio-visual aids like electronic equipment, promotion of research and teacher orientation.

The NPE, 1986 recognizes the need for improving the status of the teacher and proposes to provide opportunities for professional and career development so that teachers can fulfill their role and responsibility within the educational system. It is proposed to promote the motivation of teachers through systematic orientation in individual subjects and methodologies and thereby inculcate in the teacher, the right kind of values and interests for furthering initiative for innovative and creative work.

Establishment of Academic Staff Colleges

Professional development of teachers is one of the major approaches for ensuring quality higher education. Realizing its significance and relevance the NPE of 1986 embodied 'professional development' as its integral part. This gave birth to ASCs in

1987. Since then, these have become the epicenters for the professional development of College and University teachers and their performance has been subjected to periodic review and assessment by the UGC, its standing committee and Academic Advisory Committees.

Objectives of the UGC–Academic Staff Colleges

Organization of Orientation Programmes

Organization of Orientation Programmes is the primary objective of UGC-Academic Staff Colleges. Orientation Programmes enable the young lecturers to:

a) understand the significance of education in general and higher education in particular in the global and Indian contexts;

b) understand the linkages between education, socio-economic and cultural development with particular reference to the Indian polity where democracy, secularism and social equity are basic tenets of society;

c) acquire and improve basic skills of teaching at the College/University level to achieve the goals of higher education;

d) to be aware of the latest developments in their specific subjects;

e) understand the organization and management of a College/ University and perceive the role of teachers in the total system;

f) utilize opportunities for development of personality, initiative and creativity; and

g) promote computer literacy as well use of ICT in teaching and learning process.

Organization of Refresher Courses for In-service Teachers

Refresher Courses will:

a) provide opportunities for teachers' in-service to exchange experience with their peers and to mutually learn from each other;

b) provide a forum for serving teachers to keep themselves abreast of the latest advances in various subjects;

c) create the culture of learning and self improvement among the teachers;

d) provide opportunities to further widen their knowledge and to pursue research studies;

e) give an introduction to new methods and innovations in higher education and enlighten them so that the participants can in turn develop their own innovative methods of instruction.

Besides these kinds of courses, the ASCs provide opportunity for:

(i) motivation of teachers to understand the vital role of Information Communication Technology in the realm of higher education;

(ii) equipping the teachers to meet the challenges and demands of 21st century as a result of globalization of higher education; and

(iii) preparation of teachers to play multi-dimensional role in the society.

Other programmes conducted by ASCs include:

a) organization of Seminars, Symposia, Workshops, Meetings, etc. on related aspects of Higher Education.

b) organization of Orientation Programmes/Training Programmes for Academic Administrators.

c) organization of Principals' Meetings once or twice a year, and

d) any other academic function assigned by UGC.

Functions of an ASC

The functions of an Academic Staff College will be to plan,

organize, implement, monitor and evaluate orientation courses for newly appointed college/university lecturers. An ASC will also organize refresher courses for serving teachers, and orientation programmes for senior administrators and heads of departments, principals, officers, etc. Specifically, an ASC will:

a) formulate a programme of orientation

b) identify resource persons in various fields of specialization for running the orientation programmes and refresher courses, and familiarize such resource persons with the philosophy and guidelines for the courses;

c) set up a documentation-centre-library for reference and source materials necessary for the courses;

d) produce specially designed material required for effective implementation of the courses;

e) organize, monitor and evaluate the courses for teachers;

f) create a culture of learning and self-improvement among teachers so that it becomes an integral part of the educational system at the tertiary level;

g) organize orientation programmes for senior administrators, heads of departments, principals, deans and other decision-makers to familiarize them with the philosophy of orientation intended to facilitate reform in higher education through appropriate modification of the management systems at various levels;

h) to provide opportunities for teachers in service to exchange experience with their peers and to mutually learn from each other;

i) provide a forum for serving teachers to keep themselves abreast of the latest advances in various subjects;

j) provide opportunities to further widen their knowledge and to pursue research studies;

k) provide an introduction to new methods and innovations in higher education so that the participants can in turn develop their own innovative methods of instruction

l) bring out publications relevant for enhancing the teaching and research capabilities of teachers; and

m) conduct capability enhancement programmes for non academic staff so as to strengthen the teaching-learning environment

Education Technology for Teacher Education and the Availability of Information Technology

Most of the educational experts expressed that teacher performance is most crucial input in the field of education. In fact, teachers have the ultimate to discharge the policies of education through teaching learning process. The National Policy on Education 1986 suggested that education technology should be employed, inter alia, in 'the training and retraining of teachers' to improve quality, sharpen awareness of art and culture etc. The teacher should be provided with pre-service and in-service education by means of various media, methods and materials constituting educational technology. The quality of teaching can be improved if the technological aspects that are necessary to impart knowledge are made known to teachers.

Out of the four revolutions in education, the fourth one has commenced with development in the electronics like radio, T.V., Audio-Video recorder, Computer and Communication technology. In these days communication technology play a crucial role in teaching learning process.

The Directors of Academic Staff Colleges at their meeting held in 2004 recommended the following to train the teachers in higher education:

The computers are acquired in all the Academic Staff Colleges with the UGC funds of rupees twenty lakhs. Full-fledged and well-furnished computer center has already been developed by the respective Universities. The Computer center would be utilized to realize all the proposed objectives of the UGC. In addition to this objectives, the ASC would aim to realize all the following activities.

1. to train the teachers in the production of computer based

instructional materials availing all the facilities of the multimedia in all the subjects being taught at higher education.

2. to train the teachers in using authorware so that teachers of all subjects can develop computer based instructional materials even though they may not be experts in programming languages.
3. to encourage the teachers to become members of different netforums as per their specialization and interact with the experts at the international level through the net forums.
4. to encourage teachers to moderate different net forums in different subjects.
5. the ASC would also conduct net forums in different subjects from time to time
6. teachers' will be given training in the development of computerized question banks in different subjects.
7. teachers will also be given training in the conduct of online testing.
8. efforts will be taken to conduct teleconferencing through various media from time to time in the conduct of teaching and learning different subjects at higher education
9. train the teachers in the techniques and methods of networking.

The Directors might be given intensive training in handling autherware packages so that teachers would be better trained in production of computer based instructional materials.

Broad Agenda for XI Plan

Towards conceptualizing and operationalising the perspective of the XI Plan based on inclusive growth of higher education in India, the agenda of the programme of action has to necessarily incorporate the dimensions, some of which are:

Faculty Development

The Parliamentary Standing Committee on HRD in its 172nd Report has recommended that the conditions of service, remuneration and career advancement of the teacher be linked with their overall performance. The Committee expresses its concern about large number of vacancies at different levels in teaching community. The Committee is of the view that drastic steps need to be taken so that students are not deprived of proper guidance.

- There is a need for provision of fully staffed, equipped and functional Academic Staff Colleges in all the Central Universities.
- Professional development of teachers in higher education needs to be a continuous and an ongoing process for maintaining quality
- Vacancies in the sanctioned teaching posts must be urgently filled up all over the country
- The refresher courses and orientation programmes should be revised for, updating of the skills of the teachers in the respective fields, with coordination between the industries and the employers, where necessary.
- The faculty improvement programme should be extended to computer faculty and such faculty members should be allowed to the industry to update their knowledge.
- Principals of colleges should be given training programme in innovative leadership.
- Exchange of faculty members across the borders should be done for developing managerial skills.
- The facility of going on sabbatical leave for improving subject knowledge and skills should be extended to teachers of colleges as in the case of Universities.
- Restructuring of service conditions and salary of teachers to maintain and retain the best talent in view of the lucrative offers available in IT and management sectors.

- Financial support for faculty to present research papers abroad.
- Four to six months of sabbatical leave may be awarded for research work, projects, post-doctoral research, for completing doctoral thesis (for faculty who have not availed FIP) and for writing and publishing books and research articles.
- Colleges may be allowed to conduct the refresher courses.
- Three weeks of academic programme conducted by institutions of repute should be recognized as refresher courses.
- To arrange for Technical training programme for teaching and non-teaching staff to develop software skills.
- All affiliating Universities may have academic staff colleges and labs are to be set up for them.
- There should be four faculty members for academic staff colleges.
- Academic Staff Colleges need to be open throughout the year.
- Resource centre is need to be set up within the University.
- Academic Staff Colleges in State Universities need to be strengthened.
- The Universities and Colleges need to participate in promotion of Indian higher education abroad and attract as many foreign students as possible to study in India.

Infrastructure Development

- Classrooms need to be equipped with modern conveniences, audio-visual equipments and quality seating arrangements for students.
- In view of the rising cost of books, journals and laboratory equipments, there is an urgent need to make adequate provision in the 11th Plan for capacity building in the

libraries and laboratories in the Universities. Similar provision may be made for the colleges affiliated to Central and State Universities, particularly for those colleges, which offer post-graduate courses.

- The UGC's Inflibnet System also needs to be expanded to cover all State Universities. The same facilities should be made available to the affiliated colleges, especially those colleges that offer post-graduate courses.
- Sports facilities in Universities/Colleges need to be strengthened.
- Innovations in laboratory teaching need to be encouraged.

Curriculum Development

- There is a need for starting of interdisciplinary and integrated courses at undergraduate and post-graduate levels with flexibility in choice of courses and a system of credits that enable horizontal and vertical mobility/transfers for teachers. These courses need to be started in both science and social science streams and must be offered by the Departments of the Central Universities. Colleges should also be involved in curriculum development.
- The Curricula should be revamped to reflect the need for national development with international benchmark.
- Creativity of teachers, research fellows, students and external experts should be harnessed in order to develop multimedia teaching material.

The UGC has also provided other facilities like Library-Cum-Documentation Centre, Computer Laboratory with all ICT equipments, Seminar Hall, Hostel facilities etc. in Academic Staff Colleges to support and manage the Teacher Education Programmes without causing any inconvenience.

Since education is a lifelong process, certainly there is a need for the teachers to become lifelong learners. Due to the information explosion and rapid growth of knowledge in various disciplines, we are considered to be the learners only in the Academic environment.

REFERENCES

1) Chalam, K.S. *Modern Techniques of Teaching and Staff Development*, New Delhi, Anmol, 2006.

2) Chalam, K.S. *Performance of Academic Staff College in India*, Visakhapatnam, Andhra University Press, 1994.

3) Mohanty, Jagannath: *Current Trends in Higher Education*. New Delhi, Deep and Deep, 2000.

4) Mohanty, Jagannath: *Dynamics of Higher Education in India*. New Delhi, Deep and Deep, 1993.

5) Rajendra Pal: *Academic Orientation of University Teachers: A Qualitative Inquiry. In University News, 1996 38(2), pp. 6-9.*

6) Rao, Chalapati, I.V.: *College Teachers and Administrators – A Handbook*. Hyderabad, Booklinks, 1992.

7) Rao, P.H.S. and Palsane, M.N.: *Training for Higher Education*. New Delhi, Rawat, 1994.

8) Savita Rastogi: Academic Staff Development in Higher Education: Indian Efforts. *University News*, 37(14), 1999, pp. 5-8.

9) Sisodia, M.L. *Educating the Educators-Vitalizing from Experience*, New Delhi, Devika, 1998.

10) Verma, Yoginder: Evaluation of Academic Staff Colleges: Certain Criteria and Issues. *University News*. 36(18), 1998. pp. 9-10.

18

VISIONARY LEADERSHIP IN HIGHER EDUCATION

A. Pal Pandi, U. Surya Rao** & D. Jeyathilagar****

Introduction

The education is a confluence of research, experiment and experience. Engineering and Management education is essential to improve the technical and executive manpower of a country. Today's vision and mission statement of every institution is good. In our perceptions, the performances are not satisfactory in most of the institutions, since they fail to practice visionary leadership concept. Engineering and Management institution encompasses the understanding of the technical and managerial skills employed in the utilization and improvement of natural resources for human fitness of purpose. The ultimate aim of the institution is to assure the quality and reliability of students. So, the institutions must have good visionary leaders for enhancing faculty and student knowledge in all aspects and also improving the wealth of the institutions.

* Asst. Professor, Department of Automobile Engg, SACS M.A.V.M.M. Engineering College, Madurai, India.

** Professor & Head, Department of Management Studies, Madurai Kamaraj University, Madurai, India.

*** Visiting Professor, Department of Management Studies, Madurai Kamaraj University, Madurai, India.

Problem Statement

Due to rapid expansion of technical and management institutions, majority of them are not able to meet the requirements of stakeholders i.e. quality education, employability skills of the students and highly intellectual capital (faculty members). Many institutions have got ISO9001: 2000 and NBA accreditation certificates. Unfortunately, some of them have failed to comply with the norms of the above. The reason is not practiced visionary leadership concept in educational institution. This is the right time to put visionary leader in their institution to meet out the needs of the stakeholders.

Proposed Suggestions

The dual challenges of competition in a world market and rapid technological advancements have necessitated a redesign of the workplace into an innovative work environment known as the high performance workplace like Indian Institute of Technology, and Indian Institute of Management. These environment having visionary leaders to solve the academic related problems, create many ways to improve the methods they use, and engage effectively with their resources. The standard of IIT's and IIM's is not less than any world-class educational institution. Especially self-financed institutions are not meet out that requirement of stakeholders, because the reason is not having visionary leader. Therefore visionary leader must institute all the institution for providing the high quality culture in the working atmosphere. The success of any institution is dependent on the quality of visionary leaders. The dynamic and effective leadership is a major segment of the success. They need to be educational visionaries, instructional and curriculum assessment experts, disciplinarians, community builders, public relations experts, budget analysts, facility managers, special programs administrators, policy mandates and initiatives. The following high quality character must be comes under the visionary leadership.

- **Developing people** – Enabling teachers and other staff to do their jobs effectively, offering intellectual support (i.e. Knowledge Management practice) and stimulation to improve the work.

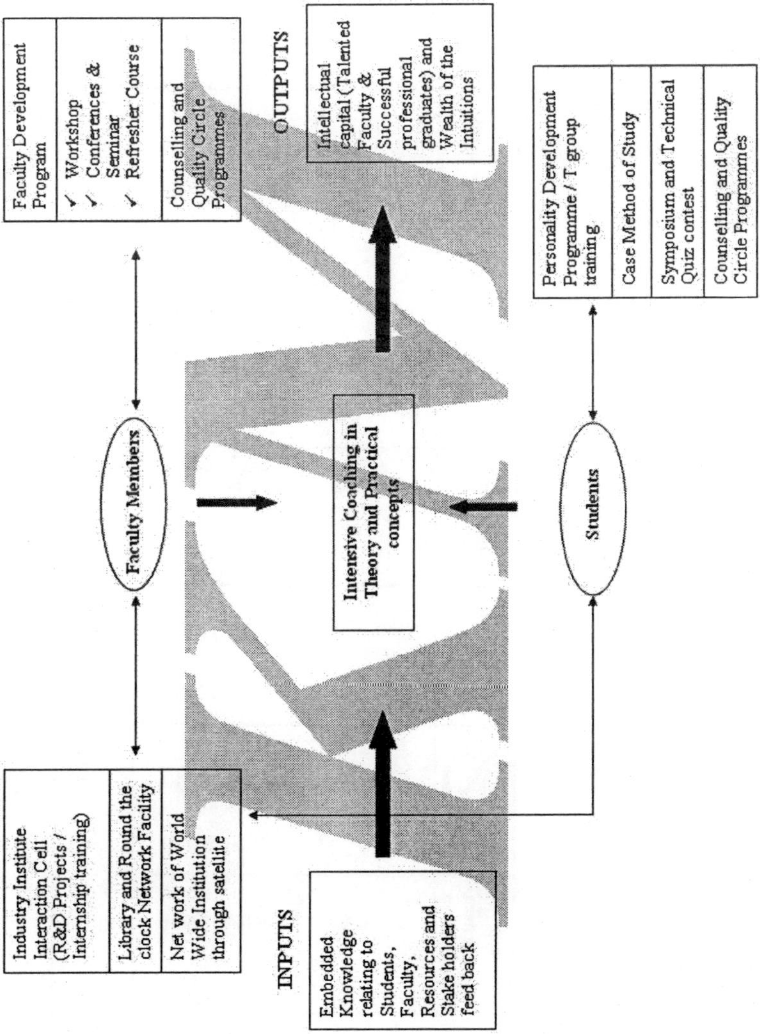

Figure 1. Knowledge Management Processes in Technical Institutions (Rao & Pandi, 2007)

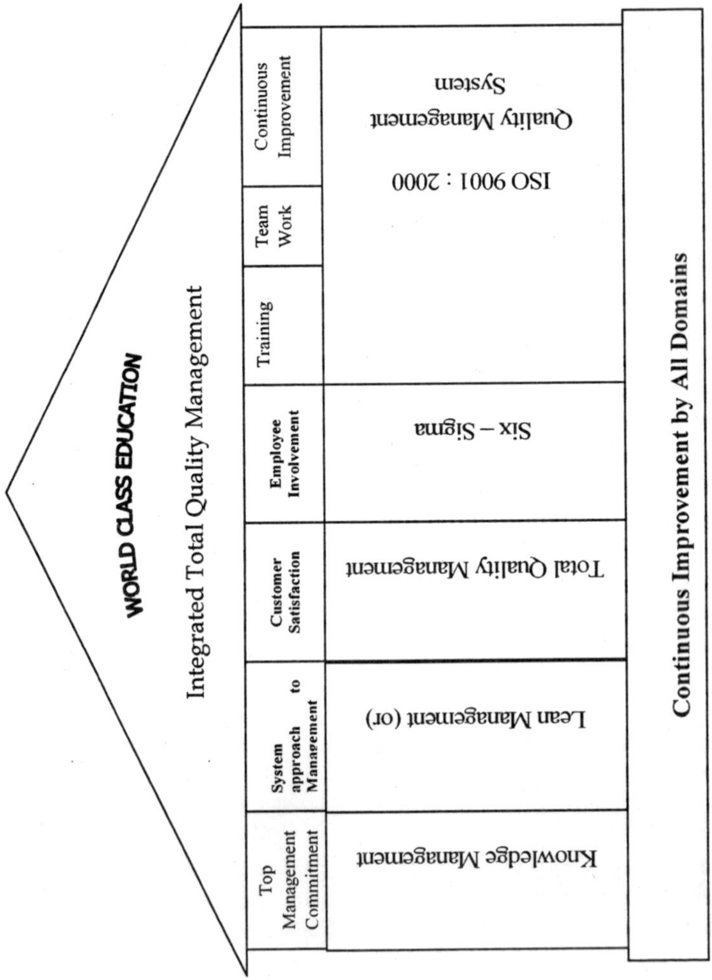

Figure 2. Proposed Framework for World-Class Education (Pandi & Rao, 2007)

- **Setting directions for the organization** - Developing shared goals, monitoring organizational performance, and promoting effective communication.
- **Redesigning the organization** - creating a high quality culture [i.e. Integrated Total Quality Management practices (ITQM)] in the system. ITQM is a bundle of global management practices such as ISO 9001:2000 Quality Management System, Six-Sigma (DMAIC), TQM, Knowledge Management and Lean Thinking.

Conclusion

The higher educational institutions are now realizing the growing disparity between what they impart to the students and their employment. Engineering and Management education in India has developed considerably; however it seems, most of the self-financing institutions are suffered to run without proper leader. The authors in this paper suggest visionary leadership concept must be instituted in the institutions and also to implement the model of Integrated Total Quality Management for improving quality level of performance in the academic activities for achieving quality assurance in institutions. Visionary Leadership is essential for educational and management system, leads to overall human development and social exclusion. Therefore Vice- Chancellors/ Principals/Administrators/directors have to be played as a visionary leader role in setting the direction for human and organization development.

REFERENCES

1. Surya Rao.U, Pal Pandi.A, (2007), "Quality Enhancement in Engineering Institutions through TQM and Knowledge Management", *Indian Journal of Engineering Education*, New Delhi, Vol.No. XX No.3, January, pp.10-15.
2. Pal Pandi.A., & Surya Rao, U. (July-September, 2007), "Achieving Global Quality in Technical Institutions through Integrated Total Quality Management", *Indian Journal of Training and Development*, Vol.XXXVII (3), 41-44.
3. Hoyle, John R. et al., (1998), *Skills for Successful 21st Century School Leaders: Standard for Peak Performers*, American Association of School Administrators, 1801 N. Moore St., Arlington.
4. Green, Madeleine, F., et al, (1988). *Leaders for a New Era: Strategies for Higher Education*. New York: Macmillan.

SECTION - C
EDUCATION OF WEAKER SECTIONS

19

WOMEN EMPOWERMENT THROUGH EDUCATION

*J. Rama Rao** & *T. Tirupathi Naidu***

Empowerment is a multidimensional process, which should enable a group of individuals to realize their full identity and powers in all spheres of life. It consists of greater access to knowledge and resources, greater autonomy in decision-making to enable them to have greater ability to plan their lives, or have greater control over the circumstances that influence their lives and free them from the shackles imposed on them by custom, belief and practice.

Literacy and access to basic education are prerequisites for taking advantage of opportunities for higher education. Almost everywhere, the literacy rates of girls and women and their access to basic education are lower than those of boys and men. In 1995, according to UNESCO, the regions with the lowest female literacy rates were Sub-Saharan Africa (47% for females compared to 66%for males), the Arab States (44% compared to 68%), and Southern Asia (37% compared 63%). For the least developed countries as a whole, the female literacy rate was 38% compared to 60% for males.

* Assistant Professor in Economics, M.R.P.G. College, Vizianagaram, Andhra Pradesh.

** Lecturer in Economics, M.R.A College, Vizianagaram, Andhra Pradesh.

According to UNESCO, women and girls are "the largest single category of persons denied equality of education opportunity in the world today". Female participation in primary, secondary and tertiary education compared to males varies considerably by regions. With the exception of developed countries and Latin America and the Caribbean, the percentage of the population enrolled in school is lower than the male population at all age levels. Sub-Saharan Africa and Southern Asia are the regions with the lowest percentages of enrollment of both school age males and females and where the gaps at each level are greatest.

Empowerment of women would mean equipping women to be economically independent and personally self-reliant, with a positive self-esteem to enable them to face any difficult situation. Moreover they should be able to contribute to the developmental activities of the country. The empowered women should be able to participate in the process of decision-making. Women empowerment is a dynamic process that consists of an awareness-attainment-actualization cycle. Again, it is a growth process that involves intellectual enlightenment, economic enrichment and social emancipation on the part of women.

Education is one factor that plays the most crucial role in empowering women. Schools, colleges and other professional bodies are persistently trying to educate, motivate and train the women in their chosen areas of career through curriculum, training, field-exposure and other practical methods. Research and publication in the areas of women's problems, social evils and their eradication and women empowerment are the hot topics of the present. Media coverage aiming at attracting the attention of the policy makers and authorities is at its highest level now.

A broad objective of National Policy on Education (NPE), 1986 modified in 1992 has been that education should play a positive and interventionist role in correcting social and regional imbalances, empowering women and in securing rightful place for the disadvantaged and the minorities. At the international level, India is committed to the "Millennium development goals and education for all". At the national level there is the commitment under the NCMP for increasing public expenditure on education to 6 percent of GDP and for universalizing elementary education. There is also an obligation, under the constitution's 86th amendment, for making available free and compulsory education for all children in the age group of 6-14 years. To achieve these objectives, a number of programmes are being implemented out of which the two flagship programmes of the government are: Sarva Shiksha Abhiyan, Mid Day Meals Programme, National Programme for Education of Girls at Elementary Education (NPEGEL) and Kasturba Gandhi Balika Vidyalaya (KGBV) of Residential schools for girls would also support universalization of elementary education. An attempt is made in this paper to study empowerment of women through education.

The Specific Objectives of the study are:

1. To estimate disparities between male and female literacy rate.
2. To estimate drop out rate at different stages of school education.
3. To examine the stages of Enrolment at different levels.

The importance of education for empowerment of women is undeniable. However, India has the lowest female literacy rate in Asia. In 1991, less than 40% of the 330 million women aged 7 and over were literate, which means today there are over 200 million literate women in India. This low level of literacy not only has a negative impact on women's lives but also on their families and on nation's development and Prosperity. Let us begin with a look at the rate of enrolment of girls as compared to boys at various stages of primary education. The data in Table 1 presents the data of sex-wise school enrolment in different Stages of the School education from 1950-51 to 2001-2002. Since 1950-51 the total enrolment at the primary, upper primary, secondary and senior secondary stages increased by 6, 14 and 20 times respectively. The girls' enrolment increased by 9, 37 and 60 times respectively during the same period in the above institutions.

As may be seen from the Table 1 the participation of girls at all stages of education has been increasing steadily through

Table 1: Enrolment by States

(In Million)

Year	Primary (1 - V)			Upper Primary (VI - VIII)			High/Hr. Sec./ Inter (IX - XII)		
	Boys	Girls	Total	Boys	Girls	Total	Boys	Girls	Total
1950-51	13.8	5.4	19.2	2.6	0.5	3.1	1.3	0.2	1.5
1960-61	23.6	7.5	24.6	3.8	1.0	4.8	2.2	0.4	2.6
1970-71	35.7	21.3	57.0	9.4	3.9	13.3	5.7	1.9	7.6
1980-81	45.3	28.5	73.8	13.9	6.8	20.7	7.6	3.4	11.0
1990-91	57.0	40.4	97.4	21.5	12.5	34.0	12.8	6.3	19.1
2000-01	64.0	49.8	113.8	25.3	17.5	42.8	16.9	10.7	27.6

Source: Selected Educational Statistics 2002-2003, Ministry of Human Resource Development, Department of Elementary Education

the years. Since 1950-51 girls participation has increased many folds in primary, middle, secondary/higher secondary stages and Higher education levels. From 28.1% to 44.1%, from 16.1% to 41.8%, from 13.30 to 39.5%, and from 10% to 39.9% respectively. However in totality their participation is still below 50% at all stages of education. Underlying factors that contribute skewed enrolment ratio and perpetuate gender inequalities in school and society between the two sexes or many.

As a result of number of initiatives and measures taken up by the Governments we notice a rise in the percentage of enrollment of women. The rate of literacy among women too has gone up from 39.29% in1991 to 54.16% in 2001. In fact, the increase in female literacy (by 14.8%) outpaced that of male literacy (11.7%). The male female literacy gap has been reduced from 24.84% in 1991 to 21.70% in 2001. Still the rate of literacy among males is higher than females. The male literacy rate has increased to 75.85%, which shown an increase of 11.72 %. On the other hand, the female literacy of 54.16 has increased at a much faster rate of 14.87%.Despite the fact that literacy and school enrolment among both males and females has increased yet the male female gap in the rate of literacy has widened and much remains to be done. At least 60 million girls lack access to primary education in India. According to a recent National Sample Survey Organization (NSSO) report, the literacy rate in India during 2004-05 was 64%, with Kerala having 83% of its rural population and 85% of its urban residents as literates.

India as a whole the gender gap in literacy has been decreasing since 1981.The data Table 2 indicates that the improvement in rate of literacy continues to be a large gap between literacy levels of men and women.

Even though the vitality of women's contributions to Social

Table 2: Literacy Rate in India

(In Percentage)

Year	*Persons*	*Males*	*Females*	*Male-Female Gap in Literacy Rate*
1951	18.33	27.16	8.86	18.30
1966	28.30	40.40	15.35	25.05
1971	34.45	45.96	21.97	23.98
1981	43.57	56.38	29.76	26.62
1991	52.21	64.13	39.29	24.84
2001	65.38	75.85	54.16	21.70

Source: Census of India

and Economic development has been well established, girls are still perceived to be playing roles mainly in non public domains. Women has whole are still disadvantaged in terms of education and enjoying benefits of Economic growth .Social and Economic systems supported by patriarchal values continue to influence women's education from the beginning. One of the major reasons for lack of education among women in India is high drop out rate among girls at the early stages of schooling as compared to boys. As per data 45% of girls and 41% of boys drop out of school between class 1 and 5. The data on school attendance by age show the proportion of girls attending school decreases with the age while for boys it remains somehow stable. In 1992-93, only 55% of girls aged 11-14 years were attending schools compared with 61% of the younger age group. The difference between the percentage of boys and girls becomes much more pronounced as we move up the level of education, this is mainly due to the higher school drop out rate among girls vis-à-vis the boys. The figures related to drop out percentages at different stages of schooling among boys and girls are presented in Table 3.

Table 3: Dropout Rate at Different Stages of School Education

(In Percentage)

Year	*Elementary*			*Primary*			*Secondary*		
	Boys	*Girls*	*Total*	*Boys*	*Girls*	*Total*	*Boys*	*Girls*	*Total*
1960-61	75.0	85.0	78.3	61.7	70.9	64.90	NA	NA	NA
1970-71	74.6	83.4	77.9	64.5	70.9	67.0	NA	NA	NA
1980-81	68.0	79.4	72.7	56.2	62.5	58.7	79.8	86.6	82.5
1990-91	59.1	65.1	60.9	40.1	46.0	42.6	67.5	76.9	71.3
1992-93	58.2	65.2	61.1	43.8	46.7	45.0	70.0	77.3	72.9
1999-2000	52.0	58.0	54.5	38.7	42.3	40.3	66.6	70.6	68.3
2001-2002	52.9	56.9	54.6	38.4	39.9	39.0	64.2	68.6	66.0

Source: Education in India, Department of Secondary and Higher Education, Ministry of Human Resources Development

Major Obstacles to Women Education

Some of the reasons for women's unequal participation in education are:

Lack of Sufficient Time

Girls begin helping out at an early age with the household chores that burden women (fetching fuel, water, preparing food, childcare and working in the fields) and these responsibilities increase as they grow holder, resulting in a decline in participation in education with age.

Customs, Traditions and Attitudes

A Combination of mutually reinforcing customs and attitudes place greater value on males than females in many societies. Preferences within families are often for boys to advance their education since social and cultural perceptions confine girls to roles that are thought to require little in any education.

Cycle of Poverty

The poorer a family is, the less likely it is that girls are sent to school because their labour is required at home and in the fields. Extreme Poverty in many Countries tends to lock illiterate women in to a cycle of early marriages and bringing up illiterate girls who continue the cycle of early marriages and illiterate children.

Conclusion

Among various reasons poverty is one of the prime cause for lack education and higher dropout rate among girls especially in rural areas. Some of the off-cited factors as reasons for dropping out as per girls are: reluctance of parents to send school, have to participate in domestic activities, helping the fields, teacher's unfair behaviour, illness, death in family, poverty and lack of interest in the studies. Spending on education, especially educating a girl child in rural areas is perceived as waste of money and resources as there is no immediate gain from education.

The Indian society has accorded differential status to women through out the history. But there has been a significant change in the status of women in modern India. Educating women is critical to socio-economic development of nation. In the words of Ex-President A.P.J. Abdul Kalam "Empowering women is a prerequisite for creating a good nation, when women are empowered, society with stability is assured. Empowerment of women is essential as their thoughts and their value systems lead the development of a good family, good society and ultimately a good nation." Women will gain power only when both men and women begin to respect and accept the contribution of women. Education would emancipate and endow women with ability to control her life, accomplish her dreams and enhance her status; the task is challenging, not impossible. Education and the empowerment of women are both essential and indispensable for a prosperous nation.

REFERENCES

1. Dr. Sheetal Sharma, "Empowering women through education: strategy for sustainable Rural Development", *Kurukshetra*, Vol.56, No.3, January, 2008, pp. 3-7.

2. Promilla Kapur, *Empowering the Indian Women*, Publication Division, Ministry of Information and Broadcasting, GOI, New Delhi, pp. 47-50.

3. Economic Survey, 2006-2007, Ministry of Finance, GOI, New Delhi, pp. 212-2.

4. Antony, "Education and Employment, the key to women empowerment," *Kurukshetra*, Vol.54, No. 4, February, 2006, p. 27.

5. Census of India, 2001.

20

WOMEN EMPOWERMENT THROUGH EDUCATION

G. Syamala Rao & M. Sanyasi Rao***

Introduction

Women's empowerment is the issue of raising awareness about rights - legal literacy, right to education and health and enhancing information sharing about basic issues. Jawaharlal Nehru had said "You can tell the condition of the nation by looking at the status of women". According to Mahatma Gandhi, "If you educate a man you educate an individual, but if you educate a woman you educate an entire family." Our predominant patriarchal system doesn't provide enough chances for women to have higher education even if they wish. Girls should be motivated to take up higher education. True empowerment will only be reached when women take part actively in the decision making process of our country. The Government of India had ushered in the new millennium by declaring the year 2001 as 'Women's Empowerment Year' to focus on a vision 'where women are equal partners like men'. In many societies Including India, gender inequality was part and parcel of an accepted male-dominated culture. Discrimination is the major problem, which the Indian women face in the present day society.

* Asst.Professor, Dept. of Management Studies, G.V.P. P.G. College, Rushikonda, Visakhapatnam, Andhra Pradesh.

** Asst. Professor, Department of Economics, G.V.P. P.G. College, Rushikonda, Visakhapatnam, Andhra Pradesh.

The traditional mentalities of India assume that the place of women is mainly concentrated to the household activities like kitchen work and upbringing of the children. They have been considered as the sex object and inferior to the men in different spheres of knowledge. The 'Sati System', 'Child Marriage', 'Dowry System', etc. have been some form of atrocities and discriminatory attitudes against the women. Now a days women are actively participating in all the fields because of their educational levels. The main objective of this paper is to highlight the importance of education in the women life and economic development.

Significance of Women Education

Education is significant for girls and women because it is an entry point to other opportunities and the educational achievements of women can have ripple effects not only within the family but for many generations to come. Educated women recognize the importance of health care and know how to take care of themselves and their families. Education helps to know their rights and they get the confidence to claim them. An educated mother plays a greater role in household negotiations and she secures more resources for her children. An educated mother can pay more attention to her children. "Education is one of the most important means of empowering women with the knowledge, skill and self-confidence necessary to participate fully in the development process" says the International Conference on Population and Development (ICPD) Programme of Action. Educated women can recognize the importance of health care and know how to seek help for themselves and their children. Education helps girls and women to know their rights and develop confidence to claim them. Recently UNFPA has supported several projects in Jamaica, Bolivia, Mali, Mauritius, to educate thousands of girls and women towards safe pregnancies, safe motherhood and other health issues towards AIDS and environment preservation. Even after fifty-seven years of Indian Independence, women are still one of the most powerless and marginalized sections of Indian society. The 2001 Census shows that the sex ratio for India is 933, which is lowest in the world. Percentage of female literacy is 54.16 (2001 Census) against male literacy of 75.85 percent.

Women's Subject Choices

By observing the above table the enrolment rate of women is increasing compared to previous years. The attitude of men towards women also changing due to the increase in literacy among women. In the above table we can observe that the women enrollment in the faculty of education is more compared to other faculty the main cause may be to get the job in the residential area.

Table 2: Women Students per Hundred Men Students

Year	*Total Women Enrolment (000s)*	*Women Enrolment Per Hundred Men*
1950-51	40	14
2005-2006	4466	68

Source: UGC Annnual Report , 2005-06.

Table – 2 shows the increase of women enrolment per hundred of men increased from 14 percent in 1950-51 to 68 percent in 2005-2006 i.e. the enrolment of women increased to nearly five times compared to 1950-51 data.

Table 3: Number of Women Colleges during the Decade 1995-1996 to 2005-2006

Year	*Number of Women Colleges*
1995-1996	1146
1996-1997	1195
1997-1998	1260
1998-1999	1359
1999-2000	1503
2000-2001	1578
2001-2002	1625
2002-2003	1650
2003-2004	1798
2004-2005	1849
2005-2006	*1902

* Provisional

Source: UGC Annual Report 2005-06.

Table 4: Proportion of Men and Women Students to Total Enrolment by Gender and Discipline/Subject (1950-51 to 2005-06)

Faculties	1950-51		1960-61		1970-71		1980-81		1991-92		2000-01		2005-06	
	Women	*Men*	*Women*	*Men*	*Women*	*Men*	*Women*	*Men*	*Women*	*Men*	*Women*	*Men*	*Women*	*Men*
Arts	16.1	83.9	24.6	75.4	31.7	68.3	37.7	62.3	41.8	58.2	44.2	55.8	45.8	54.2
Science	7.1	92.9	10.5	89.5	17.8	82.2	28.8	71.2	32.9	67.1	39.4	60.6	40	60
Commerce	0.6	99.4	0.9	99.9	3.7	96.3	15.9	84.1	22.1	77.9	36.5	63.5	37	63
Education	**32.4**	67.6	**32.8**	67.2	**36.5**	63.5	**47.3**	52.7	**50.2**	49.8	**51.2**	48.8	**51.3**	48.7
Engg/Tech	0.2	99.8	0.9	99.1	1	99	3.8	96.2	7.6	92.4	21.5	78.5	23.3	76.7
Medicine	16.3	83.7	21.9	78.1	22.8	77.2	24.4	75.6	33.2	66.8	44	56	46.7	53.3
Law	2.1	97.9	3	97	3.7	96.3	6.9	93.1	11.0	89	20	80	16.7	83.3
Agriculture	5.8	94.2	7	93	9.5	90.5	13.6	86.4	7.1	92.1	17.4	82.6	21.6	78.4
Veterinary Science*									8	92	20.9	79.1	21.8	78.2
Others									38.3	61.7	37.7	62.3	37.5	62.5

Source: *Economic and Political Weekly*, Feb 17th , 2007 & UGC Annual Report, 2005-06.

Establishment of women college is also increasing continuously year by year, it indicates the demand of women education is increasing hence the education facilitators are also interested to start women colleges.

Women as Professionals

By improving educational opportunities for girls and women, World Education helps women develop skills that allow them to make decisions and influence community change in key areas. The educated women settled in various fields in the society. According to industry statistics, the number of employed women grew by almost 200 million over the last decade, and reached 1.2 billion in 2007 compared to 1.8 billion men. However the number of unemployed women also grew from 70.2 to 81.6 million over the same period. Today women professionals outshine their male counterparts on a variety of measures and feel well equipped to grab the opportunities of the multi-polar world. Most companies have started realizing that integrating women into their business will present an enormous opportunity to help foster business. Until about three years back, most Indian women put in not more than 48 hours in work. Now, Indian women are spending longer hours and putting in 60 hours of work, partly due to improved in work culture. It is pleasing development as they are competing with their male counterparts to get an equal footing. The latest finding of Grant Thornton International Business Report reveals that the percentage of women in senior managerial positions globally has grown slightly from 19 to 22% since 2004. Surprisingly, every four in ten business worldwide has a dearth of women in senior management positions. India is leading at 14% followed by countries like Taiwan and the Philippines at 13% and Hong Kong at 9% respectively. (Ravindra Reddy N, 2008). The more women on a company's board of directors, the more women are likely to be among that company's senior management. Firms with 30% of women board directors in 2001 on average had 45% more women corporate officers by 2006, compared with ones with no female board members, according to the study by catalyst. Women, though have proved their versatility for ages and have donned the multiple facets simultaneously, be it of a loving and caring mother or daughter, an obedient wife and a good manager of her life and family, there are still finding it difficult to cross the boundaries of their home.

Conclusion

In recent years, the empowerment of women has been recognized as the central issue in determining the status of women. Education in the main source to the empowerment of women. Gradually organizations are realizing that it is better to treat women as a whole people rather than just creative human resources. Around the globe, women are joining the workforce in record numbers. Women earn a fraction of what their male counterpoints earn, often work longer hours, continues to have the same home responsibilities as before they went to work, and face the challenges of learning to balance both their home and work lives and try to be successful in both. The organization and government must treat women as equal to men and give them the respect responsibility to grow in leadership positions. Parents and Family members also should encourage the girl child education equal to their boys.

REFERENCES

1. Divya Nigam, "Women Executives", *HRM Review*, The Icfai University Press, Vol.VIII Issue- IX Septermber, 2008.pp18-25
2. Karuna chanana, "Globalisation, Higher Education and Gender", *Economic and Political Weekly*, Vol. XLII, No. 7, February 17, 2007. pp. 590-598.
3. Kathleen Patterson, Myra Dingman and Myra Robinson-Davis, "Women in the Workforce", *HRM Review*, The Icfai University Press, Vol.VIII Issue- IX Septermber, 2008. pp. 14-17.
4. Ravinder Reddy.N, "Women - on the Road to the Top", *HRM Review*, The Icfai University Press, Vol. VIII, Issue- IX, Septermber, 2008, pp. 26-31.
5. Syed Vazith Hussain and P.R. Sivasankar, "Women Empowerment and Prime Minister Rojgar Yojana", *The Indian Journal of Commerce*, Vol. 58, No. 2, April-June, 2005. pp. 101-107.

6. UGC Annual Report 2005-06.

7. http://www.sdpi.org/help/research_and_news_bulletin/march_june_06/wome_empowerment.htm.

   http://www.worlded.org/WEIInternet/projects/ListProjects.cfm?Select=Topic&ID=16&ShowProjects=No&gclid=CLyI4dWuj5YCFQ5aegodB3VvDw.

21

EMPOWERMENT OF WEAKER SECTIONS THROUGH EDUCATION

E. Vanilla Kumari, E. Sharmila Hymavathi** & G. Ratna Priya****

Indian society has been suffering from deep rooted inequalities and differences based on culture, caste, creed, region, religion and social stratification.

After the attainment of Independence in 1947, India committed to remove all kinds of inequalities and establish an egalitarian society through education and economic action. The preamble to the Constitution bears the testimony of the nation's solemn promise to secure social, economic and political justice and equality as well as opportunity for all. The constitution guarantees equality before law, removal of discrimination on grounds of caste, creed, sex, race or place of birth, abolition of untouchability, prohibition of traffic in human beings and forced labour prohibition of employment of children in factories, protection of interests of minorities, right of minorities to establish and administer educational institutions, promotion of welfare of people in general a minimum living wage, full employment and social as well as cultural opportunity to all workers, provision of free and compulsory education for children up to the age of 14 years, promotion of educational and economic interests of scheduled castes, scheduled tribes and other weaker sections provision of

*, ** & ***Department of Education, Andhra University, Visakhapatnam.

facilities for instruction in mother tongue at primary stage and Disability Act 1995. The present paper discuss about the inequalities regarding women education, adult education, elementary education, education of physically challenged and education of scheduled castes and scheduled tribes and minorities especially the Muslims and neo-Buddhist still exists despite many fold increase in the educational facilities in our country.

Views of Commissions and Committees

Since Independence a number of commissions and committees were setup to review the progress of education at different levels of education and make' recommendations for further achieving the unachieved objectives of education. Three commissions were set up in the span of 24 years (University Education Commission (1948-49), Secondary Education Commission (1952-53) and Kothari Education Commission (1964-66)). Kothari Education Commission (1964-66) emphasized five main factors responsible for existing inequalities of educational opportunities in our country. These are— (i) imbalance distribution of educational institutions, (ii) man's poverty (iii) varying standards of schools and colleges, (iv) difference in home environments, and (v) disparity in sex and class structure. It further emphasized that inequalities of educational opportunity also arise due to physical and mental handicaps of the people. Keeping in view of the existing inequalities the Commission stipulated that "0n grounds of social justice as well as for the furtherance of democracy, it is essential to make special efforts to equalities educational opportunities between these groups."

The National Policy on Education (1968) is a great landmark in the history of providing equal educational opportunity in the country. The policy emphasized the need to adopt common school system for promoting social cohesion and national integration. It calls for removal of regional imbalances' in the provision of educational facilities and provision of good educational facilities in rural and other backward areas. It also stressed the need of girls' education not only for ensuring social justice but also for accelerating social transformation. Emphasis has also been Iaid to further enhance efforts to develop education among backward classes, specially, among tribal people and for disabled children. National Policy on Education (1986) also paid special attention to equalization educational opportunities. It has clearly stated that "the new policy will lay special emphasis on the removal of disparities and to equalize educational opportunity by attending to the specific needs of those who have been denied equality so far". Regarding the education of women, the said policy stressed that education will be used as an agent of basic change in the status of women. The National Education system will play a positive, interventionist role in the empowerment of women. For promoting equalization of educational opportunities among scheduled caste and scheduled tribe students, the NPE (1986) has promised for providing special incentives like scholarships, remedial courses, new curricular innovative methods as well as media and suitable learning materials. It further specified that suitable incentives will be provided to all educationally backward sections of the society including minorities, particularly in the rural areas. It clearly stated that Muslims and Neo-Buddhist are the most backward both educationally and economically. Thus, greater attention will be paid to the education of these groups for promoting equality and social justice. The policy also laid emphasis on the education-of physically challenged students and the adult education. International Commission for the Twenty first century (1996) or Delors Commission also emphasized that the triple goal of equity, relevance and excellence must prevail in any policy of education, and the search for harmonious combination of these goals is a crucial task for all those involved in educational planning and practice.

In spite of the constitutional guarantees and positive intentions of the government to promote equality and social justice through various schemes and programmes suggested in different educational policies and commissions, the inequalities still persist in our educational system. Even after fifty eight years of planned efforts in the sector of education, we are still far away from achieving the goal of 100% literacy in our country. At the time of independence, 14% of the population in India was literate but now literacy rate has increased to 65.38% (75.96% for males and 54.28% for females) as per 2001 Census Report. It is quite evident that more than one third population or nearly 346 million persons in the age of six and above are still illiterate. A country which is projecting its prowess in Information Technology, Engineering and Science has a shameful statistics in the field of general education. About 35 million children, in the age group of 6-10 do not attend primary school 37% drop-out before reaching class V. The rate of enrolment at the secondary level is half of the primary level, showing a large number of students' dropout at the initial stages of their education. India's tertiary enrolment is only 6%. The drop-out rate in classes I to X is over 68%/. The drop-out rate among four groups - the Scheduled Castes, Scheduled Tribes, Other Backward Classes and Muslims is very high. Girls fare worse than boys. (Times of India, 17th May 2005). It is astonishing that we are among the few · in the global market in Information Technology, and yet we could not achieve the goal of universal elementary education. Moreover, the widening gap between the learning opportunities available to the haves and have nots is creating a kind of apartheid in education. The most deprived are rural poor, and socio-economically disadvantaged groups which are marginalized and excluded from enjoying the present exceptional economic resurgence taking place in India.

In India, equality between men and women does not exist specially in the field of education. Although there has been a gradual increase in the participation of women in education since independence because of the significant policy initiatives taken by the government to fulfill constitutional guarantees provided to them, the gender disparities still exist at each level of education. According to 200I censes, the sex ratio was 933 per thousand males. The percentage of girl's enrolment to total enrolment was - in primary 43.6%, middle 40.4%, secondary 38.6%, and higher education upto degree and above level 36.9%. (Selected educational Statistics 2000-200I). However, in professional courses like Engineering, B Ed. and MBBS it was 223%, 42.8% and 40.6% respectively in the year 2002 (Srivastava, 2003). These statistics seems to be satisfactory on paper but reality some what different. These figures are due to the participation of urban women belonging to educated classes and the higher socio-economic groups. Girls belonging to the urban slums and rural and remote arears continue to lag behind or even deprived to receive primary and secondary education what to talk about higher education.

In developing societies the children with special needs were thought to be not suitable for receiving education. This was despite the fact that many distinguished persons with disabilities have made significant contribution to science, arts and literature. The planning commission has now accepted that about 10 percent population of age group 6-14 has some physical, mental or sensory impairment. Thus, there are 30 million children with special needs in India (Advani, 2002). Despite such large numbers, the physically challenged children are one of the most neglected and mistreated groups in almost every society. They are denied the right to education, the right to equality of opportunity, the right to participate in society, and the fundamental right to lead a dignified life in the society. The children with special needs are children first and only their special needs are to be considered. They have the equal right to develop their potentials through education and training in order to adjust themselves emotionally and socially. Scientific and technological advancements in different fields including medicine can transform the entire life of exceptional children and they can lead a decent life and can be productive members of the society. In developed countries ameliorative steps for differently abled people enabled them to lead dignified life.

The National Policy on Education 1986 has observed, "The whole Nation must pledge itself to the eradication of illiteracy, particularly in the age group of 15-35 years; The central and state governments, political parties and NGOs, the mass media and educational institutions must commit themselves to man literacy program of diverse nature". But unfortunately the impact of adult education program as a supportive measure to eradicate illiteracy is far from satisfactory. Regional disparities in literacy rates between states, between districts in a state, between males and females and between tribal and non-tribal areas are significant. It is because of the lack of participation of educated masses, lack of enthusiasm among volunteers, socio-economic and cultural backwardness of some states, and campaign about actual planning and quality. In the areas, where total literacy target has been achieved lack of sufficient post literacy campaign to convert the neo-literates to 'functional literates' has made the task much more difficult.

In the light of the above facts it may be inferred that inequalities regarding women education, adult education, elementary education, education of physically challenged and education of scheduled castes and scheduled tribes and minorities especially the · Muslims and neo-Buddhist still exists despite many fold increase in the educational facilities in our country. Equal educational opportunities especially quality education at each stage of education does not exist in rural and urban slums. There are different types of educational institutions available to the students belonging to higher and lower socio-economic backgrounds specially in terms of quality education. Moreover, the concept of equal opportunity of education is being jeopardized by private educational institutions which offer quality education and proved to be boon and bane to the society. It leads to sectorial development. The microscopic section of Indian society which was first to enjoy the benefits of higher education during the post independence period, occupied the available avenues that gave them economic prosperity. Their accrued economic well being motivated them to invest the surplus money in education of their children. It resulted in spiraling advantages to already advantaged section of Indian society. With the increasing number of students looking for higher and professional education, compelled institutions to go for certain eliminating devices or entrance examinations. There has been a rapid growth of higher education in the world during last 50 years but India could not keep pace due to the lack of budgetary al1ocations which always hovered around three to 3.7%. This resulted in two types of educational institutions of higher learning which may be termed as white elephants which caters the elites of the Indian society and other inferior institutions in rural and semi urban areas for the poor masses. The existing system of education represents a gloomy picture as it does not cater the needs of different sections of the society, and therefore elitist in nature. Moreover, the haves of the society are in more advantageous position in this age of globalization and privatization where money plays an important role in purchasing quality education. In the present scenario, it is extremely difficult to empower the socio-economically weaker sections of the society through education. However, our commitment for an egalitarian society compels for providing equality of educational opportunity to empower the have nots too for a balanced and harmonious development to make India a forward nation by 2020.

In a country like India where one third of the population lives below poverty line and nearly 50% of the world's illiterates live, the claims of the government to make India a forward nation by 2020 seem to be a gigantic task because of the inequalities of different types lie at the base of each stage of education. The strength of the Nation lies in the fact that every individual gets a chance to nurture and groom his potentialities to the fullest irrespective of all the social and economic barriers which are deeply embedded in our social system and psyche of the people. The Indian Constitution guarantees every help and support to all the socio-economically weaker 'sections and disadvantaged groups so that they be transformed into quality human resource to shoulder the responsibilities of motherland to make it a forward nation as early as possible. Therefore, vigorous ameliorative steps should be taken for redressed of the injustice of the past. The universities should come forward to play the leading role and pledge for the transformation of Indian society.

22

POLICIES AND PROGRAMMES AND CHANGING EMPLOYMENT OPPORTUNITIES FOR WOMEN IN SCHOOL EDUCATION – A CASE STUDY OF ANDHRA PRADESH

R. Vijaya Krishna, D. Pulla Rao** & P. Jayanand Kumar****

Introduction

Education plays an important role in the process of development of human resources. Education and modernization are the two wheels of the same cart. Both, when combined together, lead to a rapid socio-economic development of a nation. While study of advanced science and technology helps achieve modernization, the basic education helps the poor masses to take advantage of scientific and technological development, and hence, of modernization. It is, therefore, not by accident that the provision regarding education of the poor masses form an integral part of the Constitution of India enforced on 26th January, 1950. The Article 45 of the Constitution provides for free and compulsory education for all children in the age group 6-14 years, up to a minimum level. The whole idea has been woven around the

---

* Research Scholar & ** Professor, Dept. of Economics, Andhra University, Visakhapatnam

*** Lecturer, Govt. Junior College, Chagallu, West Godavari, Dt. A.P.

concept of universalization of elementary education. The level of compulsory education as envisaged in this Article corresponds to the elementary education of eight years duration from Class I to Class VIII for the children aged 6-14 years. Primary education constitutes a very important part of the entire structure of education. It is at this stage, the child starts going to a formal institution and formal education starts. And it is at this stage that the child empowerment starts to build up. This is not to underplay the fact that Andhra Pradesh is among the educationally backward states in the country.

Education of girls has been high on both national and state agendas. Special commissions and committees were set up from time to time to assess the progress of girls' education and to propose suitable interventions to promote their educational participation. Several strategies were adopted to promote education of girls as an integral part of the planned socio-economic development of the country. The removal of women's illiteracy and obstacles inhibiting their access to, and retention in primary education will receive overriding priority, through provision of special support services, setting of time targets, and effective monitoring.

History of Women's Education

The history of India as well as the history of Andhra Pradesh records that women enjoyed a high status in the society. They were provided educational opportunities comparable to men. The social evils like purdah, sati, enforced widowhood and child-marriage crept into the society much later and resulted in the degradation of their status. There were no institutions for education of girls during Muslim period, but girls did receive religious education in the recitation of the *Quran* in their homes.

Under the British rule, the East India Company was reluctant to take up the responsibility of girl's education for a long time, due to the doctrine of religious neutrality, which was adopted by the Government so as not to offend the natives even on social customs that had nothing to do with religion. The Indian Education Commission (1882) took a serious note of the status and education of women and rated it to be extremely backward, and recommended measures for improvement. But, because of certain socio-political reasons, no noticeable progress could be made.

After Independence, the University Education Commission (1948-49), set up by the government of India, laid special emphasis on the education of women and recommended that in view of the similar fields of activity for men and women, and some specific requirements of women, maximum facilities should be given for education in Home Economics and Home Management.

During the post-Independence period, the main strategy adopted to achieve equalization of educational opportunities has been to make school accessible to every child. It was thought that expansion of educational facilities, as a part of providing universal elementary education for all would make education available to the weaker sections of the society including women.

Gender inequality has become one of the major areas of concern for educationists and policy makers in the developing countries in the 21st century. Gender inequality in India stems from two important sources of differences between men and women i.e. (1) earning capacity that make women utterly dependent upon men and (2) cultural taboos and traditions that greatly restrict the autonomy of women. Biological differentiation has perpetuated a structure, which has deprived women of normalcy of life chances available to men.

As long as Indian society remains male dominated, the constitutional provisions for legal equality of women with men matters very little. Perhaps, in no area are the laws so openly and widely violated as in the case of women, whether it is a question of education, health, and securing employment or equal wages for equal work. The prevailing mindset of the people of the society is primarily responsible for the gender inequalities, which force women to be submissive.

Women are discriminated against notwithstanding the important role in several aspects of human life and materially contribute significantly for the development of the family, society and the country. Women account for a large percentage of unpaid work, both at home and outside. They actively participate themselves in work on the family farms and in household enterprises. Where they do participate in paid work, their earnings are low employment, irregular and insecure, support services inadequate, opportunities for improvement and growth few and collective organization weak.

It is a well-known fact that women play a very important role in agriculture, as it is largely a household enter-prise. They are engaged in agriculture both as main workers and as marginal workers also. Women perform a variety of tasks in agriculture transplantations, such as fertilizer application, weeding harvesting. Their role in the allied activities like management of dairy, poultry, sheep breeding etc is also well known. Indian women are major producers of food in terms of value, volume and hours of work.

Women, of late, have been increasingly involving themselves in work outside agriculture - in the secondary and tertiary sectors. Increasing levels of educational attainments have facilitated such involvement. To carry forward this trend, it is necessary that education of females should continue to be accorded greater and greater priority. Fortunately, the changing norms in the society are now enabling more and more women to actively seek education. Now they can be found in large numbers in the fields of Information Technology, science and space research and in other such fields that demand high level of skills.

As per the National Policy on Education (NPE) - 1986, the government of India launched several programmes. One such programme was the Mahila Samakhya, whose main emphasis was empowerment of women. The programme endeavours to create a learning environment where women can collectively affirm their potential, gain the strength to demand information and knowledge and move forward to change and take charge of their lives.

The government of Andhra Pradesh has taken up certain pioneering initiatives such as Operation Black Board (OBB), Andhra Pradesh Primary Education Project (APPEP), District

Primary Education Programme (DPEP), establishment of School Education Committees, Village Education Committees, Mandal Education Committees, Maa Badi (our school), Chaduvula Pandunga (festival of studies), Akshra Sankranti (literacy festival), Sarva Shiksha Abhiyan (SSA), Vidya-Volunteer Scheme, Mid-day Meal Scheme, etc. to provide quality primary education for all. Due to the existing programmes, and some initiatives on the part of the government, the girls' education has developed faster than that of boys in Andhra Pradesh.

Objectives

This paper address itself to the quantification of advances made by females in respect of primary, upper primary and secondary education in Andhra Pradesh from 1959-60 to 2004-05.

The Specific Objectives are:

1. To estimate disparity index between male and female literacy rates.
2. To estimate the growth of enrollment of girls vis-a-vis boys in primary, upper primary and secondary education, and
3. To examine the increase in the number of women teachers employed in primary, upper primary and high schools.

The Data

The secondary data relating to the enrollment of students by sex in primary stage and the number of teachers by sex working in primary schools for the period from 1959-60 to 2004-05 in Andhra Pradesh are obtained from the Directorate of Economics and Statistics, Government of Andhra Pradesh, Hyderabad and the Commissioner and Director of School Education, Government of Andhra Pradesh, Hyderabad.

The Structure of School Education in Andhra Pradesh

Andhra Pradesh has accepted a uniform structure of education popularly known as 10+2+3 pattern of school and college education. This pattern visualizes 10 years of general education including 7 years of elementary followed by 3 years of secondary education, 2 years of senior secondary / Intermediate followed by 3 years of college education leading to the award of first degree. A child is admitted to Class I, normally, at the age of 6 years and is supposed to complete primary education up to Class V at the age of 11 years, and elementary education up to class VII, at the age of 13 years; up to this stage the state is constitutionally obliged to provide for free and compulsory education to all children under Article 45. At the end of VII class there is a district common examination. Elementary education is followed by three years of secondary education popularly known as 'High School'. At this stage also there is no diversification of courses and there is common curriculum for all children. The main purpose of this stage is to build a strong foundation in the fundamental principles of all basic subjects. At the end of this stage, that is, after 10 years of general education, the first public examination is held. This stage is followed by two years of senior secondary/ Intermediate education. The senior secondary or +2 stage consists of two streams, academic and vocational.

Special Schemes and Programmes for Promoting Education of Girls

Several strategies were adopted to promote education of girls in Andhra Pradesh. Theoretically, all formal and non-formal education and training programmes are open to women also along with their male counterparts. However, separate provisions are made for opening of separate institutions or separate wings for girls exclusively. Education is free for girls up to the higher secondary stage and several states have made education free for girls right up to the university level as well. Besides, there are other incentives like free noon meals, free books, free uniforms, scholarships for good attendance, bicycles etc.

In the first three Five Year Plans, girls' education covered under special component plans with additional allocations. In the Eighth Five Year Plan, a central scheme was introduced to provide funds to the state governments to hire a woman teacher for all single teacher primary schools and also towards cash awards and prizes for villages, blocks and districts with good performance in female education/literacy. Girls belonging to

Scheduled Castes and Scheduled Tribes received additional benefits for showing better school attendance. As a result of the protective discrimination policies under constitutional provisions, the enrollment of the SC and ST girl children as considerably improved.

Progress of Female Literacy Rate in Andhra Pradesh

As per the figures based on 2001 census, women constitute about 49.44 per cent of the total population of Andhra Pradesh. In fact this percentage should have been 50. The sex ratio is adverse. In the field of education these disparities between males and females are still larger. Table-1 shows the gap between the literacy rates of males and females. It shows how the gap has been persisting since 1961. In 1961 the female literacy rate was 12.03 per cent as against 30.19 per cent among males. The disparity index (ratio of male literacy rate to female literacy rate) in 1961 was 2.51. The literacy rate of females rose to 51.17 per cent in 2001 even as the rate for males increased to 70.85 per cent. As shown in table-1, the literacy rate among females has increased at a faster rate than among males. This is evident from the successively decreasing trend of disparity index from 2.51 in 1961 to 1.38 in 2001. In Andhra Pradesh females responded far more enthusiastically than males to the total literacy campaigns launched by the government with the help of non-governmental organizations and the cooperation of NGOs.

Table 1: Gender-wise Literacy Rates in Andhra Pradesh (1961 to 2001)

Year	*Male Literacy Rates*	*Female Literacy Rates*	Disparity Index
1961	30.19	12.03	2.51
1971	33.18	15.75	2.11
1981	39.26	20.39	1.92
1991	55.13	32.72	1.68
2001	70.85	51.17	1.38

Source: Handbook of statistics, Bureau of Economics and Statistics of the respective years, Hyderabad, Andhra Paradesh.

Progress of Girls' Enrollment in Different Stages of Schools in Andhra Pradesh

Table-2 shows the progress of girls' enrollment in primary, upper primary and secondary stages. In 1959-60, the enrollment of girls was 37.88 per cent (10.63 lakhs out of 28.06 lakhs) at primary stage, 22.94 per cent (61,752 out of 2.69 lakhs) at upper primary stage, and 17.88 per cent (39,594 out of 2.21 lakhs) at secondary stage. By 2004-2005, the situation had considerably improved with girls' enrollment reaching 49.37 per cent (37.98 lakhs out of 76.92 lakhs) at primary level, 47.61 per cent (12.26 lakhs out of 25.76 lakhs) at upper primary stage and 46.19 per cent (13.09 lakhs out of 28.35 lakhs) in secondary stage.

Table 2: Percentage of Girls Enrollment to Total Enrollment by Stages 1959-60 to 2004-05

Year	*Primary (I - V)*		*Upper primary (VI-VII)*		*Secondary (VIII-X)*	
	Boys	*Girls*	*Boys*	*Girls*	*Boys*	*Girls*
1959-60	62.12	37.88	77.06	22.94	82.12	17.88
1969-70	59.72	40.28	70.49	29.51	75.91	24.09
1979-80	58.67	41.33	66.38	33.62	69.91	30.09
1989-90	57.45	42.55	63.37	36.63	66.18	33.82
2004-05	50.63	49.37	52.39	47.61	53.81	46.19

Sources: 1. Commissioner and Director of School Education, Hyderabad, Andhra Pradesh.

2. Statistical Abstracts of Andhra Pradesh, Hyderabad, for various years.

The enrollment of girls has increased at a faster rate than that of boys at primary, upper primary and also secondary stage. During our study period (1959-60 to 2004-05) the Annual Compound Growth Rate of enrollment of girls was 10.25 per cent as against 0.87 per cent of boys in primary stage. The corresponding figures were 9.04 and 6.34 in upper primary stage and 6.83 and 2.88 in secondary stage respectively. The foregoing analysis shows that during the whole period of 45 years after formation of the state of Andhra Pradesh, the growth rate of enrollment of girls has been higher than that of boys as shown clearly in Table - 3.

Table 3: Annual Compound Growth Rate of Enrollment by Stages (1959-2005)

Stage	*Annual compound growth rate during1959-60 to 2004-05*	
	Boys (%)	*Girls (%)*
Primary	0.87	10.25
Upper primary	6.34	9.04
Secondary	2.88	6.83

Note: Computed on the basis of enrollment of boys and girls in different stages.

Progress of Female Teachers in Different Types of Schools in Andhra Pradesh

Table - 4 shows the percentage of female teachers to total teachers in primary, upper primary and high schools. The female teachers constitute only 18.20 per cent in primary schools, 22.49 per cent in upper primary schools and 16.10 per cent in high schools compared with the corresponding percentage of 81.80, 77.51 and 83.90 among male teachers in 1959-60. These figures increased to 45.02 per cent in primary schools, 41.43 per cent in upper primary schools and 40.10 per cent in high schools as against 54.98 per cent in primary schools, 58.57 per cent in upper primary schools and 59.90 per cent in high schools among male teachers in 2004-05. One should consider that increase in the number of women teachers is a healthy sign for the reasons (1) that it contributes to gender equality, and (2) the women teachers exhibit care and patience, their general traits, in teaching in primary, upper primary and secondary schools.

Table - 4: Percentage of Female Teachers to Total Teachers by Type of Schools

Year	*Primary schools*		*Upper-primary schools*		*High schools*	
	Males	*Females*	*Males*	*Females*	*Males*	*Females*
1959-60	81.80	18.20	77.51	22.49	83.90	16.10
1969-70	78.56	21.44	74.91	25.09	80.73	19.27
1979-80	73.81	26.19	70.52	29.48	75.18	24.82
1989-90	72.15	27.85	67.86	32.14	69.89	30.11
2004-05	54.98	45.02	58.57	41.43	59.90	40.10

Sources: 1. Commissioner and Director of School Education, Hyderabad, Andhra Pradesh.

2. Statistical Abstracts of Andhra Pradesh, Hyderabad, for various years.

During the period of our study (1959-60 to 2004-05) the Annual Compound Growth Rate of female teachers was 3.79 per cent as against 0.83 per cent of male teachers in primary schools. The corresponding figures were 7.39 per cent and 5.29 per cent in upper primary schools and 6.32 and 3.41 in high schools respectively. These data indicate that the participation of women has been increasing. It shows clearly in Table -5.

Table - 5: Annual Compound Growth Rate of Teachers by Type of Schools–1959-2005

Stage	*Annual compound growth rate during1959-60 to 2004-05*	
	Male teachers (%)	*Female teachers (%)*
Primary	0.83	3.79
Upper primary	5.29	7.39
High schools	3.41	6.32

Note: Computed on the basis of male and female teachers appointed in different stages of schools.

To repeat, the number of women teaches reached an all time high at primary, upper primary and high school stage in 2004-05. The number of both male and female teacher in primary, upper primary and high schools shows as increasing trend over the period of our study. It is particularly noteworthy that the index of female teachers recorded a much higher increase than that of the male teachers. This may be due to implementation of 33.33 per cent of reservation policy in Andhra Pradesh in favour of women.

Conclusion and Suggestions

At the time of the formation of the state, females were way behind males in terms of educational attainments, as elsewhere in the country. This is not a surprise given the cultural taboos that come in the way of educating females and given the son preference that is so glaring in our society. However, as time passed by, females made rapid progress especially in school education, the constitutional provisions and special efforts at the state level coming in handy. A process has set in motion where by the gap between males and females in literacy rate is getting reduced, the growth rate of enrollment of girls at the school level is exceeding that of boys, the gender disparity index is fast decreasing and, more importantly, large number of females are taking to teaching in schools. Though women share is about fifty per cent in the total population, their involvement in the education system is quit far far behind. Mother as the first teacher of the child, herself being an illiterate and one cannot expect miracles from her. It is a shame that we have kept mother India illiterate, ignorant and second grade citizen of the society. Unless, all the women are totally educated we cannot expect them to play any effective role in the society.

Therefore, it is time that we concentrate on women education as a first priority. If resources are scarce it is highly advisable that the women educational needs are satisfied first.

REFERENCES

1. Altekar, A.S. (1951): *Education in Ancient India* (fourth edition), Nan Inshore And Bros., Banaras (variance).

2. Chalam, K.S. (1988): *Education and Weaker Sections*, Inter India Publications, New Delhi.

3. Chalam, K.S. (1993): *Educational Policy for Human Resources Development*, Rawat Publications, Jaipur.

4. Gopinathan Nair, P.R. (1981): *Primary Education, Population Growth and Socio-economic Change*, Allied Publishers, New Delhi.
5. Government of India (1969): *Education and National Development*, NCERT, New Delhi.
6. Naik, J.P. (1975): *Elementary Education in India – A Promise to Keep*, Allied Publishers, Bombay.
7. NCERT. (2000): *National Curriculum Framework for School Education*, New Delhi.
8. Nurullah, S. And Naik, J.P. (1943): *History of Education in India during the British Period*, MacMillan, Bombay.
9. Pulla Rao, D. (1998): *Economics of Primary Education*, Rawat Publications, Jaipur.
10. Rajaiah, B (1987): *Economics of Education*, Mittal Publications, New Delhi.

23

STATUS OF EDUCATION AND EMPLOYMENT OF WEAKER SECTIONS IN INDIA (IN RELEVANCE TO ACCESSIBILITY OF RESERVATIONS)

S. Pulla Rao & P. Usha***

Despite the Constitution of India provided equality for all irrespective of gender, caste, religion, race and place of birth, which aimed at socio-economic emancipation of millions of Indians, the Indian society suffers from substantial inequalities in education, employment and income, based on caste and ethnicity. The economic condition of SC and ST continues to be worse off than the other sections of Indian society. In fact one can correlate the socio-economic deprivation which SC/STs faced from centuries as the major cause of poverty. Weaker sections in India have no access to good socio-economic opportunities and therefore get deprived of the right to adequate standard of living. Invariably, they are employed in unorganized/traditional occupation that have very low wages and have no regular employment.

At All-India 35.8 percent of the SC and ST population is below poverty line while for the rest of the population it is around 24.5 percent only in 1999-2000. It is evident in the Report of United Nations Economic and Social Council, which reveals that the poverty ratios for SCs and STs were significantly higher

* Reader in Economics, Mrs.A.V.N College, Visakhapatnam.

** Asst.Professor of Women Studies, Andhra University, Visakhapatnam.

than the national poverty ratio. In 2004-05, the decline in poverty ratio was 24 percent for the whole population where as the decline is 23 percent for SCs and only 9 percent for STs.

The objective of this paper is to examine the economic status of weaker sections and their accessibility in availing reservations in education and employment. This paper mainly focused on educational attainment and employment of weaker sections, as reservation is a means to increase representation of hitherto under privileged caste group and helps the marginalized people to lead a successful life.

The problem of illiteracy was more acute with SC/ST and some other backward castes. Though the government has allotted seats in educational institutions including professional courses under reservation quota, the literacy level of SCs and STs is comparatively lower than the others. In rural India, where 80% of SC/ST and backward castes reside, in 2001 the literacy rate is a mere 59.4 in contrast to 80% in urban India where the majority of the population comprises of the so called upper castes.The Constitution laid down 15% and 7.5% of vacancies to government aided educational institutes and reserves 27% of higher education. Reservation in most of states is at a maximum of 50%, and for jobs in the government/public sector, as reserved quota for the SC and ST candidates respectively for a period of five years, after which the situation was to be reviewed. In central government funded higher education institutions, 22.5% of available seats are reserved for Scheduled Caste and Scheduled Tribe students (15% for SCs, 7.5% for STs). In AIIMS 14% of seats are reserved for SCs, 8% for STs. In addition, SC/ST students with only 50% scores are eligible. This ratio is followed even in Parliament and all elections where few constituencies are earmarked for those from certain communities. In Andhra Pradesh, 15% of seats in educational institutions and in government jobs are reserved for SCs and 6% for STs.

The status of education and employment among members of SC, ST and other backward classes as per the NSS on employment and unemployment situation among social groups in India in 2004-05 revealed that the literacy rate is the lowest among the STs (52%) with 42% for females and 62% for males population of STs. Among the SCs, the literacy rate is 57% with 46% for females and 68% for males. In other backward classes, the literacy rate is 64% with 54% for females and 75% for males. For all these social groups, the literacy percentage in urban areas is almost 18 percentage points higher than in rural areas for SC and Other Backward Classes whereas it is about 24 percentage points higher for ST population. As per the NSS 2004-05, the number of persons currently attending in educational institutions per 1000 population of various social groups and age groups was much higher among the children and the youth belonging to others category (other than SC, ST and OBC) of households. However, among the urban male youths of age 20-24 years, the current attendance rate was highest among the STs (32%) followed by others (28%). In rural India, the current attendance rate among the OBCs was higher than that among the STs and SCs. Between the SC and ST population of rural India, the current attendance rate of both males and females excepting the age group 20-24 years, were higher among the households belonging to the SCs than that among the STs. Contrary to this, in urban India, current attendance rates were much higher for STs than for SCs for both males and females. In urban India, though the current attendance rate among the STs were higher than OBCs for the age group 15 years and above, the rates were lower for the age group 5 to 14 years. It may further be observed that the school attendance rates, in general, had steadily increased during the period 1999-2000 to 2004-05. The increase has been faster in rural areas than in urban areas.

The rate of decline in respect of the percentage of SCs living below the poverty line was marginally higher than that of the total population between 1993-94 and 2004-05. The gap between the total population and the SCs also decreased during the same period, both in urban and rural areas. This is primarily due to the fact that a large number of SCs who are living below the poverty line are landless with no productive assets, no access to sustainable employment and minimum wages. The women belonging to these groups suffer even more because of the added disadvantage of being denied equal and minimum wages.

The overall poverty ratio for the rural areas was 37.3% in 1993-94 and it decline to 28.3% by 2004-05. The corresponding ratios for the urban population were 32.4% and 25.7% respectively. The poverty ratios for SCs and STs were significantly higher than the national poverty ratio, both in 1993-94 and 2004-05. Against 37.3% of the total population living below the poverty line in rural areas in1993-94, 48% SC population and 52% ST population live below the poverty line. In 2004-05, the decline as compared to 1993-94 in poverty ratio was 24% for the whole population whereas the decline is 23% for SCs and only 9% for STs. In urban areas, the poverty ratio in 2004-05 has declined by almost the same rate for SCs & STs as that for the whole population. Thus, it is evident that the decline in poverty is much lower in case of rural STs. The proportion of SC population living in poverty is higher in urban areas than in rural areas. The urban population below poverty line has declined from 32.4% in 1993-94 to 25.7% in 2004-05. The SC population below poverty line in the urban areas has declined from 49.5% in 1993-94 to 39.9% in 2004-05."

As a result of the special measures the status of SC/ST women has registered quantifiable improvements. However the Government has a lot more to do to fulfill the Constitutional commitment of raising the status of SC/ST to that of the rest of the population. Towards the economic upliftment of SC/ST, the Government commits to make all efforts not only to endow every landless SC/ST family with a minimum piece of land with ownership rights but also to maximize their productive capacities through up- gradation of their skills, modernization of methods and equipment and supply of seeds and pesticides. Special legislative measures are also being taken to ensure payment of minimum wages and equal wages for women, with no gender discrimination, especially in the informal/un-organized sector to make more concerted efforts for bringing SC/ST above the poverty line. The Government also commits to organize landless and agricultural labourers on the pattern of swarozgaris of the SGSY with special focus on women for bringing the SC/ST women above the poverty line.

Statistics based on NSS on status of education and vocational training in India in 2004-05 revealed that the proportion of persons who received formal vocational training is highest among the unemployed and that too, among the unemployed females, being as high as 12 percent in the rural areas and 17 percent in the urban areas as compared to 7 percent among rural unemployed males and 12 percent among urban unemployed males. The proportion is around 2 percent for persons not in the labour force and 2 to 3 percent for the employed. As regards non-formal vocational training received through hereditary sources or otherwise, the survey revealed that the proportion is 9 percent for males and 5 percent for females, being around 9 percent for both rural and urban males but around 6 percent for rural females and 5 percent for urban females.

Education, being the most important instrument for empowering weaker sections of the society, every effort has been made to improve the educational status of SC/ ST on a priority basis. Several educational schemes have been implemented by the Ministry of Social Justice and Empowerment for children belonging to the disadvantaged sections, like the SCs, socially and educationally backward (other backward classes), street children and those with disabilities. The Government provides pre-matric scholarships to SC children on a 50:50 basis to State Governments and 100 per cent to UTs to pursue education upto the matriculation level. During the decade 3.7 million children have been assisted of which a large proportion are girls. Post-matric scholarships to pursue studies beyond the matriculation level has been provided during the period with 100 per cent Central assistance to 13.8 million SC children of which around 25 per cent are girls. Under the Central Sector Scheme of upgradation of merit of SC/ST students, 100 per cent assistance is provided to States and UTs for providing remedial and special coaching to remove deficiencies in school subjects and to prepare them for competitive examinations. Between 1997-2004, 8,807 students including girls benefited from this scholarship. Hostels for SC girls have been set up to facilitate them to pursue their education beyond the upper primary level. As of 2003-04, 731 hostels were set up and 55,799 SC girls benefited from the facility. Pre- and post-matric scholarships and hostel facilities for girls have also been provided to motivate and promote education among the OBCs belonging to low income families. Between 1998-2004, around 4.5 million OBC students, including girls have benefited from the scholarships and 21,336 girls have availed of the hostel facilities.

The Ministry of Rural Development plays a vital role in raising the status of the people living below the poverty line and improving the quality of life in rural areas through the implementation of various poverty alleviation programmes and providing avenues for self/wage employment to the most disadvantaged groups, viz., the SCs, STs and others. Under SGRY, which provides wage employment and food security in rural areas, 22.5 per cent of the funds earmarked for programmes implemented at the District and intermediate level Panchayats are earmarked for individual beneficiary schemes for SCs/STs and 50 per cent of the funds earmarked for programmes being implemented at the village panchayat level are for taking up activities in the habitations of SCs/STs. For taking up self-employment and income-generation activities, Swarnajayanti Gram Swarozgar Yojana (SGSY) stipulates that at least 50 per cent of the swarozgaris will be from SC/ST. Subsidy under the scheme to SC/STs and disabled persons is 50 per cent of the project cost as against 30 per cent to others. Under SGSY, 1.4 million SC swarozgaris accounting for 30.4 per cent of the total number of swarozgaris benefited upto March 2004.

In addition to these poverty alleviation programmes, the Indira Awaas Yojana (IAY) is being implemented with the objective of providing dwelling units to the people below poverty line living in rural areas mainly belonging to SCs/STs. 60 percentage of the total allocation during a financial year is to be utilized for construction of dwelling units for SCs and STs. During the year 2003-04, 42.8 per cent of the dwelling units constructed were for SCs and 19.3 per cent were for STs. The National Scheduled Castes Finance and Development Corporation has introduced a new micro credit finance scheme called Mahila

Samriddhi Yojana, exclusively for women belonging to SC/ST from very poor families. Under the scheme, Rs.1130.70 million was disbursed during 2003-04 to 59,826 beneficiaries. The same scheme is also being implemented by NSKFDC for women, who are scavengers and the dependent daughters of scavengers.

The National Social Assistance Programme (NSAP), comprising the National Old Age Pensions Scheme (NOAPS), the National Family Benefit Scheme (NFBS) and the National Maternity Benefit Scheme (NMBS) introduces a national policy for social security assistance to the poor SC/ST families and represents a significant step forward. The Ministries of Social Justice and Empowerment and Tribal Affairs promote educational and economic development for SC and ST respectively. In addition, the Planning Commission in May 1999 set up a Central Standing Committee for assessing and monitoring the Special Component Plan (SCP for SC) and Tribal Sub-Plan (TSP for ST). For the economic development of SC/ST, OBCs and Minorities, the following National level Apex bodies were set up to act as catalytic agents in developing schemes for employment generation and financing pilot projects: (i) The National Backward Classes Finance and Development Corporation (ii) The National Minorities Development and Finance Corporation and (iii) The National Scheduled Castes and Scheduled Tribes Finance and Development Corporation (NSFDC).

The National Backward Classes Finance & Development Corporation is implementing a scheme, 'Swarnima' for improvement of credit facilities for women belonging to backward classes living below poverty line through State channelising agencies. The Corporation is implementing Mahila Samridhi Yojana, exclusively for women belonging to backward classes living below the poverty line. The National Minorities Development Finance Corporation also introduced Mahila Samridhi Yojana for women particularly in the Northeast region. Since its inception, NMDFC has helped 44,804 women in formation of self-help groups and 57,875 women for establishment of self-employment venture. During 2004-2005, 3,086 women have been provided micro credit and 3,268 have been provided with term loan.

Participation of SCs in decision-making is a positive indicator of progress made by them. Representation of SCs in All India Services of IAS, IPS and IFS stands at 10.6 per cent of the total in the IAS, 12.4 per cent in the IPS and 11.5 per cent in the IFS in 2000 which is still below their expected level. Although the percentage of SCs in IAS and IPS declined between 1996 and 2000, the actual number has increased over the same period. However the number of women SC/ST in these categories is very negligible. The rise in total representation of SC in Central Government services covering A to D groups from 13.66 percentage in 1974 to 16.70 percentage in 1999 is marginally higher than their share in the total population. Though their representation in the Government service has shown an increasing trend from 3.25 per cent in 1974 to 11.29 per cent in 1999, in group 'A' service it is still low and does not reflect the impact of affirmative action and special measures adopted. The representation of SC/ST in political decision-making is quite impressive - their share stood at 14.3 per cent (2001) in PRIs , 13.8 per cent (2000) in the State Legislative Assemblies and 14.5 per cent (2001) in Lok Sabha.

As a result of the special measures the status of SC/ST women has registered quantifiable improvements. However the Government has a lot more to do to fulfill the Constitutional commitment of raising the status of SC/ST to that of the rest of the population. Towards the economic upliftment of SC/ST, the Government commits to make all efforts not only to endow every landless SC/ST family with a minimum piece of land with ownership rights but also to maximize their productive capacities through up- gradation of their skills, modernization of methods and equipment and supply of seeds and pesticides. Special legislative measures are also being taken to ensure payment of minimum wages and equal wages for women, with no gender discrimination, especially in the informal/un-organized sector to make more concerted efforts for bringing SC/ST above the poverty line. The Government also commits to organize landless and agricultural labourers on the pattern of swarozgaris of the SGSY with special focus on women for bringing the SC/ST women above the poverty line.

To conclude, though the government has opened the doors of reservations in educational institutions, the levels of education among members of SC, and ST is low. Enrolment, sustenance and drop out are some of the problems continue to exist which lowered the literacy rate among these groups. The SC-ST in general is unaware of provisions under the reservation policy. Inadequate publicity, lack of positive and proactive attitude among common people is the reason for their non-accessibility of reservations. In addition to that, inadequate planning and budget allocation is also responsible for this low literacy and employment levels. The desired progress can be achieved only when these people are well aware about all those programmes initiated by the government which is possible through extended publicity towards the provisions available to these sections.

REFERENCES

1. Population " Registrar and Census Commissioner,India. Retrieved on 2005, 2006, 2007.
2. de Zwart, The Logic of Affirmative Action;caste,class and quotas in India, *Acta sociological*, 2004;43;235.
3. Reservation in India from *wikipedia*, August 2008.
4. Alternate Report submitted to UN Committee on Economic, Social and Cultural Rights, Geneva, during state party (India) Report by ACJP-India (Mumbai, India)
5. National Sample Survey report.

24

EDUCATIONAL STATUS OF SCHEDULED CASTES IN INDIA

E. Vanilla Kumari, E. Sharmila Hymavathi** & G. Ratna Priya****

Indeed, education is a process of human enlightment and empowerment for the betterment and quality of life. It not only enhances man's knowledge, skills, competences, potential, values and attitudes but also transforms his belief and thoughts. At the same time, it is assumed as the training of the human soul in the persuit of truth and the practice of virtue. (Dongaonkar, 2004).

The present millennium is witnessing phenomenal global changes and no nation can isolate itself from the process. In the process of global changes and development India has achieved success in various field i.e., agriculture, industrialization, science and technology, production and so on. With the result of these phenomenal changes education are expanding at every corner in India, as it is assumed as the Human Resource Development (HRD) in the country. However, after Independence, the country has become more conscious to educate people, therefore, it has introduced various educational schemes and programmes to attain higher level of education and also to achieve socio-economic as well as overall development. But their education expansion or changes has not taken place for everyone and all sections of

*, ** & *** Department of Education, Andhra University, Visakhapatnam.

society. The scheduled castes and underprivileged people are still lagging behind in all stages of education. Despite constant efforts both by central and state governments to spread the education of scheduled castes and other weaker section, the level of .education among scheduled castes is very low in comparison to general castes and other community. It seems that people belonging to scheduled castes still have to go a long way to come up to the general level in the field of education. These can be compared through number of enrolments at various stages of education ad in turn the probe the permeability and spread of education.

According to Ministry of Human Recourses Development (MHRD) Annual Report, 2002-0:3, total number of scheduled caste students' enrolment all stages of education is 32,407,378 which accounts for less than 20% of total scheduled castes population while they constitute more than 16% of country's total population (16.66 crore in 2001). However, majority of SC population (i.e., almost 80%) are still away from educational accessibility. The reasons behind this low education are due to:

- Poverty and backwardness,
- Social discrimination and exploitation,
- Lack of aspiration and awareness,
- Marginalisation in the society,
- Lack of political will,
- Faulty education system,
- Absence of a balanced, sensible and realistic approach,
- Negative approach in handing educational programmes, and
- Non-implementation of education policies for the progress of SC education level.

Enrolments at Different Level

Enrolment in primary and middle levels of education is the most important indicator which always determines the future of educational development. Therefore, it is necessary to analyse number of scheduled caste students enrolled at various levels of education and can be compared with (Non-SC) (general) population. The enrolment of scheduled casts and general castes (Non-SC) students in various courses from primary to higher education are given in the Table 1.

Table 1: Percentage of Enrolment of Scheduled Caste and Non-SC Students by Stages, 2001

Stages	*General'*			*ScheduledCastes*		
	Girls	*Boys*	*Total*	*Girls*	*Boys*	*Total*
Primary or Basic (I -V)	43.48	56.52	10042.12	57.88	100	
Middle (VI-VIII)	41.45	58.55	10039.50	60.50	100	
Sec/H.Sec Or Pre degree	39.00	61.00	10036.58	63.42	100	
Higher Education	40.53	59.47	10031.98	68.08	100	

The above table reveals that there is a variation in the enrolment of general and scheduled caste students at different stages. Up to primary and middle stages enrolment ratio is very high but after that, it declines rapidly, especially in higher level in both categories. This is precisely because of high dropout ratio at this level. Similarly, there is a wide disparity in the level of education between boys and girls in general and SC students in particular. The enrolment of girl students is much lower than that of boys in both cases i.e. SC as well as general students. This is because of gender biasness and social discrimination against girl child. Further, it also illustrates that there has been substantial increase in the number of students belonging to scheduled castes at all stages of education, particularly in the primary level. This can be judged from the fact that the enrolment of SC students in primary level has increased from 1.13 crore in 1980-81 to 1.74 crore in 1992-93 and it is 2.05 crore in 2001-02.

Even after 60 years of independence, these people are struggling to achieve higher level of education. The constitution of India promises free and compulsory 'education to these community and more than 60 years have passed, yet majority of the SC population are illiterate. What does it indicate? A constitutional fraud? This has a serious implication for a country like India. Why have the promises not been kept? Was there any shortage of resources or management problems? This is very alarming and need immediate intervention. Low education level of these people is not only hampering the socio-economic development but also raising several issues and challenges. These challenges can be discussed as:

- It is creating manifold socio-economic disorder in the society;
- Lower education level is deteriorating the condition of all well-being and other sections seriously;
- Socio-economic backwardness, unemployment, mass migration and many more problems are attributed due to low education level among these people and in general;
- Lower education level is accentuating discriminations and deprivation among these peoples;
- It is not only generating problems and miseries in the country but effecting society at all levels and scales; and
- If these evolving trends continue, it will accelerate the number of illiterates in the country.

Education is an important indicator of socio-economic development and also a prominent component of population studies. Equally, it is considered as an essential trait of civilization, and overall development of human beings. Emancipation and empowerment of people can be achieved only through education. Indeed, the country's advancement and development largely depends upon the level of education as it provides enlightenment, power, privilege, protection and prestige to the people.

The study of nature and extent of education level for scheduled castes in India reflects pathetic scenes. Their level of education is fairly very low and it is lower at higher level. Despite the constitutional provision and persistent efforts to improve the levels of education since independence, there exhibit high degree of dispersion and disparities. In fact, it is a matter of serious concern and worrisome for the whole nation as it effects each and every individuals of the society. However, it makes obvious that educational strategies in India should aim at achieving higher level of education to the scheduled castes and deprived people. It is imperative that measures proposed for the country is education level should be in harmony of scheduled castes and underprivileged people as we all know that Ignorance is disastrous and leads to irrationality.

Therefore, following measures can be taken effectively:

- There is a need of major shift of attention to make education as a priority sector in respect to scheduled caste people;
- Education development among scheduled castes in India urgently requires a shift in focus to · bring out intensive educational programmes to achieve higher level of education;
- There is a need of quick implementation of strong and effective education policies in the country. For this, a monitoring body should be constituted under the supervision of high cabinet level and action should be taken on the persons and officers' who show any negligence;
- Higher proportion of the country's budget needs to be spent towards scheduled castes related educational programmes.
- As education among scheduled castes suffers due to acute poverty, unemployment and lack of awareness, there is a need of mass campaign and creating awareness, providing full financial supports and scholarships, counseling and guidance to parents;

- Lastly, it is also essential to create a congenial atmosphere in the country. For this, government and people's participation is equally required.

The whole study demonstrates a very complex scenario and suggests that there is a need of change of people's mind and attitude and put collective efforts to improve education level of scheduled castes in the country. The realization of dream can come true if the government takes strong and effective steps in the implementation of country's education policies with this assumption that education is the essence of human beings and the best contraceptive to socio-economic development.

25

EDUCATION OF WEAKER SECTIONS IN INDIA

V. Krishna Murthy & R.V.L.N. Ratnakara Rao***

Introduction

Considering India's enormous problems – its large population, widespread poverty, rampant illiteracy and deep rooted traditional beliefs, the six decades of achievements are indeed significant. Few other developing countries can claim such successes. But a lot still remains to be done like the following:

a) The burgeoning population needs to be checked. b) Illiteracy needs to be stamped out. c) Fallacious beliefs in irrational thoughts have to be eradicated. d) Agricultural production that seems to have hit a plateau needs to be given another push. e) cutting edge the research needs to be funded and pursued with more vigour. f) wasteful expenditure and corruption needs to be routed out from all sections of the society. g) Education of weaker sections like Scheduled castes, Scheduled tribes and women to be improved.

CAG Report on SC, ST Dropouts

The Central Government may have put in place several educational schemes for the benefit of students belonging to Scheduled Caste (SCs) and Scheduled Tribes (STs). Yet, these

* Retd. Professor, Dept. of Education, Andhra University, Visakhapatnam, Andhra Pradesh.

** Department of Physical Education, Andhra University, Visakhapatnam, Andhra Pradesh.

do not seem to have benefited those belonging to these two categories, which is evident in their declining enrollments and increasing dropout rates in many states. In its audit on the educational status of SC and ST students, CAG has noted: "The gap in the Gross Dropout Rate (GDR) between the general candidates and SC and ST candidates which was 6.7% and 15.1% in 2001-02 deteriorated to 10.4% and 16.6% in 2003-04 respectively".

It is a fact that has prompted CAG to suggest that independent evaluation and review of the educational schemes for SC and ST students be carried out through Non Governmental Organizations (NGOs). For as the CAG report makes it clearly evident, the schemes have failed to either increase the enrollment of SC/ST students or help arrest their dropout rates. This scenario has also prompted CAG to suggest to the Union ministries that they take urgent measures to ensure educational schemes that it has for SC, ST are effective.

Percentage of Enrollment

1. Upto Primary and Middle stages, the enrollment ratio is very high but after that it declines rapidly, especially in higher level in both general and scheduled caste categories.
2. There is a wide disparity in the level of education between boys and girls in general and SC students.
3. The enrollment of girl students is much lower than that of boys in both cases of general students as well as SC. This is because of gender bias and social discrimination against girls.

Stages	*Enrollment of General*			*Enrollment of Scheduled Castes*		
	Girls	*Boys*	*Total*	*Girls*	*Boys*	*Total*
Primary or basic (I-V)	43.48	56.52	100	42.12	57.88	100
Middle(VI-VIII)	41.45	58.55	100	39.50	60.50	100
Sec./Hr Sec orPre-Degree	39.00	61.00	100	36.58	63.42	100
Higher Education	40.53	59.47	100	31.98	68.08	100

The SC and ST population constituted 16.33% and 8.01 % respectively at the 1991 Census.

Percentage Share.of SC/ST children in Total Enrollment at elementary stage in 1997-98:

Category	*Primary Stage Classes (I-V)*			*Middle Stage Classes (VI-VIII)*		
	Boys	*Girls*	*Total*	*Boys*	*Girls*	*Total*
SCs	17.27	16.60	16.96	14.99	14.04	14.59
STs	8.40	8.13	8.28	6.26	5.52	5.96

Source: Dept. of Education MHRD, GOI.

Percentage Share of Girls in Total Enrollment at elementary stage in 1997-98:

Category	Primary Stage Classes (I-V)		Middle Stage Classes (VI-VIII)	
All communities	43.62	47.45	40.12	15.84
Scheduled Castes	42.59	Million	38.49	million
Scheduled Tribes	42.82	in 1997-98	37.09	in 1997098

Source: Development of Education, MHRD, GOI.

Due to persistent effort, enrollment of girls at the elementary stage has grown steadily over the last 5 decades. The number of girls at primary stage has gone up from 5.38 million in 1950-51 to 47.45 million in 1997-98. The number of girls at middle stage has increased from 0.53 million in 1950-51 to 15.84 million in 1997-98.

Enrollment Ratios by Stages Sex, Scheduled Castes and Scheduled Tribes

Category	*Primary Stage Classes (I-V)*			*Upper Primary Classes (VI-VIII)*		
	Boys	*Girls*	*Total*	*Boys*	*Girls*	*Total*
SCs	102.25	81.60	92.36	72.84	37.59	56.17
STs	102.93	78.34	90.73	50.03	32.93	43.24
All groups	97.5	81.2	89.7	66.5	49.5	58.5

Source: Selected Educational Statistics (relevant years) DOE, MHRD, GOI.

Enrolment ratios for all groups were 81 girls and 97 for boys at the primary stage as well as 49 for girls and 66 for boys at upper primary stage in the year 1998-99.

According to *The Economic Survey (2007-08)* of the Government of India, the Gross Enrollment Ratio (GER) among girls in the age group of 6 to 14 years is very less i.e. 89.87% compared to the GER among boys in the same age group i.e. 96.91%. The gender gap in literacy needs to be reduced to zero through 100% enrollment of girls in order to achieve the development goals of the XIth Five Year Plan.

Conclusion

Although there is evidence of substantial increase in literacy rates during the last three decades, still India has to go a long way. Education plays a vital role in the process of development of human resource and hence the ministry is also called Ministry of Human Resource Development (MHRD). For the over all development of economy, development of education in general and universalisation of elementary education in particular are given a high priority in India. Primary Education as the foundation occupies an important position in the entire structure of education. Therefore, a high priority has been given to invest in education. This is perhaps the reason that Article 45 of the Indian Constitution guarantees provision of free and compulsory education to all children up to the age of 14 or 7 years of schooling i.e. 4-14 years of age.

INDEX

□□□